turmoil to turning points

building hope for children
in crisis placements

ERRATA

The publisher regrets that figures 5.2 and 5.4 are incorrect in the book and asks that you substitute the following on pages 110 and 118:

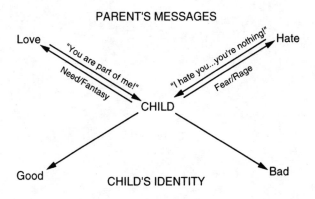

Figure 5.2. Splitting messages and a child's identity
(after Masterson, 1976)

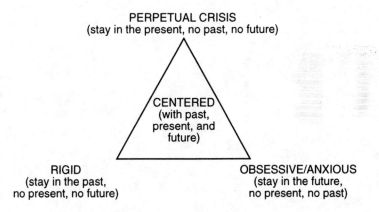

Figure 5.4. Time orientation

turmoil to turning points

building hope for children in crisis placements

richard kagan, ph.d.

W · W · NORTON & COMPANY · NEW YORK · LONDON

Printed in the United States of America

First Edition

Composition by Eastern Composition
Manufacturing by Haddon Craftsmen, Inc.

For information about permission to reproduce selections
from this book, write to
Permissions, W. W. Norton & Company, Inc., 500 Fifth Avenue,
New York, NY 10110.

Library of Congress Cataloging-in-Publication Data

Kagan, Richard.
    Turmoil to turning points : building hope for children in crisis
placements / Richard Kagan.
        p.   cm.
    "A Norton professional book."
    Includes bibliographical references and index.
    ISBN 0-393-70218-9
    1. Family social work—United States.   2. Family counseling—
United States.   3. Problem families—United States.   4. Foster home
care—United States.   I. Title.
HV699.K35   1996
362.7—dc20   96-11005   CIP

W. W. Norton & Company, Inc., 500 Fifth Avenue, New York, N.Y. 10110
    http://web.wwnorton.com
W. W. Norton & Company Ltd., 10 Coptic Street, London WC1A 1PU

1 2 3 4 5 6 7 8 9 0

To my Mom, who taught me that there was nothing more important in life than raising children

To my Dad, who taught me to push the limits of our understanding

and

In memory of Gilbert Alpert, my first father, who showed me courage and hope against all odds

contents

preface   ix
acknowledgments   xvi

part one   turmoil

1   solomon's quest   1
2   no one heard   21
3   writing to mom   46

part two   practice strategies

4   setting a course toward change   71
5   centering in the storm   105
6   staying the course   131

part three   turning points

7   speaking up   159
8   saying "no"   174

part four   the quest

9   from practice to policy   185
10   building a better future   209
11   breaking through the storm   230

appendix: split message exercise   249
references   253
index   263

preface

AS I APPROACHED THE ROW OF UNIFORMLY BLEAK APARTMENTS, I COULD feel a growing knot in my stomach. My years of graduate school education had prepared me to work with clients who had at least enough motivation to get them to come into an agency or clinic. But here I was knocking on the door of what was then, to me, the unknown.

One of the Williams* family boys opened the door and screamed for his mother, "They're here, Ma!" "Come in," he muttered, waiting neither for his mother's reply nor any introduction from us. The boy turned and left without even looking back to see if we were coming. My colleague and I were just another team of social service people, part of the regular stream of visitors who came into his house, looked around, talked, and left. "The Welfare . . ."

I had just finished my internship and started work at a child and family services agency with my freshly printed Ph.D. proudly hung on the wall. Family therapy meant parents and children coming in to see me in a professional office environment. Most of my work consisted of psychological evaluations of children who were not getting any better, stuck cases where any help was appreciated. I was able to work with a few children in play therapy and occasionally participated in a family session or two involving kids I had seen.

The week before I had been asked to see Martin Williams, a rather sullen and angry 13-year-old who was about to be expelled from his

---

*In order to protect confidentiality, individuals described in this book represent composites from different families, agencies, counties, states, and time periods. Families, practitioners, agencies, cities, and counties described in this book are not intended to represent any real people or organizations. Quotes are not exact; however, issues, dynamics, and critical dilemmas have been maintained to reflect my experience working for two decades in child welfare, mental health, substance abuse, and special education programs.

junior high school for fighting with peers and threatening teachers. I had him draw pictures of people, houses, trees, his family, and make up stories for pictures of children and families. To no one's surprise, his stories described parents yelling, screaming, and hitting their children, who were involved in everything Martin was reported doing.

"You should see his family. It's chaos," urged a colleague in my agency's newly developed prevention of placement program. My agency, a pioneer in developing family-centered residential treatment in the late 1960s, had initiated a home-based family counseling program in 1976, the same year I joined the staff. In essence, the program sent practitioners from the residential treatment center out to families in crisis. A social worker, child care worker, and special education teacher were sent to work with each family for what was planned to be short-term interventions. Families would be given the help they needed to nip crises in the bud, prevent children from going into foster homes or residential treatment centers, and save the state millions of dollars with a reduction in out-of-home placements.

The Williams family, of course, had a different view of our entry. The Williamses were one of those legendary families that every agency knows. With five or more family members in some form of crisis at any one time, the family was well known to mental health centers, the police, child and family services, and child protective services. The children were usually on the verge of being kicked out of school and were already well known to judges for truancy, vandalism, and petty thefts.

While I wondered about the impact of another stranger in their home, the Williams kids showed me this was just "more of the same." We stood awkwardly for a few minutes waiting for the children's mother to come in from the kitchen where she was screaming at a 2-year-old to pick something up. After a perfunctory "Hello" to my colleague, she screamed for her husband to come downstairs and ordered Martin and his two older brothers to "Sit!" Within minutes, the 14- and 16-year-old sons were jostling with each other. Mrs. Williams yelled again at the 2-year-old. A 10-year-old curled herself up into what looked like a fetal position in the corner and began filling in animals in a coloring book.

As the teenagers moved from verbal threats to throwing small projectiles, Mr. Williams came down the stairs. He was a short, graying man with a weathered face which made him seem 20 years older than he was. He grabbed a scratched black metal lunch box from the kitchen, mumbled a "Got to go" to my colleague, growled at his old-est son to "Shut up!" and was out the door, all in about 20 seconds.

With Mr. Williams's speedy entry and exit, the kids picked up their tempo. Cries became screams. Mrs. Williams never budged from her chair but her tense smile changed into a deep scowl and her voice became bitter and sharp. Each of her yells seemed to punctuate a new outburst of animosity from one or another of her five children.

Meanwhile, the knot in my stomach was getting tighter. I was sup-posed to comment on what Martin had shown me in our short ses-sion the week before and somehow engage the family to work to-gether on ending the fighting, truancy, and thefts. "He's in big trouble now," Mrs. Williams said. "He's suspended for the third time this month. His principal wants him out and I don't blame him," she added with a glare at Martin. I was impressed with how quiet Martin was. Compared to his siblings, he appeared calm and almost angelic, the quiet center of today's family hurricane.

My colleague reminded the family of the psychological evaluation. "So, what's wrong with him?" his mother demanded as she slapped one of her youngest on the rear. For a brief second, silence descended and all eyes focused on me. I could feel my stomach tighten one more notch. I tried to point out the positives as well as my concerns but, after my first words, no one seemed to be listening. Within a few minutes, the din had resumed.

I worried that the whole notion of reporting on Martin was just feeding the conflict. That he would be in trouble seemed accepted as a given. The only question was how much and my presence simply sup-ported the presumption of his being in big trouble. His mother had been threatening placement for months and I had no clue how we could interrupt the cycle of her children acting out and being placed.

My words of insight had no impact and I felt as powerless as everyone else to change things. I was frustrated when my colleague announced that we had to be going but relieved to get out of the Williams battlefield before one of the projectiles struck me.

Obviously, we weren't performing any miracles today. The teenage boys were just as close to placement today as yesterday, with the younger children following right behind. The parents and children seemed mired in patterns of yelling, screaming, fighting, and crisis that went back through years of child protective reports of abuse and neglect, multiple mental health therapists, and countless evaluations like my own.

No one's needs were being met. Martin would very likely be on his way to a residential treatment center as soon as he was brought back to family court. He would be placed for 18 months and then sent back home until he was old enough to fend for himself. By that point, he most likely would have started his own family.

I left that home visit with little hope of change for this family. Whatever was propelling their behavior remained a mystery. Scores of practitioners had already tried to work with the kids, the parents, and the family. I could feel Martin's desperation to get away from the chaos and tension and his need at the same time to stand by his mother. Mrs. Williams seemed on the verge of exhaustion with repeated threats to give up and get out herself. I worried most about the silent girl in the corner and the youngest children not getting what they needed. The younger children seemed doomed to repeat the experience of their older siblings. Two had already been placed.

It would be easy to write off the Williamses as an "unworkable family." Yet, even in their fighting a certain appeal remained. The 10-year-old girl in the corner had a mournful smile, suggesting that something, sometime had been better for her. Her younger siblings were playful and engaging with bright eyes and occasional flashing grins. The teenage boys were quite handsome. The family had two parents and was filled with energy. Mr. Williams had maintained a job and his wife assembled her children for the family sessions. In short, the Williamses had a lot going for them compared to many of the families served by child and family services.

Visiting the Williams family was like sailing into a storm. Whatever direction we had was quickly lost. Our own balance and safety seemed precarious at best. After all, when things are flying through the air, anyone can be hit. Yet, my colleagues and I did not want to give up on the Williams and the many families like them. We would keep searching for ways to help Martin and his family pull out of the storm and gain the direction and hope that were so lacking.

Child welfare has become a major national issue. In Florida, a 12-year-old successfully sues his mother for divorce. In Chicago, a judge orders adoptive parents to turn over custody of the 4-year-old boy they raised from birth to the biological father he had never seen. In Texas, foster parents fight for the return of a toddler who had been removed from their care and placed in another home because he was of a different race. A New York adoption agency is sued for allegedly withholding information on sexual abuse of a child placed for adoption. The evening news televises the arrest of parents in

Illinois for leaving their children home alone while they jetted off
on a nine-day vacation. Newspapers headline accounts of battered
and starving children living with crack-addicted mothers. In 1993,
the *Chicago Tribune* listed the year-to-date count of Chicago
children found murdered. Child and family services are now front
page news.

The statistics alone are staggering. The number of children in foster
care swelled in the 1980s with an estimated 450,000 children living in
foster homes, hospitals, residential treatment programs, and detention
centers by 1993 (American Public Welfare Association, 1994). In 1987,
2.2 million children were reported to be abused or neglected and each
year 1.5 million children run away from home (Wylie, 1990). Re-
searchers have found evidence linking early childhood experiences
with violence to biological changes in children which in turn lead to
violent behavior (see Kotulak, 1993). The nightmare of abused/ne-
glected children has become everyone's nightmare as our cities, small
towns, and suburbs have been caught up in an epidemic of violence.

Every day, children are removed from their homes by child protective workers or placed into foster homes, residential treatment centers, or psychiatric hospitals because of their behavior. Family court
judges are asked to make decisions that have tremendous impact on a
child's life and a family's future. Yet, judges often have little information and hear conflicting viewpoints.

The power of the judge comes with a terrible pressure to make the
right decision and provide for "the best interests" of the child and the
community. Decisions are driven by statutes that guarantee parental
rights. Judges are limited to legally admissible evidence, which often
doesn't match the dangers perceived. The claims of parents may not
match the expression of fear on a 4-year-old's face. The alternatives
presented (e.g., another foster care placement, a return to a home
with questionable parenting, group care) all appear detrimental in
one way or another for a 10-year-old who has already been placed
into a dozen foster homes or group care facilities.

The pain and pressure on the judge are too much for any one person. "Experts" are called in to evaluate, to assess, to recommend. The
power, pressure, pain, and responsibility for the "best interests of the
child" are shared by child protective, probation, and mental health
staff in public, private, and nonprofit agencies.

No amount of graduate education, workshops, or seminars can prepare you for the reality of seeing photographs of a battered 3-year-
old's corpse, meeting his siblings and mother, and being asked along

with colleagues to develop a plan to ensure the safety of the remaining children. And this is just the beginning of the work that must take place to help a child and his family overcome longstanding problems and traumas reenacted over multiple generations. The process of change and the effort to bring in hope requires person-to-person relationships and interventions, which tax the skill and perseverance of the most seasoned practitioners.

Behind the headlines and statistics, real life dramas of parents, children, grandparents, judges, lawyers, child protective workers, probation officers, educators, foster parents, child care workers, and therapists are played out with high stakes. Interventions are guided by the dominant theories of our time and controlled to a large extent by economic and political factors. Today's conception of good practice, evidentiary requirements of the judicial system, regulations of competing state, local, and federal agencies, and politics of governments, public agencies, and private service organizations all come to bear on the lives and futures of people in crisis—crises which have become so dangerous to children, to parents, or to communities, that outside authorities have been called in.

Turmoil to Turning Points shows how practitioners work on a person-to-person basis to help families who have lived with chronic trauma in their lives, children and parents who typically are not asking for help and for whom crises and violence have become a way of life that impacts everyone around them. This book presents a look from "the trenches" at what is happening to children and parents, what leads a teenager to become violent or to turn to drugs, what triggers regression to infant-like behavior, and what resources exist that can empower individuals to survive traumas and cope with adversity. Descriptions of evaluations, coordinating sessions, and interventions with parents, children, administrators, and staff in child and family services are included to illustrate how the child welfare system works, as well as its successes, its failures, and the consequences for children, parents, and practitioners.

Stories of trauma and change are used to depict what I learned from each family about their struggles, motivation for change, and what was needed to make their lives better. The impact of children's and parents' actions on my colleagues and myself, our assessments, the thinking behind interventions, what helped, what didn't help, and what I learned about myself are portrayed as part of family sessions and review conferences.

I have learned from all of the children and parents who have shared their lives with me and allowed me to see what happened over time. From them, from the insights of my colleagues, and with the foundations of theory and practice from the family systems and child welfare movements, I have learned how to engage families and work with them to change the crisis cycle leading to placements of children. This is not a miracle approach, but rather a different perspective, a different focus, and a collection of understandings that have come from watching what helps, what has no effect, and what leads to more crises.

I am writing this book to share what I have learned in the last 20 years from work with families where children and adolescents have been placed away from their homes, families like the Williamses who seemed hopelessly locked into lives filled with traumas and crises. This book is a tribute to foster parents and practitioners* who have struggled to make child and family services work for children and families revolving in chronic and destructive crises. Much more needs to be done and I hope this book will promote the innovative policies, programs, research, and person-to-person interventions that are needed to help these families and our communities.

---

*Practitioners include child care workers, foster parents, child protective workers, teachers, social workers, psychologists, psychiatrists, probation workers, art and music therapists, nurses, and lawyers for child and family services.

acknowledgments

NO ONE CAN DEAL WITH THE STORMS AND TENSION OF THIS KIND OF work without a safe port to return to after a hard day's work. My wife, Laura, brought me back to earth each time I would come home "spacey," obsessing about cases, agency problems, workshop presentations, or how to write what I had learned. She and my children, Michelle, Joshua, and Michael, rewarded me with the affection that kept me going and made writing this book a reality.

My training in graduate school taught me to understand emotions, how perspectives and thinking lead to all kinds of behavior, and how families work. Twenty years in child and family services taught me how to engage families like the Williamses, to understand what their behaviors were saying, and to work with colleagues to help families to change. Without the help and guidance I received from my colleagues and teachers at Parsons Child and Family Center, I would have remained just as lost as I felt in the first minute of my first home visit as a psychologist. I have learned from each family we worked with and from the staff of the Albany, Schenectady, Rensselaer, Schoharie, and Saratoga Departments of Social Services who joined me in this effort. I am grateful to Andrea Burger and Barbara Comithier for bringing consultants such as myself into Albany County Child Protective Services. I also wish to thank Nadia Finkelstein and John Carswell and their successors, Ray Schimmer and Kathryn Gerbino, for supporting my writing and mobilizing Parsons staff to face the challenges of managed care and fiscal cutbacks.

The foundation for this book rests on the premises and interventions described in *Families In Perpetual Crisis* (1989), which was written with Shirley Schlosberg. Shirley became the Director of the Prevention Program at Parsons Child and Family Center and developed this program into a national model for what can be done to help families immersed in repeated crises. I learned from her messages, which have helped me to engage families who expect every visit by social services practitioners to shame them once again with all of their deficits, failures, and problems. I learned to tell families up front that "I'm nosey" and that I was counting on them to stop me if I went too fast or asked about things they did not want to talk about. Shirley modeled persistence. She has never stopped working for permanency for children, no matter what obstacles stood in the way. I owe a great debt to her as my mentor through 17 years of work in Parsons' Prevention Program. She has always challenged me to do nothing but my best for parents and children and my work is filled with interventions I gained during our work together.

The approaches I and my colleagues developed stemmed from the pioneers in family therapy, child welfare, and network therapy. Their ideas are part of everything I have done. I was greatly influenced by a core of contemporary leaders in family systems who contributed to Parsons' professional development programs: Guy Ausloos, Joel Bergman, Eliana Gil, Evan Imber-Black, Judith Landau Stanton, Cloé Madanes, Monica McGoldrick, Michael Rohrbaugh, Paul Steinhauer, David Waters, to name just a few. Michael Nichols has been a long-standing friend and adviser.

Many colleagues and friends helped keep me on track and focused by reviewing and editing my endless drafts. I am very grateful to Nathaniel Bracey, Christine Celmer, Suzanne d'Aversa, Kathryn Gerbino, Barbara Henderer, Sudha Hunziker, Natalie Nussbaum, Seth Rigberg, Ray Schimmer, Robin Sorriento, Cindy Szypulski, and Joan Valery for their insights and suggestions. I would like to thank Ivor and Terry Moskowitz and Ellen and Pat Green for reviewing early drafts of chapters and encouraging me to persevere in the effort that led to this book.

My sons, Michael and Josh, edited my manuscript line by line. Michael deserves special thanks for teaching me how to put life into my writing and to develop a consistent voice. Josh helped me to catch multiple errors and to clarify the meaning and the context of my work. Regina Dahlgren Ardini carefully edited this book in its final stages and helped me catch repetitions, streamline sentences, and eliminate digressions. Vicki Santiago and my daughter, Michelle Kagan, helped with typing. Sue Parnes helped me locate innumerable references and Mary Abrams helped me gather statistics on children in placement. Rabbi Scott Shpeen helped me with a citation from the Talmud and Kate Charbonneau contributed information on Native

American culture. My brother, Jim, provided a photograph with a difficult subject. None of this, of course, would have been possible without the support, guidance, and direction of Susan Munro, my editor at W. W. Norton. I am grateful to all of them for their encouragement and help.

turmoil

chapter 1

The monsters did mean things to the girl and the
girl just lays there scared in the dark. . . . She
yelled for her mother (but) her mother never
comes.

*From a story by a 14-year-old girl in a long-
term substance abuse facility*

solomon's quest

"STAY AWAY FROM ME!" YELLED A THIN BLONDE GIRL AS I WALKED INTO
the crisis shelter. The girl turned and darted off before I could reply.
"Off to a good start," I thought to myself. I was 42 years old, precipi-
tously balding, and a Ph.D. I didn't usually think of myself as frightening young children.

Several child care staff greeted me with knowing smiles. "Seeing Rebecca today? She woke up all the kids again last night . . . screamed
about the monster at the foot of her bed. . . . She's been hyper since
she heard you were coming this morning. . . . Good luck!"

I welcomed the chance to get some coffee and read several reports
we had received from clinics that had previously worked with Rebecca
and her family. I sat down at a long table in the eating area and read
about a 9-year-old girl who had told her fourth grade teacher four
months earlier that she saw and heard a monster coming into her room
every night and climbing on her bed. She was placed in a private psychiatric hospital for two weeks, then transferred to a state-run facility
100 miles from her home when the private hospital discovered that her
parents' insurance would not cover the charges for hospital treatment.

At the state-run facility, a tranquilizing medication was administered. After three months of hospitalization she calmed down until the staff began talking about sending her home. Rebecca then told another girl in the hospital that the monster she had told her teacher about was really her father and that he had forced her to have sex with him. The girl told hospital staff who in turn called the state's child abuse hotline.

Rebecca's father, Mr. Burns, visited her in the hospital, denied that there had been any sex abuse, and told hospital staff that this was just more of the heartache Rebecca had caused him over the years. He shared with hospital staff that at age 4 Rebecca had told a daycare teacher that he had forced her to perform oral sex and that as a preschooler she had been soiling herself and smearing feces in her room. He reported that when she was 6 she had again told a teacher that he was forcing her to have sex. This followed placement of her older sister into a residential treatment facility.

Mr. Burns explained that Rebecca's older sister was saying similar things, which he attributed to "auditory hallucinations and central nervous system impairment." Mr. Burns's four daughters had shown other strange sexual behaviors in his opinion, including inserting objects in their vaginas as preschoolers. Mr. Burns told hospital staff that he was confident that this latest charge of sex abuse would be seen as just another manifestation of Rebecca's disorder and dropped like all of the previous allegations.

"Don't yell at me!" I looked up to see Rebecca standing 10 feet away and glaring at me with her little hands clenched in fists. One of the child care staff came up. "Rebecca, this is Dr. Kagan. He's going to be seeing you today." Rebecca's whole body appeared to tense up and she frowned. The girl appeared not so much angry as defiant, searching for some sense of control.

Who could blame her? Unsubstantiated sexual or physical abuse allegations were typical of the children placed in this facility. The kids were placed away from their families and their parents usually remained at home demanding that the children change their behavior. These were children under age 12 who had become dangerous to themselves or others. Rebecca had told hospital staff that she would kill herself if they sent her back to live with her father. Instead, she was placed in a shelter for children in crisis, children who were seen as too disturbed and too dangerous to live at home.

Child protective services (CPS) staff had conducted interviews with

Rebecca, her sisters, and father. Their reports noted insufficient evidence to take her father to court and ask a judge to rule that Rebecca had been abused and needed to live in a foster home for her own protection. Instead, Rebecca was sent to our facility with the hope that she could be "stabilized" before being sent to another institution, a residential treatment center for children, where her problems could be treated. Mr. Burns had approved this plan.

I took it as a good sign that Rebecca didn't immediately run away from me this time and told her that I was a psychologist who worked with some of the kids in the program every Monday morning and that I hoped to talk with her in a few minutes. Her frown turned into a forced smile and with a loud, high-pitched giggle she was gone. I wondered if I would actually be able to talk to her for more than two minutes. Staff had noted that she hated men because they reminded her of her father. She had told several staff that he would kill her for telling about the abuse and she was terrified that he would come after her.

Mary, Rebecca's social worker, brought her back a few minutes later and I described how I would like to have her draw some pictures and make up some stories. Rebecca giggled with a silly, high-pitched laugh more typical of a 3- or 4-year-old and whispered into Mary's ear, keeping Mary between herself and me. "She says she's worried about her three sisters," Mary said as we walked into Mary's office. Mary asked Rebecca to talk with me and left us alone with the door slightly open.

"I love them a lot!" Rebecca said referring to her sisters. She began crying softly. Rebecca had not been able to see them in four months and believed she was living away from home because "I talked about it."

Rebecca drew a picture of a girl with no neck, large eyes, no hands, and no feet. In response to drawings of children that I showed her, she made up stories about girls who were "scared . . . just like me." One of the pictures I used showed a girl sitting up in her bed. In her story, Rebecca said that the girl had the same nightmare that she had every night. Her "Daddy was coming . . . He was hurting me . . ."

"How was he 'hurting' you?" I asked. Rebecca looked away. "I can't say it!" I told her that was okay; I didn't expect her to tell someone she had just met.

"Can I write it?" she asked a few minutes later. I nodded and Rebecca ripped off a small piece of paper and printed: "Daddy made me have sex. . . . He put his thing in my private part." Rebecca said that her father was sometimes nice and sometimes mean. She didn't love him anymore. "He likes what he is doing!"

"I really want to see my sisters and my mother," Rebecca continued with a sad look. I asked whether she thought her mother believed what Rebecca had said about her father forcing her to have sex. Rebecca looked down and shook her head. "My Daddy decided that he should have us kids and my mother signed the agreement. . . . She's going to leave our house again with her new boyfriend, as soon as they get the money."

Rebecca went on to describe finding her mother clutching a bottle of pills in the bathroom. Rebecca said she called the ambulance. "The reason why she did it is because something happened to her . . ."

"What happened?" I asked. Rebecca said she didn't know, but in another story she described a girl who felt sad because the girl's "daddy hurt the mother and the mother killed herself."

I showed Rebecca a picture of a girl seated at a desk looking at a book and some papers. "That's just like me at school. I told my teacher that I was seeing a monster with a big horn on his head." Rebecca's eyes seemed to glaze over as she went on. "The monster came every night and said he was going to kill me. He climbed up on my bed." Rebecca's voice faded. She looked down and her breathing became heavy. Her chest seemed to shudder slightly as she continued in thought.

"What was the monster like?" I asked very softly. Rebecca frowned and looked at me, coming out of her trance. "It wasn't a monster. It was my Daddy. I just told the teacher it was a monster. . . . Daddy said that if I told, he'd kill me!" Rebecca's voice rose in pitch and her eyes widened as if she was feeling once again the shock of being abused. "He's really going to do it!" I felt a tremor in my chest.

I showed Rebecca several other pictures of children and parents. She described girls in her stories who had been hurt by their fathers and were too afraid to tell someone what happened. Some ran away. She then added in a monotone: "Whenever someone tries to hurt you, you have to tell other people."

I showed Rebecca the Rorschach inkblots, asking her to tell me what she thought each one looked like. "It's a monster. See, it's got two horns," she said about the first inkblot. Her voice rose in pitch and her eyes again began to glass over. "It's a devil."

"Do you believe in monsters and devils?" I asked. Rebecca glared at me for a second. "The monster is my father . . . a real person. . . .

He's like a monster!" Her voice became determined and her face tightened. "If I have to go home, I'm going to kill myself . . . I really mean it!"

After Rebecca rejoined the other children, I asked Mary what had happened with the child protective investigation of sex abuse. "Well," Mary replied, looking morose, "Rebecca denied anything happened when CPS staff talked to her in the hospital. She told them her family was 'beautiful' and that she had no problems at home. Her sisters said everything was 'wonderful' at home and child protective staff said that Mr. Burns did not fit the profile of a sex abuse perpetrator. They found him very pleasant, concerned about his children, and willing to take part in family counseling if Rebecca was placed in another treatment facility closer to his home. If he was an abuser, they said he had put on the best cover-up that they had ever seen."

"But what about her statements since she came here?" I asked.

"She's told me five or six times about her father coming into her room at night and demanding sex. Her story is basically the same. She talks about oral sex and intercourse . . . that he'd belt her if she complained. Every day, she seems to add a little more. Now, she's talking about him forcing her to have sex with her mother's boyfriend who's been living with them for about a year. She's said the same things to other staff here, too, but when her child protective worker comes, she clams up."

"What's the plan, right now?" I asked.

"Her father placed her in the custody of the county Department of Social Services. The plan is to find a residential treatment center where she could get therapy. You know she was diagnosed as having 'childhood schizophrenia' when she was in the state hospital. And she still sometimes starts talking about monsters with horns coming after her when she gets upset."

"And after she's in the next facility?"

"Back to her father, I guess. She said she'll kill herself if they make her go back. I'm really worried she'd do it too."

I asked for a meeting with her child protective worker. I saw Rebecca as a terrified girl who desperately needed to be validated and who was literally scared to death about being sent back to her father now that she had disclosed sex abuse again. Sending her to a residential treatment center without any validation by her parents or child protective services would just confirm that she was the problem, that she was crazy, and that she needed to change. As soon as she heard she would have to go home, Rebecca would lose the little balance she

had and would have to go back to her nightmares of monsters telling
her to kill herself.

This was a girl who had disclosed sex abuse three times, beginning
at age 4. Rebecca watched her older sister try to talk about what happened and learned that nothing stopped the abuse. Girls were sent
away temporarily but the sex and threats went on. She really had no
one she could count on to protect her. It was no wonder she was
clinging to staff like a 2-year-old.

Mary agreed and I felt sure that we could get help from Rhonda,
the child protective worker assigned to investigate this case. She was
coming to see Rebecca in a few minutes, as it turned out. Mary and I
met with her and outlined what Rebecca had disclosed and our assessments that this was a case of ongoing, chronic sex abuse, a girl
who had grown up traumatized with no one she could count on to
protect and care for her.

Rhonda disagreed. "Don't you think her schizophrenia has something to do with it?" she questioned. I was taken aback. Rebecca's
behaviors from age 4 (soiling, talking in detail about oral sex), her
sisters' behaviors, her consistent and detailed statements to our staff
about what her father did to her at night, her night terrors, and her
telling us that her father had threatened to belt or kill her if she talked
all fit together as typical signs of sex abuse and neglect.

"Listen, I'd like to believe her, really I would, but she never told me
any of this. Even if she told you about sex abuse, Rebecca would
never be believed in court. She giggles. She cries at the drop of a hat.
She runs up and hugs people like me that she hardly knows. The
girl's just not credible. I ran this by our lawyer. He said we didn't
have enough to go to court. Mr. Burns won't even talk to us without
his lawyer present and he'd shoot down what we have. The county
won't go to court on sex abuse if we're going to lose."

Mary and I went over the details of the case again and I tried to
understand what was holding Rhonda and her supervisor back from
pursuing this as a case of sex abuse. Rhonda remained focused on the
diagnosis of schizophrenia and she had a hard time with Rebecca's
clinging and demanding behavior. Rhonda saw Rebecca as a girl who
needed months or years of individual therapy in a professionally supervised institution.

I tried to convince Rhonda to at least file a petition citing Rebecca's
parents' failure to protect and appropriately supervise her. Rhonda
shared with us that a gynecological exam had revealed vaginal scarring. Surely that plus Rebecca's statements would be enough for a

petition of neglect. Rebecca needed to hear that someone with some power believed her fears and that she and her sisters could be safe.

"We don't know what caused the scarring," Rhonda replied. "She supposedly was inserting objects from age 4. How do you know Mr. Burns did it? I'm sure something was happening at home and she wasn't safe before. But he took her to the psychiatric hospital. He's willing to cooperate with treatment for Rebecca at an institution. That's not neglect. We even took Rebecca to a specialist on sex abuse investigations last week. Rebecca didn't give her enough information to validate a sex abuse charge against Mr. Burns. She giggled, went wild when she was shown pictures of naked kids, and said 'I don't know' when she was asked about what happened before and what happened after. It just won't hold up. There's nothing we can do. I'm sorry. We've got to listen to our attorney!"

Rhonda said she couldn't do any more and was about to go. I asked her to at least share with Rebecca that she knew Rebecca had not been safe at home even if she didn't know what had happened and to tell Rebecca that she would work to keep her safe. Rebecca knew Rhonda had come to see us and I thought she'd be frantic by now, wondering what was happening. Rhonda agreed to talk with Rebecca, who just about ran in the room when she was called.

Rebecca gave Rhonda a spontaneous hug and showed her silly smile. "Can I see my sisters?" she asked. Rhonda gently but firmly unlocked Rebecca's hands from her back and asked her to sit down.

"How do you like it here?" Rhonda asked.

"It's okay. Can I see my sisters? I really want to see them. Please. Please. Please. Can't I?" Rebecca pleaded almost falling off her chair as she leaned toward Rhonda. She was becoming more excited as she went on.

"I'll look into it. We might be able to work it out." Rhonda replied.

I asked Rhonda to share with Rebecca what she was doing with the investigation and what she thought about what Rebecca had said. "I don't think you were safe in your father's home before." Rhonda said looking at Rebecca. "I'm not sure what was going on. I want you to stay here and then we'll find another program where you can stay for now."

"But do I have to go home?" Rebecca begged, tears forming in her eyes.

"Not for now," Rhonda replied.

Rebecca looked down at her toes and started swinging her legs. I asked Rhonda to be as clear as she could about what she saw as unsafe in Rebecca's home. Rhonda repeated that she knew Rebecca had not been safe. "That's all I can say."

We discussed the interviews, etc. that were planned to happen next and asked for a meeting with Rhonda and her supervisor again the next week so that we could all continue to work together and show Rebecca what was happening. The meeting ended.

Rebecca gave Rhonda another long hug and ran out to join the other kids, a silly smile back on her face. I stood up to say "goodbye," but inside I suddenly felt sick in my stomach. This was not supposed to be how it worked. Placing Rebecca in a fourth treatment facility would certainly push her deeper into her fantasies as her only refuge. She needed to receive some validation of the terror and abuse she had experienced and CPS was the only agency involved that had the legal power to show Rebecca she would not have to return to sex abuse and fears of being killed.

The system of services set up to help children like Rebecca was breaking down. Winning in court seemed to be the bottom line rather than helping children and parents. CPS became stymied by the threat of lawsuits. Family crises were to be played out in an adversarial process with great risks for everyone. Mr. Burns could go to jail if sufficient evidence was obtained. Sex abuse was a felony offense. Conversely, Rebecca's condition would worsen if she was not believed by child protective services or the judge.

Even the process of a formal sex abuse evaluation seemed cruel and uncaring. A fragile girl had been transported to her hometown very close to where her father lived in order to take her to the offices of the local sex abuse specialist. Rebecca had felt safe enough to disclose in our facility which was some distance from her home and after getting to know our staff over several weeks. However, her statements to us were not sufficient. She had to go to a stranger's offices and meet privately with another person to tell again what had happened.

Most counties in NY state have designated one or two specialists as "validaters" who are asked to conduct assessments of sex abuse and report whether a case would hold up in court. Validation is equated with being able to convince a judge to believe the charges and to refute typical challenges that the charges were lies by the children or that the children were led to make up stories by professionals. These designated specialists are required to conduct interviews with a second person watching in order to verify that the specialist didn't use any prompts or language that could lead a child to make false allegations.

While the specialist who saw Rebecca told us informally that she believed Rebecca had been sexually abused, she couldn't substantiate any accusations against Mr. Burns from the little Rebecca had shared in her office. We needed to recognize the reality that contributed to Rhonda's message. She had to be able to win in court in order to maintain a placement based on abuse or neglect and Rebecca was a poor witness.

The investigative process worked to protect a parent's rights against false charges. False accusations have occurred most often in custody disputes where a young child's memory could be swayed by one parent to bolster an attack on the other parent or in cases where a youth had a significant motive for getting a parent in trouble. The procedures and time involved in lengthy investigations are an ordeal for the children and parents involved. Children can end up losing one or both parents and have their worst nightmares come true. Children looking for help for themselves and their families can end up ostracized by their parents, siblings, and relatives, and labeled as liars, troublemakers, crazy, or simply evil.

Children like Rebecca who act like much younger children when stressed and can't express themselves well in words often end up hearing that they are not believed. Rebecca needed to provide a consistent story of what happened before, during, and after the alleged abuse occurred. Without detailed descriptions, her case would be difficult to substantiate. Rebecca had told us what happened in graphic terms, but not the "before and after."

This didn't surprise me. After all, this was a girl who woke everyone up each night with terrifying screams from her nightmares and who had to greet everyone she knew with clinging hugs and a silly smile. She was desperately searching for someone that she could count on and had not yet heard that CPS believed her. While staff at the crisis shelter supported her, she knew that we were all just temporary figures in her life.

The sex abuse Rebecca described was not the worst thing she experienced. Judging by the terror she showed every night, her fantasies of monsters, and her stories to me in our session, the "before and after" were the most traumatizing parts of Rebecca's experience. "Before and after" would have been when she was threatened with beatings and much worse and when she felt the terror of having no escape. These parts of her experience would be the last things she would remember and only if she was provided with enough security so that she could let down her guard and allow herself to again feel what happened.

It was a classic "catch 22" or "double bind." Rebecca needed to feel safe enough to share what happened. However, she had never known this kind of safety and ability to trust parents or parent-figures. She was being asked to make a clear, detailed, and accurate statement of everything that happened in order to be protected by child protective services or family court. The system worked well for those children who were secure enough and had the abilities to express themselves well enough to make a credible case for court. The children who were most in need of protection often got the least.

The words "for now" echoed in my ears. Rebecca was two years behind her age level in most skill areas, yet she was smart enough to know that being sent to a residential treatment center "for now" meant that she was not believed and that she would probably have to go home not believed or protected.

I felt another twinge in my stomach. Once Rebecca heard this message, she would very likely revert back to talking about monsters coming after her or worse. The hospital had described her as easily falling apart and becoming wild. Our facility was not locked and lacked the level of staffing of a hospital. We could lose her (or any other upset child) very quickly.

THE SEARCH FOR SOLUTIONS

Historically, when facts were obscure and the risks were high, the challenge of finding the best solution was given to kings, religious leaders, and judges. In the biblical world, King Solomon became legendary for his ability to break through deceit and get to the essence of a dilemma. I often remember the story about two women who had both recently given birth and shared a house. One infant had died and both women came before the King claiming the surviving infant son as their own. The truth was unclear. Someone was lying.

The first woman to speak claimed the other woman had accidentally rolled over on her own baby in the night and smothered him. The first woman went on to accuse the other woman of stealing her baby and replacing him with the dead baby during the night. The second woman cried out that this was a lie; the dead baby belonged to the first woman. Solomon ordered that the child be cut in half and divided equally between the two competing women. One woman cried out to stop the swordsman and pleaded that the child should be spared and given to the other woman. The woman's pain and concern for the child convinced Solomon that she was the true mother.

The legend is melodramatic by twentieth-century standards but remarkable for the King's focus on who cared the most for the child as the determinant for who was the real parent rather than on competing claims of legal ownership. The King's decision rested on the boy's needs for a parent who cared more for his needs than for her own.

When a court or social services agency requires an evaluation and recommendations on what would be in a child's best interest, the child is often at high risk of neglect, injury, or death. This risk typically reflects a lack of a nurturing relationship with a parent who children can count on to protect and guide them as they grow up. These are children, parents, and often grandparents who typically lack the basic sense of security and predictability that most Americans take for granted. Just starting a family tradition of having breakfast or dinner together can be a major change. And living without the ever-present worry about Dad or Mom getting drunk or hitting someone may seem like an impossible dream.

Our challenge in evaluations and therapy is to involve lawyers, judges, child protective workers, therapists, physicians, and community leaders to work together with nuclear and extended family members to face dilemmas and to mobilize a network of people who can spur and maintain needed changes. We need to validate that we have heard family members' frustrations, anger, needs, and fears. We look for and support positive moves toward making things better and work to help family members break out of the cycles of crises and emptiness that have put everyone at risk. This means touching their pain without becoming overwhelmed, frozen, or traumatized ourselves. We have to maintain our focus on children's needs for nurturing, bonded relationships with parents who will raise them and protect them now and into the future.

Children and parents involved with family court, CPS, mental health clinics, or probation departments are often agitated, moving from crisis to crisis. Judges are often appointed or elected with little background or training on what children need. County lawyers commonly begin working with little background in child welfare law and feel pressured to make whatever deal they can out of court. Recommendations from child protective and probation workers often seem to get lost and child and family services staff often leave family court hearings feeling slighted and discounted. The turnover in the field is enormous. Cases pile up; too few services are provided too late.

We feel pulled in to rescue, to find some common ground, to heal. We walk in full of energy, heads held high, eyes clear, with a desire to help. Two hours later, we may leave a session feeling muddled, sullen, and jumpy, shoulders sagging under the strain of knowing that the risks are high yet so much remains unclear.

Stress has been defined as high-risk and low-control—the essence of work in child and family services. Unlike health services, we can't order a specific procedure to be administered in a controlled setting, like a dose of medicine or surgical removal of a cancerous tumor. Most parents of children in crisis have already received and rejected advice and directives. Change is painful and risky.

At the same time, crises can be addictive for everyone involved. We feel a "rush" of adrenalin and later a downside of exhaustion. Service providers like myself quickly become caught up in the crises they have sought to prevent and can become just as addicted to crises as their clients. Practitioners become overwhelmed with the responsibility inherent in their jobs. We wake up in the middle of the night wondering if we neglected to ask the right questions, made the right decision about the safety of a child, or arranged for the right services. When morning comes, we feel the exhaustion from too much strain and feel a need for a vacation, to get away from the job. We can become irritable, demanding, and even abusive. In professional circles, this is recognized as "secondary posttraumatic stress disorder." Most of us call it "burnout."

Yet, something keeps many of us going day after day, year after year. Perhaps it is the glimmer of hope in a child's eye, the pleas of a young child like Rebecca for help for herself and her sisters, the plaintive cry of a young parent wishing to reunite with her* child, the signs of strength we learn to discern in the midst of a crisis. Our challenge is to understand a family's dilemmas, strengths, and traumas and to mobilize efforts by family members and service providers to create long-term solutions for a child's terror and a family's strife.

I get reenergized when I can talk with a family about painful issues and help them to do more than just deny that anything is wrong. I can see the impact of our work when children settle down after we discuss in front of everyone involved the fears, caring, and pain that they never dared to say themselves.

---

*Rather than refer to his/her throughout this book, I will alternate from chapter to chapter between references to boys and girls.

Seeing or hearing about clients who have done well reaffirms our mission and work. When I am feeling frustrated, I remember some of our success stories: the workaholic and disengaged woman who won back the trust of her sexually abused children, another mother who made the choice to free her children for adoption so they could get what she never had and knew she could not give, the girl who was sexually abused and diagnosed with attention-deficit disorder who had been soiling, running away, and defying everyone but settled into her adoptive family and was able to move out of a small, highly supervised special education class into a mainstream classroom.

The children and adults we work with still have a long way to go. We don't have miraculous recoveries in this work. Yet, small gains are enormous for these families and make the difference between perpetuating histories of trauma and giving the next generation a chance at a better life. We have the opportunity to mobilize family members and practitioners to create turning points in the lives of children and parents who have almost given up hope.

This is painful and difficult work but it is needed to break cycles of abandonment, neglect, and violence. Real life dilemmas can be addressed in therapy for these families. Evaluations and assessments can help us to understand what has led a family to today's tragedy and what is needed to help them change and build on their own strengths.

FORMING A PLAN

It was time to pull our little team together and plan the next step to help Rebecca and her family. I knew I lacked the wisdom or power of Solomon but we could still help make Rebecca's placement in our facility a turning point for the better. This was a crisis shelter and crisis by definition meant both risk and opportunity. Our challenge was to find the opportunity.

A week after the sessions described above, we met again. This time, Rhonda's supervisor joined our group at my request. We were still lacking Rebecca's court-appointed legal guardian, but we had spoken to her on the phone. We also had Rebecca's mental health case manager with us. Mary and I again outlined our concerns and how Rebecca's disclosures from age 4, the vaginal scarring, the night terrors, and her need to cling to people all supported her consistent and repeated descriptions of sex abuse to our staff. Rhonda's supervisor said she didn't know whether she could believe Rebecca and Rhonda again asked, "Couldn't this all just be from the schizophrenia?"

I was supported by Rebecca's mental health case manager in arguing that Rebecca's fantasies and nightmares about monsters with horns at the foot of her bed were the result of traumas, lack of support, and terror. Even if she had a neurologically based mental illness, this would not lead her to consistently show and talk about fears of her father. Everything she was showing us appeared directly related to her described experiences of terror in her home. She needed CPS support to have any chance.

I thought we had won the support Rebecca needed but Rhonda's supervisor ended the meeting echoing Rhonda's statements a week before: "I just don't know. Our lawyer says it's still not enough to win in court. We can't even prove lack of supervision."

It would be easy to give up at times like this, to say, "We did our best," go on to the next case, or change jobs. I don't know anyone who can handle watching young children like Rebecca move from bad to worse without wanting to get away. Perhaps that would be better for our own mental health, but most of us in this field don't like to give up.

Most of the adolescents and young adults I have seen in long-term psychiatric facilities have reports of physical and sexual abuse at young ages that were never proven. I could imagine Rebecca a few years from now still in an institution but totally locked into her fantasies and without hope of making things better for herself or her sisters. When the hope is gone, little change can occur. Children may grow physically into adult bodies but remain thinking and acting like terrified, angry, and abandoned children inside.

Rebecca still clung to a fragile thread of hope. You could see it in the way her eyes brightened if you went up and said "hello" to her. Despite the slight tremor in her smile, which told me that she was still feeling the terror and loneliness she had deep inside, Rebecca knew that Mary, the child care staff, and I had heard her terror, believed her, and wanted to help her.

Rebecca's demands to be hugged by everyone she knew turned off many people but also reflected her search for someone to be there for her. I didn't accept the silly smile and asked her for an age-appropriate hand slap instead of a hug. She gave me a shocked look at first but responded in a much more age-appropriate manner when I saw her the next time. Rebecca desperately needed a parent to hold her but she was strong enough to learn other ways to act with adults.

Rebecca's desire for connections to staff and her wish for a new family was most likely a tribute to her mother or father. Someone had given her enough love and caring as a young child that she wanted to attach herself to other parent-figures. A child who didn't get this basic caring would not be looking for affection and closeness. Rebecca still had a chance.

I asked Rhonda's supervisor what her gut feeling was. "I just can't believe her," she replied. "And we have nothing proving her behavior is tied in with anything that happened in her home."

I told Rhonda's supervisor that my psychological evaluation, an evaluation by a psychiatrist from our facility, and Mary's reports would be sent to her, the law guardian, and the judge who would preside over the case. I wanted Rhonda and her supervisor to know that I understood the reality of the pressures for validation that they faced and their need to have sufficient evidence of neglect and abuse. In the past, Rebecca had not shown the ability to be a good witness.

At the same time, I stressed how everything Rebecca had shown us, from her first disclosures as a young child to her current nightmares, all fit together to support her statements about being abused. Her stories and terror all appeared directly related to her experiences in her home. Rebecca's mental health case manager supported our assessments and believed that our reports would probably be accepted by the judge.

"We'll look them over," replied Rhonda's supervisor, and the meeting ended.

Two days later, I received a call from Mary. "Rhonda's supervisor called. They're going to file a petition in court asking for placement based on sex abuse. She said they thought about it and were moved by what you said and your report." Rebecca's law guardian had also received our reports, agreed to come out and see Rebecca, and said she'd also support a petition.

Rebecca got another chance for herself, her sisters, and even her parents. She later disclosed more details about the sex abuse and her gynecologist offered to testify that the vaginal scarring was the direct result of sexual intercourse. With the sex abuse out in the open, Rebecca's mother and father would be asked to work in counseling on what happened, to admit that sexual and physical abuse had occurred, to participate in an appropriate treatment program, and to work on providing a safe home for their children.

Most of all, Rebecca heard that she was believed and was not just considered crazy or bad. She would not have to live every day wondering if she would be sent back to the life she knew before and had so desperately sought to escape. She would have the opportunity of moving into a foster or adoptive family if her parents could not (or would not) provide the home she needed. Rebecca's fragile thread of hope grew a little stronger. The system had not let her down.

THE QUEST FOR HOPE

I have worked with children, adolescents, and their families for two decades. Most of my work has been with families of youths placed (or about to be placed) into foster families, small group care facilities, or institutions because they were at high risk of hurting themselves or others or being seriously hurt themselves. I am introduced as "Doctor Kagan." The "Doctor" title reflects the limited but real power that my assessments and recommendations can have on family court decisions and on how services are provided to family members.

In my view, "doctor" means *teacher* from the ancient Greek rather than the more popular image of a physician dispensing medications or carrying out surgical procedures. Teachers must engage their students in a joint effort to learn and make things better. For me, doctors never stop learning and sharing what they have learned. This view shapes my work as a psychologist. I look for strengths and ways to engage healthy behaviors rather than focusing on problems and pathologies.

I invite you to join me on a journey into a world that is filled with strife and to help in the search for hope. This book is part of a quest to understand and to help children and parents for whom crises and violence have become a way of life that impacts everyone around them. This is not a systematic study with surveys, charts, trend analyses, or statistics. It is, rather, a close-up look at what is really happening to children, parents, and practitioners dealing with crises.

My colleagues and I strive to help parents who grew up with no one they could rely on for ongoing nurture, safety, and caring. We help the next generation avoid the terrors of abandonment and annihilation experienced by their parents and grandparents. Like Solomon, we look for parents who care enough to meet a child's needs. This means working with parents to achieve their goals while meeting their children's need for safety and attachment to parents they can count on to nurture, protect, and care for them now and into adulthood.

Every time I work with a child and family in crisis, I learn a little bit more about how we can all become mired in crises, what helps people survive, how we can help children and parents tap into their strengths and build new resources, and how cycles of despair and violence can be replaced with acts of courage.

Rebecca was not miraculously cured by our interventions. She did, however, leave the crisis residence with the hope that she would get a family in which she could someday live without terror. Eighteen months later, I testified at a court hearing in which a family court judge ruled that her parents had failed to protect her from sexual abuse and that she had been neglected in her parents' care. The judge would not rule, however, on who had sexually abused her.

Rebecca's parents refused to see her or allow her to see her sisters who remained at home denying any sexual abuse. This left Rebecca feeling torn, missing her sisters, worrying about their safety, and growing angrier at her parents. Nevertheless, Rebecca was supported and believed by her foster family, her county social services workers, and her law guardian, as well as by the agency staff who continued to work with her. After months of hospitals and group care, she was able to live without medications in a foster family and attend public school.

Meanwhile, foster care staff and I continued to urge Rebecca's county worker, law guardian, and the judge to rule on permanency issues. We worked along with her foster parents to help Rebecca develop her confidence, age-appropriate social skills, and to understand her experience. Two and a half years after her placement in our crisis residence, the county filed an abandonment petition citing the failure of Rebecca's parents to meet with any workers, to participate in any counseling program, or to make any effort to contact or help Rebecca. By the end of that school year, the girl who had been called schizophrenic had earned a position on the honor roll of her school. That summer, her parents surrendered their parental rights, freeing Rebecca to find an adoptive family.

This is a book about what it's like to work in child and family services day by day: the successes, the pain, and the frustrations. It's about how professionals work together for better and for worse, the forces that impact our work, and what keeps us going in jobs filled with high risk and little control. I would like to share what I have learned through a series of stories about trauma and change (Parts One and Three), a discussion of principles and strategies that guide my work (Part Two), and a look at what can make the system work better for children, families, practitioners, and communities (Part Four).

We may lack the wisdom and power of Solomon but we can build on the hope that lingers in the most crisis-addicted families and engage children, parents, extended family members, community leaders, and service providers in the quest for healing and a better future.

chapter 2

Monsters don't like cameras.

*Eleven-year-old girl in a foster home who
was sexually abused by her father*

no one heard

I KNEW IT WAS GOING TO BE A TOUGH MORNING WHEN I SAW THE WORN, tense look on my colleague's face. "I almost called you . . . Have to look at the photos . . ." Robbie, a 3-year-old boy, had been brought to the emergency room with reddish brown welts on his face and shoulders. Some were dark and of recent origin while others appeared faded, suggesting that they were several days old. The boy's testicles were black and blue with splotches of dried blood and swollen to twice their normal size. The photographs were grotesque, with close-up shots of the boy's genitals. Emergency room physicians reported that they were damaged by blows inflicted with a blunt object. The child looked strangely numb, peering out from the photograph like a frozen body drained of all feeling.

Looking at photographs is part of a day's work at CPS, a way of sharing horrible images with staff whose daily lives are filled with reports of neglect and cruelty. The threshold for shock rises with every month we work. It's easy to become calloused to acts that would horrify most people. Reports and photos of a boy with multiple cigarette burns or a girl covered with bruises are studied and discussed with what might appear to an observer to be an insensitive, even noncaring attitude considering the pain these children must have endured.

"Just another day on the job." But you can see the underlying tension that builds with each day's series of tragedies. Men and women from CPS return home to their own families carrying grim memories of the day and often the on-call beeper, which inevitably links them with the crises of the night.

Greetings move from friendly interchanges to jokes with barbed edges about oneself or taunts to colleagues: "I think we'd better have Dr. Kagan evaluate you today, Bob." Frustrations with judges, lawyers, and other social services workers are vented more and more as each day and each week goes on. The strain of working day by day with children at risk shows up in frowns, anxious looks, and impatience. And, every few months new shockwaves seem to ripple through the building as the worst cases of molested, cut, or mortally battered children shatter the artificial sense of calm and order.

I have never seen a more tense work environment in any medical or human service organization than exists in the intake unit where new cases of reported abuse and neglect come into CPS. Before smoking was curtailed, you could smell and breathe the level of tension from department to department. The intake unit was the smokiest. This staff has the job of responding to hotline calls and making quick assessments of whether a child was in imminent danger. They have the power to temporarily remove a child when necessary. Hotline calls require careful and timely visits with families and children. Few parents welcome a visit from a CPS worker and staff often encounter the rage of parents upset over allegations of neglect or abuse.

These were the people with whom I worked one morning a week as a consulting psychologist. A clinical social worker, a CPS staff member, and I met with parents and children who did not ask for our services and most often would have preferred we stay away. We usually went to a family's home where we talked with family members, tried to find out what was working well, and shared our concerns about risks for children and parents. I would then write a formal report for use by CPS, family court, and other service providers. In sessions and reports, we shared what we learned and what we thought needed to happen.

Each week we made interventions into the lives of people living on the edge of crises. I have often met them again months or years later through my involvement with other family service programs. Chil-

dren will come up to me in a waiting room with shy smiles or spontaneous hugs. "I remember you. You came to our house . . ." Parents
will usually smile as I say "Hello." I look into their faces to see how
they remember me: someone who cared, someone who helped, or just
another person from social services that they battled with in the past.
I may not remember their names, but the images, words, and feelings
connected with each family remain.

Despite several years of this work, it was hard for me to look at the
photographs of Robbie. His face alone was appalling. I turned
abruptly to Susan, the child's CPS worker, to find out what she knew.
"I met the Mom in the hospital two weeks ago. She was screaming
and carrying on with the nurses. She swore that no one was going to
take her child. She kept on screaming. All the while, Robbie just lay
there looking at her with this numb look on his face. She hardly
looked at the boy . . . just kept on screaming. I thought he looked
scared, like he was in shock or something. So I put my arm around
him, stroked his head, and asked her to calm down, take a walk if she
needed to. She left the room and in a few minutes, Robbie fell asleep.
Then, she comes back into the room with an even bigger tirade,
swearing she'd sue me, the county, the doctors. I've got to tell you,
she gave me a real bad feeling."

The boy had been placed on an emergency basis in a foster family
after an overnight hospital stay. Contact with his mother had been
suspended because of the severity of his injuries. The judge didn't
want to traumatize the boy any further and told Susan not to allow
any visits to take place between the mother and her son until the
perpetrator had been identified. Yet, if Robbie had been attached to
his mother, separation for long periods of time would be experienced
like a death. I worried that this 3-year-old boy was being unneces-
sarily traumatized by the judge's order.

Everyone at CPS understood the risks behind these questions.
"This reminds me of the Hopkins case," Sharon, a clinical social
worker, interjected. I nodded. All of us remembered the murder of a
child only a year earlier, a child of the same age who had been treated
just a few weeks before his death for less severe injuries to his genitals. Hospital staff had accepted the parent's explanation that the injuries were accidental and had not reported the incident to the state's
child abuse hotline. I had been involved in work with that child's
family after his death. Thinking about him brought back a shiver as I
remembered the photographs of his battered corpse. We had become
involved with that family to assess the risk for the remaining children

and to develop a plan for helping the family. Now, we were looking at a battered boy from another family who could end up the same way.

Only ten minutes into the day's work and I felt an urge to leave and a nagging question on my mind: "What was I doing here?" I found myself studying the photograph of the mute boy and imagined him looking at the stranger who was taking his picture that day in the emergency room of a local hospital. Looking at his face reminded me of the force that keeps us in this work and the impact we can have helping children like Robbie gain a chance for a better life.

Crisis interventions can and do lead to real changes in people's lives. Psychological assessments have been described as detective work—uncovering the mysterious forces that move people to behave as they do and putting together the pieces of a puzzle that can help explain how people act. Most of all, we look for positive forces and a way to empower and mobilize people to make their lives better. This family, as with so many others we see at CPS, pulled practitioners like myself to give them everything we had. Decisions about treatment and services could have life or death results.

"Listen," Susan told us, "the judge ordered an evaluation to determine whether any visits should occur with the child's mother and her boyfriend. You're also supposed to write up recommendations for the judge about what needs to happen to keep him safe. The mom and her boyfriend and the boy will be here any minute."

What happened to this child? Was this an early point in an abusive cycle that could lead to more devastating abuse and death? Or, as the mother and boyfriend complained, was this just another accident with an accident-prone boy for whom they had appropriately sought medical treatment?

The police investigation was inconclusive and no charges had been filed thus far. Susan and police detectives had interviewed the mother, her live-in boyfriend, and the child. "They deny anything to do with hurting Robbie." Susan said. "They said he fell on the stairs a few days before and slipped into the toilet the day before his testicles were found swollen. His mom brought him to the emergency room. We haven't been able to get the boy to say anything."

Looking at the photographs again, I wished I could turn to someone for the wisdom I surely lacked—for a sure way to break through the deceit, to find out who had hurt the boy staring mutely out of the pictures, and like Solomon to discover who cared enough for this boy to protect him. Instead, I looked around the office and felt the eyes of

Sharon, Susan, and two other child protective workers looking at me. They knew the risks; they felt the pain that this child did not show. Their faces were drawn and strained, reflecting a sense of urgency and the reality that once again a child was in danger, a child whose safekeeping and, in many ways, whose future had become their responsibility.

Someone was lying. CPS staff had the job of protecting this child. The likelihood that the perpetrator (or perpetrators) would admit to battering the boy was almost nil given that any admission to CPS staff or consultants could lead to criminal prosecution, conviction, and a prison sentence. We thus faced the usual dilemma in child protective services: tremendous risks, little certainty about what happened before and what could happen in the future, the parents' rights under the law to maintain custody, and every child's need for a safe, nurturing, and consistent home with parents they can count on as they grow up.

Centuries after Solomon, we lacked instruments and protocols to find the truth with certainty. Our interview strategies and psychological tests could enrich the judge's perspective on how the individuals in this family functioned, but there was little chance that we would come out of a family or individual evaluation with indisputable findings about who hurt the boy.

"We can't get psychological assessments through the county mental health department for four months," the CPS unit supervisor told me. "The judge was furious at this mom. He wants to cut off visits until someone confesses." Susan, the family's CPS worker, believed that the mother had hit the boy but lacked proof. "See if you can find out who did it," she told us.

I needed to reassert the limits of what we could do and to remain focused on our contract with CPS, which did not include forensic assessments for criminal court. And, if I were to plan a forensic assessment, I would set up a series of sessions beginning with individual evaluations of the boy, his mother, and her boyfriend before seeing all of them together. The crisis of this boy and the pain he could not express demanded much more attention than we were able to provide within the few hours we had to work with CPS that week.

The primary objective in our contract with CPS was to engage family members in the difficult work needed to provide a safe home for a child at risk. We assessed how family members interacted with each other and the risk this posed for children like Robbie. We looked at how a child or parent acted within the context of their family, including aunts, uncles, grandparents, their ethnic group, and community. We considered with family members and CPS staff what could be done to best help a family. I worked within a program dedicated to strengthening families to make necessary changes, face difficult decisions, and, whenever possible, keep children in their families and out of foster homes, residential treatment centers, and psychiatric hospitals.

LOSING FOCUS

I knew that I needed to stick to our assigned role. Yet looking around the room at my colleagues, I was struck by the urgency of the case, the judge's demand for a report in five days for the next scheduled court hearing, and requests from CPS staff to determine who was the perpetrator. I felt a pull to do much more than our usual family assessment.

Why couldn't I evoke the wisdom of Solomon? Why couldn't we end this boy's nightmare or at least find out what had really happened, as Susan asked? This, too, is typical of work in CPS: the pull to rescue and the urge to find a perpetrator. Red flags went up in my head warning of impending disaster.

It's easy to become overwhelmed with cases like these where the risks are severe and the facts are unknown or disputed. Parents typically expect an adversarial process and will do their best to present a positive image especially if criminal prosecution is possible. Children hear a powerful message to keep quiet for the good of the family.

For a young child like Robbie, nothing is more powerful than the threat of being cut off or losing his parents. For an infant, such a cut-off means death. "Keep your mouth shut!" has been a longstanding mandate in many families and for a young child there often is no choice. Loyalty is equated with belonging. Telling what's really going on can mean banishment.

CPS staff and other service providers take on the responsibility for managing the risks and crises that family members cannot talk about. Even after 18 years of working in child and family services, I find myself pulled to take on unreasonable responsibilities. We see and feel the pain of distraught parents who feel unfairly treated and the terror of children who cannot express what they most fear.

I was losing sight of my primary objective for this session: to engage Robbie's mother, any supportive family members, and helping professionals to work together on providing the safety, caring, and bonded relationship this boy needed as he grew up. This is painful work. We all wish we had some elixir or some magic words that would heal the wounds we see and make everything better in a few days, the way an antibiotic can cure pneumonia: "Take 10 sessions of family therapy and you should be feeling a lot better."

Sharon and I agreed to meet the mother, the child, the boyfriend, and the foster parent, make recommendations to the court and CPS about visits and further evaluations, and give feedback to the family that day or in a subsequent session. Sharon reminded me that we only had to address the visitation question but both of us knew that assessments can have a much greater impact. Our session was just the beginning of a long process of work with this family. Our challenge was to start this work in the best possible direction.

LOOKING FOR ATTACHMENT

I wanted to see what attachment this boy had to his mother, her boyfriend, and any other family members. The foster mother told Susan that Robbie had not asked about his mother, her boyfriend, or anyone else since placement. The numb look on his face raised troubling questions about his level of trust. He not only couldn't talk about what happened but had also learned that he couldn't even show feelings of distress.

Children learn not to talk or even to feel when they live with parents who respond harshly or in a frightening way when their child gets hurt. Children learn to separate themselves from what happens to their bodies. They block out feelings, memories, thoughts, and even their own actions. Children (and adults) living with repeated traumas begin to operate in what has been called an "as if" manner where little is real and you do whatever you have to just to get by. This is the product of living without the basic validation of one's feelings and experiences that every child needs in order to move beyond an entirely self-focused orientation.

Robbie, like every child, needed someone to say, "I hear you," and show that they believed him and would always be there when he needed them. The quest for a safe home for Robbie reflected the fact that he needed to feel attached to a parent who validated his feelings so that he in turn could grow up, manage himself competently with others, and someday provide the parenting his own children would need.

WORKING IN THE SYSTEM

"Assessments need to take place very quickly so that family work and visits can begin," I said to my colleagues. "Waiting months will harm Robbie even more than the beating." This was my way of venting frustration and didn't contribute anything new for anyone. I knew we didn't have the time to do what was being asked of us and at the same time I felt we had no choice but to go ahead. I ignored another red flag going up and walked with Sharon and Susan to meet the family.

Our family session took place two weeks after Robbie was placed into a foster home. The system of child and family services in which we operated was inadequate to carefully assess each parent and child and provide needed services in a short period of time. A 3-year-old child who was bonded to his mother would almost certainly experience the secondary traumatization of prolonged separation. This was a disservice to everyone involved but it was the best the county's hard-pressed child protective system could provide.

Welcoming families at many county office buildings is a paradox in itself; the offices are neither a warm inviting atmosphere for parents and children in turmoil nor a comfortable and safe place for staff. We usually hold our sessions in a room intended for staff meetings or between dividers in a large impersonal conference area where privacy is impossible. The furniture is worn and discolored. Toys for children are old, missing parts, and sometimes broken.

THREATS AND VIOLENCE

Families entering the reception area pass by a security guard sitting in the hall, a reminder to all of us of the risks involved in working with people who have been violent. Five social services workers were killed in my state in the preceding two years. Most of these fatalities took place in public assistance offices. But CPS and foster care workers have often been threatened by angry parents and relatives when a child was removed from a family or parents were mandated to participate in services (for example, alcohol or drug treatment programs).

Most of us have experienced personal threats. One of my first involved a man who I had to report to CPS when his 5-year-old daughter graphically demonstrated the "wedding night game" she played at home. First, she rubbed a stuffed snake and other animals together with a rocking motion. Then she used family puppets and dolls to demonstrate sexual intercourse between male and female figures. I stopped the session when she tried to act out the "wedding night game" with me. Before I had met this girl, her father ranted about sexual perverts being everywhere. That was enough to make me feel anxious and to question the safety of his daughter. A child hearing that kind of talk every day would have to be terrified, a form of emotional abuse in itself.

When this father found out that a hotline report had been made, he angrily told his social worker that he was going to kill me. He was enraged with the subsequent child protective investigation and removal of his daughter from his home. I told my colleagues (and myself) that the man was frenetic and certainly paranoid but not likely to carry out his threats. Yet I couldn't help but worry when a local police officer and service providers who had worked with this man for several years told me they believed he was dangerous, especially when upset and threatened with a sex abuse conviction. Most sex abusers can become violent (Madanes, 1995a). Were my own impressions of the man wrong? What made the situation especially difficult was that I could not talk to him about the hotline report until a sex abuse investigation by CPS was completed.

The protocol for sex abuse reports in our area precluded telling suspected perpetrators of any report or talking to them about suspected sex abuse until the investigation was completed. In this case, that meant waiting seven weeks before I could even ask to meet with him—Weeks in which I and other staff could not work with this father and deal directly with his and our concerns, weeks in which I could only keep reminding myself that I did not think the man was dangerous and in any case it would be impossible to do much about it anyway. Still, I found myself thinking about him and quickly looking around when I walked outdoors in the dark or stepped in front of an open window at night. I could only wait out the time and allow him to vent his anger with others. While this man was not a real threat to me, I learned how easy it was for fear to spread. My colleagues and I were feeling the terror with which this man and his children had always lived.

A more ominous threat for me involved a former marksman recently discharged from the Marines who repeatedly described how he would eliminate (and was trained to eliminate) anyone who got in his way or interfered with his girlfriend and daughter. He was accused of breaking his girlfriend's neck a few weeks after an interview we had with him concerning injuries suffered by his 2-year-old daughter.

Parents typically come into the offices of the county's child and family services department expecting to be accused and attacked. Practitioners come into this field seeking to help. We begin as rescuers and find it necessary to take stands for children at risk. Voicing the needs of children can threaten a parent's delicate balance and frighten parents that secrets may come out that could lead to the breakup of the family, a parent leaving, or a child going into placement. A parent may have to decide between maintaining a relationship with an occasionally violent paramour and the need to provide a safe home for a child. This is a terribly difficult question for a parent who grew up battered, homeless, and frequently desperate for his or her next meal. A boyfriend or girlfriend who showed a need for the parent and who has provided a home, some security, and hope for the future may look like the best chance for love the parent has ever had. Talking about what was really going on in his or her life could mean losing this person, their home, and ending up on the streets again. Telling the truth, in cases of physical or sexual abuse, could also lead to someone's going to prison.

MEETING THE FAMILY

Robbie did not run up to his mother in our waiting room but walked solemnly over to her with his head held down after she called to him. He looked small for his age and thin with blue eyes and light blonde hair. Robbie would have been seen by many as very cute except for his stern countenance.

Karen, his mother, also had light blonde hair, blue eyes, and an attractive face. She wore a low-cut shirt and jeans that were too tight for her weight. Karen picked Robbie up and embraced him. Robbie laid his head on her shoulder and put his arms rather stiffly around her, neither clinging to her nor pulling himself toward her.

"I would never hurt my son," Karen said as we began the session. "Everyone knows I love him more than anything in the world. I give him everything . . . Since he left, I haven't been able to sleep . . . I'm sick to my stomach all night . . . I'm going to be fired from my job."

Sharon and I explained our role in this session, the court order for a family assessment, and that we worked for a private agency and consulted with CPS. We appreciated her talking with us and wanted her to know her right, if she wished, to ask to meet with someone else.

Karen begged us to help her get her son back. "It's not fair! No one hears my side. No one cares!"

Karen noticed Robbie's sniffles, the small cut on his elbow, and how he avoided eye contact with her. "He's mad at me for leaving him in the hospital." She held him in her lap and rocked him, saying again that she would never hurt him. I felt an urge to help her. Despite being 32 years old and accused of maiming her son, Karen looked and sounded like a young girl in trouble; she seemed like a child with a child.

We asked if she would tell us what she thought happened leading up to Robbie's injuries. Karen held Robbie and begged him to say who caused his "boo-boo." "Was it Mommy? Was it Daddy (her 35-year-old boyfriend, Ralph)? Was it Dee-Dee (her 40-year-old girlfriend, Diane, who shared her apartment)?" Robbie responded with a scared, tense face but said nothing.

Karen urged Robbie to "tell Susan (their CPS worker) who hurt you." He climbed off his mother's lap, walked quickly over to Susan and hugged her for several minutes. Robbie had only met her once before this session. He said nothing but climbed onto Susan's lap.

"He got the bruises (on his face and shoulders) when he tripped and fell down our stairs," Karen continued. "That happened a week before he went to the hospital. Ralph was watching him while I did the groceries. . . . I don't know what happened to his privates . . . he must have slipped in the toilet . . . he's done that before."

Karen also remembered hearing Robbie scream the evening before she took him to the hospital. She had briefly left him in the care of her girlfriend, Diane, while she showered. "He was shrieking at the bottom of the stairs. I ran down the stairs, picked him up, and held him for a while. . . . He never liked staying alone with Diane. He always wanted to be with me . . . wherever I went. That was the only time he was alone with Diane that weekend."

I asked about how Robbie got along with Diane and Karen remembered finding a small burn mark on him several months earlier when she had left him in Diane's care. "He always tried to get away from her. Diane tried to make him sit at the kitchen table and he'd never want to stay. . . ." Still, Karen asked Diane to babysit whenever she went out and Ralph was not around.

Karen went on with her view of what happened that evening. "After a couple minutes, he stopped crying. He always cries when I leave him alone for a few minutes. . . . I didn't think anything of it. Then Diane said she had to walk over to the grocery. So I took Robbie and went with her . . . Diane would never go alone. I had to go with her. She was mad at me already that weekend because I wouldn't go shopping with her the day before."

Karen said she had been having a fight with Diane during the previous week. "She knew how to hurt me!" Karen said with an aching voice. "When we got back, about 9:00, I got him ready to go and spend the night at my mom's place . . . he'd always smile when I told him my mom was coming. Robbie always liked going with his grandma . . . then he'd cry when she dropped him back off at our apartment."

"I had him all set to go that evening when my half-sister, the bitch, called. She said my mom couldn't take Robbie that weekend, that my mom needed to get to bed early. My mom had things to do and wanted to rest up for a party the next day. My half-sister and brother-in-law were giving a party for their 1-year-old baby. . . . I was so mad! But, I couldn't do anything. I couldn't even get hold of my mom."

Karen remembered nothing else unusual that evening. She, Diane, Ralph, and Robbie remained at home for the rest of the night. "I found Robbie black and blue the next morning. I was changing his diaper. I didn't know what to do. It was horrible. I couldn't even look. What could I do? I called my doctor. I called my brother-in-law to get over there fast and give me a ride to the hospital. . . . Then they took him away. . . they made me leave him there . . . I couldn't stop crying . . . ." Tears formed in Karen's eyes. I got her some tissues and she sobbed quietly for a few minutes.

"How would you feel if they took your baby?" she complained. "I'd be furious," I answered.

Robbie roamed around the room and began to put his fingers into an electrical socket, eliciting a spontaneous "Don't touch!" from Sharon. Robbie collapsed on the floor and began to sob quietly. He began to shake like he was shivering and I could see sweat form on his forehead. Sharon picked him up while Robbie's mother sat looking at him sadly but never speaking or moving. Robbie calmed down quickly, responding to my colleague's soothing hug despite again being in a stranger's lap.

Several minutes later, Robbie was again playing by himself on the floor with some toys when Susan had to leave. He began to whimper like a small hurt animal as she got up from her chair. This time, Karen called to him and hugged and rocked him. After about 10 minutes he calmed down and climbed off her lap.

Karen described Robbie as the only person who ever truly meant anything to her. "He was always there for me. The only one. . . . He'd come over and give me a hug when I was crying." Karen explained that Robbie was a long-sought child she had conceived at age 29 with a previous boyfriend after a series of miscarriages. She had wanted a baby since she was 16 and had run away from her fourth placement in a residential treatment program.

"I wanted someone I could love, someone to love me. Robbie was all I ever had. He's always loved me. He's all I've got." Karen liked how he used to follow her around the apartment, never allowing her to go out of sight. She had left Robbie's biological father shortly after becoming pregnant and accused him of having a violent temper and using drugs. He had never been involved in Robbie's care and contributed no child support. "I don't know where he is. And I don't care! I don't want him in Robbie's or my life. He's an asshole."

Alone and Screaming

"No one ever cared about me," Karen complained again with a soft moan. "I still have dreams where I wake up screaming and sweating. It's always the same thing. I'm about to get hurt or something. I don't even know what's happening. I try to scream but no one ever hears me. Nobody."

"My mom just left me in foster homes. She put me in detention centers, girls' homes . . ." Karen went on, sounding angrier as she described growing up in institutions and foster homes beginning at age 9 when her mother first placed her, citing Karen's "ungovernability" and running away. "She never visited. They had to make her come for family meetings. Then she'd leave early. All we did was scream at each other."

Susan had told us that past records on the family supported Karen's stories of growing up with years of neglect along with physical and sexual abuse by a stepfather and an uncle. Agency staff had believed her reports of being beaten, molested, and raped but her mother had denied that anything had ever happened to Karen. Twenty years later, her mother still doubted whether Karen had been sexually abused. Nevertheless, Karen said, "We're getting along great since Robbie was born." She let her mother take Robbie for visits a couple times a week and most weekends. In Karen's eyes, her mother was giving Robbie the love that she never received.

I asked Karen to change Robbie's diaper during the session and

Robbie appeared, as before, solemn and mute, showing neither fear nor comfort. Ralph, Karen's boyfriend, was later invited to join our session. Robbie walked quickly over to Ralph when Ralph called him. Robbie gave Ralph a little hug and sat in his lap showing a small smile for the first time in the session. However, when Ralph was later asked to check Robbie's diaper, Robbie began to cry as Ralph laid him on the floor to take off his pants. Ralph said he had helped take care of Robbie many times, including diaper changing.

Could Karen have battered her son? She had good reason to feel deep-seated rage against males in general after years of physical and sexual abuse as a child and being raped as a young adult. While describing herself as never violent and unable to protect herself against abusive people, she had yelled, screamed, and verbally de-meaned Susan almost every day since Robbie was placed. Her expla-nation of how Robbie got hurt did not make sense given the medical report, and Susan told us that Karen had told at least three conflicting versions of what happened the weekend that Robbie was hospitalized.

That weekend was a very difficult time for Karen. She was in the midst of a fight with her live-in girlfriend who had been threatening to move out of their apartment and leave Karen, another abandon-ment. She was enraged at her mother, who abruptly canceled her plans to take Robbie for the weekend, choosing instead to help Ka-ren's half-sister with a planned party for this sister's baby.

Karen most likely saw her mother's change of plans as a rejection of both her and Robbie, rekindling the longstanding rage at her mother she had never been able to resolve. Her mother had refused to believe Karen's disclosures of being abused, failed to protect her, placed her in institutions as a young child, and then rarely visited, blaming Karen's years of placement on Karen's defiant behavior. Yet, despite all of these rejections, Karen had continued to look for her mother's love and had gladly sent Robbie to her mother every week as a way of keeping a link to her mother.

Despite the abuse Karen experienced from men, her rage appeared almost exclusively directed at women and at her mother in particular. Records of Karen in institutional placements backed up an image of an abused/neglected teenager who would verbally threaten but who never actually hurt anyone; she was described as a fragile and often volatile girl who tended to run away when upset. In this session, Karen appeared very much like the young, neglected, and abandoned child she had been when she was first placed into institutional care. She looked and acted like a very needy young girl who could barely hold herself together.

In our session, Karen was distraught and desperate to end this ordeal. She appeared to have rehearsed her explanation of what happened and seemed to have genuine difficulty grasping the meaning of a few common words as well as the CPS and legal process that was ensuing. Karen tried hard to be sensitive to her son. Robbie, in turn, put his arms around her in a stiff and formal fashion, showing that at age 3 he understood that he needed to comfort his mother when she was upset.

Robbie never relaxed in her presence. In fact, he became noticeably upset when his CPS worker left the room and was far too easily comforted by people who were strangers to him. He seemed accustomed to going to other adults for comfort. While most 3-year-olds would be angry at their parents after a two-week separation and would be likely to initially reject them when they were reunited, Robbie showed a need to comply with his mother's requests.

Robbie's collapsing on the floor and whimpering when he was reprimanded by Sharon for touching the electrical socket was also disturbing. This was the kind of behavior young children show when they are used to being severely punished for misbehavior. While he did not seem afraid of his mother, he also did not look to her to protect or comfort him, nor did he show any signs of feeling safe with her in the room. For Robbie, having his mother present did not mean being protected.

Karen expressed a tremendous need for her son. But was Robbie attached to his mother? Robbie's ease in going to strangers and his lack of talking or asking about his mother suggested that he did not see her as a primary source of comfort, safety, and affection. Attachment is based on a child's learning over time that his parent is sensitive to his feelings, responds to his needs, and diminishes his pain and fears (Bowlby, 1969, 1979).

Robbie was used to depending on many people for help when his mother was unavailable. Karen's description of him constantly trailing behind her would fit with a young child's need to keep an eye on his mother for fear of losing her or of something bad happening. A more secure and attached 3-year-old would have been pushing the limits and boundaries of his home, going off to play by himself in different areas of the apartment, and pulling his parents to set limits.

Karen's accusation that Diane could have hurt Robbie was also disturbing. Karen had found him screaming while briefly in Diane's care. Yet, if Robbie had been bludgeoned in the groin by Diane, he would have been in agony and miserable for more than a few minutes. For Karen to have then taken him along a couple minutes later on a walk (to appease her friend) would have meant a callous disregard for her son's condition. Whether or not the story was true, Karen did not appear truly empathetic to her son's needs or even to recognize what he would have felt or needed. Karen seemed intent on finding someone outside of herself or Ralph to blame for Robbie's injuries rather than on protecting her son.

Could Karen's boyfriend have hurt Robbie? Robbie's "accidental" fall down the stairs was described as taking place when Ralph was babysitting a week earlier. Karen's conflicts with her friend and her mother the weekend Robbie was hit would have likely provoked her to become preoccupied with her own fears and anger, leaving her with less energy and sensitivity than usual to keep an eye on her son.

In contrast to Karen's overt and sometimes out-of-control emotionality, Ralph was extremely controlled and careful in what he said in our session, showing almost no feeling. He was a tall, rather handsome man who had grown up with an alcoholic and distant father who left him and his sisters for weeks at a time in the care of his mother. His mother had had a series of "breakdowns," which he would not describe.

Ralph was proud that he had learned to keep hardships in his life from touching his inner feelings and he worked hard to keep himself tightly in control. His father's broken promises of personal help or financial assistance had continued through his life, but Ralph said he felt no anger or resentment toward him. As a teenager he had become heavily involved with alcohol and was placed on probation for petty thefts and truancy. He was sent to several alcohol rehabilitation centers, had a few relapses, but claimed to have maintained his sobriety since moving in with Karen.

Ralph had three previous children with two other women with whom he no longer had any contact for reasons he did not want to discuss. He wanted to maintain his relationship with Karen but was unsure how it would work out. At this point, Karen was dependent on Ralph as her only support, especially following her fight with her girlfriend and renewed feelings of being abandoned by her mother. While Karen had spoken of an upcoming marriage to Ralph, Ralph said he was not making any commitments. On the other hand, he wanted to stay with Karen and described supporting Karen that weekend when she was upset with her mother.

Ralph said he was at work when Karen discovered the bruising on Robbie's genitals. Ralph wanted Robbie returned to their home immediately and said he missed him and wanted to continue to care for him. Nevertheless, his inability to deal with feelings, past history of alcoholism, lack of contact with his other children, Robbie's history of getting hurt while in his care, and Robbie's crying when Ralph changed his diaper were all significant risk factors suggesting Robbie would not be safe with Ralph present in Karen's apartment.

Our time for meeting with family members was quickly used up. We had learned a lot, but nothing that clearly delineated what had happened to Robbie or what was the best plan for him in the future. Three adults had access to him during the weekend in which he was hurt. Susan and other CPS staff were most suspicious of Karen. She certainly had a long history of victimization by males, a fragile emotional balance, frequent angry outbursts, and appeared desperate to come up with a story absolving herself and Ralph.

On the other hand, Karen's rage was consistently directed at females. Toward males, she was at times seductive, typically looked for support, and in past relationships had ended up victimized again and again. Robbie showed no fear of her, even when she changed his diaper. Yet, Robbie's trust, comfort, and emotional attachment with his mother appeared very weak. He seemed to act in many ways like a parent to Karen with a need to care for his mother and to watch out for her emotional outbursts.

Ralph could have hurt Robbie and pressured Karen to support him. The brutality involved in this beating, Ralph's history of alcohol abuse, and Ralph's repeated relapses suggested that drug or alcohol use was likely and that drug/alcohol evaluations were needed for both Ralph and Karen. Diane, the live-in girlfriend, could not be interviewed by us, but would presumably be questioned by the police investigating the case. Much more could be learned through individual psychological evaluations of all three adults. An assessment with Robbie alone, using human figures, dolls, toys, pictures, etc., was especially needed as he had shared little in previous verbal interviews.

VISITATION?

Should Robbie's mother have visits and, if so, what kind of visits: supervised or unsupervised, at the agency or her home, and how often? A copy of our assessment and recommendations was needed in family court in just a few days. I left the family assessment feeling exhausted by the tension and had only a few minutes to talk with Sharon and Susan before we each ran off to a week of scheduled family work. Susan felt more than ever that Karen had battered her son and believed that she should have no visits.

For 3-year-olds with an attachment to their parent, I recommend frequent visitation (at least two or three times a week, whenever possible) in order to maintain the bond between parent and child. In Robbie's case, however, his attachment to his mother seemed very weak and I wanted a psychological evaluation with Robbie alone before he received more pressure from his mother to see and communicate things the way she saw them. Sharon and I also wanted to see that Karen was cooperating with her own evaluations and thus showing some effort to work on helping her child before further visits were scheduled. In a rushed telephone conversation, we agreed with CPS staff and the judge that visits should be held off until CPS finished with their evaluations and the perpetrator was identified or Karen was found innocent, with the hope that a temporary cut-off of visits would lead Karen or Ralph to disclose what had really happened.

A few days later, I was still feeling anxious about our role with this family, a sure sign that I had taken on too much of the pain in a case and quite likely constricted my own perspective. I was angry at myself for accepting the pressure to come to a quick decision about visitation without the time we needed to examine critical issues and meet individually with Robbie. Karen, to our surprise and disappointment, canceled her own upcoming appointment for a psychological evaluation, saying she was doing this on the advice of her lawyer. At the same time, she called Sharon, begging for help in getting counseling for herself.

Sharon and I reviewed what had happened. We, like the judge and CPS staff, had become caught up in finding the perpetrator(s), fearing that without this Robbie would end up returned home with nothing really changed and the very real risk of being sexually abused, severely beaten again, or killed. I felt we had reacted to Robbie's unspoken agony, the screams that no one seemed to have heard. We had absorbed the shock of the case, which was limiting our own understanding of what had happened and what was needed. It's hard to be objective and to address a child's long-run needs when you're thinking of life-or-death risks and feeling constrained by demands to make a quick decision and move on to the next case.

WORRIES FOR THE FUTURE

I worried that delays in starting visits and services would prolong the time Robbie had to remain in temporary placements. Foster home placements are by definition limited in duration and Robbie could easily end up moved from one foster family to another as the criminal investigation dragged on over a course of months or years. It was unlikely that the actual perpetrator(s) would be identified, even with the judge's order barring visits until a perpetrater was identified. And, if no one was convicted, Robbie would probably be sent back to Karen and Ralph and lose whatever attachments he made to his foster families.

Under the law, Karen had a year from the date of placement to do whatever was necessary to provide a safe and nurturing home so that she could reunite with her son. During that year, the law stipulated that she would be provided with all possible assistance (for example, individual, family, or drug counseling) to make this possible. Karen's rights as a parent would only be terminated if she failed over the course of a year to make the changes and plans necessary to provide Robbie with a home where he would be cared for and not beaten.

If visits were delayed, the time frame would have to be extended in order to allow her a year to work on reuniting once visits were started. Robbie would have to remain in temporary foster homes longer, without knowing whether his mother would be taking him back.

This is much more than a legal requirement. Whether Robbie returned to live with his mother or not, he would need to know that she had been given help and had chosen through her actions to do what was necessary to take him back or conversely to have him grow up with another family.

Children naturally cling to the wish (even if it's a fantasy) that their biological parents will provide the care they need. Often, the less care the child has received the more they need to continue their hope and struggle to get their parent to care for them. If Robbie, now or in the future, heard a message from his mother that CPS or a judge summarily kept him away, he would likely grow up believing his mother had been treated unfairly and fight to return to her even if she had hurt him or left him in danger. Robbie would not be able to attach to a new family without feeling that he had betrayed his mother, even if it later proved impossible for him to return to (or even find) her.

Karen needed to work on winning Robbie's trust that she would protect him and provide a safe home. I talked with Susan about Sharon's and my misgivings about our initial recommendation and the judge's order barring visits. I urged her to advocate in family court for supervised visits with his mother once a week, provided that Karen was meeting with CPS and complying with court-ordered evaluations and after Robbie had been seen individually for a psychological evaluation scheduled for the next week.

Weekly visits at the county office building seemed to be the best option given Robbie's weak attachment to his mother and the lack of proof of Karen's complicity in battering Robbie. More frequent visitation would have burdened CPS staff who lacked the time needed for transportation and supervising visits on a more frequent basis. Visits would also provide an opportunity to see if Karen could gain her son's trust and would be a necessary part of the services mandated under the law to help her to bring her son home.

"Don't believe her," I was cautioned by Susan. "She's always been seductive with men. Did you see that low-cut shirt she was wearing? That girl really scares me! I think she could do anything." Susan angrily described Karen calling her and cursing, threatening lawsuits, and showing little attention to her son's well-being. Karen's statements to CPS appeared to be self-serving and very likely untrue. Yet, I knew that we had to look at Robbie's need for a permanent family he could call his own. Susan reluctantly agreed to support visits at a court hearing in a couple weeks and I put this recommendation into reports that were sent to the judge after I saw Robbie and Karen for individual psychological evaluations.

No miracle occurred in our family assessment. No clear proof "beyond a reasonable doubt" emerged to identify what had happened and who had done what. Robbie saw his mother for the first time after two weeks of placement and heard people talk with his mother about making a safe home where he would not be hurt again. He would, if the judge agreed with us, begin seeing his mother again as soon as a play therapy evaluation was conducted. Sharon and I rearranged our schedules so that I could see Robbie alone, as no other psychological evaluation could be arranged for several months. This meant juggling our list of CPS evaluations which already were set up for the next three months. Meanwhile, Robbie's foster parents reported that he had begun to warm up, to smile a little, to play, and to talk in two or three word phrases in their home.

THE SEARCH FOR HOPE

Robbie was just entering the foster care system, a time when things typically look bleak for everyone involved. It would be easy, even natural, to see this as another horror story with no hope. Yet, we had learned a great deal from this limited session and had a chance to use what we had learned in recommendations to CPS and the judge for the work that was beginning with Robbie and his family.

Robbie, Karen, and Ralph, in fact, had taught us a great deal. Each of them was a survivor. Robbie, despite the terrible battering he experienced, was still looking to adults for comfort. The way he was soothed by his CPS worker and Sharon showed that he still wanted to be held, to be cared for by a parent, and to be protected. Robbie had not given up and neither should we.

Robbie's ability to be comforted was in itself a testament to the care he had received in his first years from someone, most likely his mother or grandmother. A boy who had not received some regular nurture in his first three years would have avoided contact with adults, showed little affection to caretakers, not be comforted when held, gotten into a lot of trouble, and provoked anger from foster parents or other caretakers. Robbie was still seen as an appealing little boy despite his experiences of trauma and neglect.

We needed to recommend what kind of services would be most helpful for Robbie and it helped me to think about what typical preschool children need from their parents. Parents of 2- to 4-year-olds face a new world as their baby becomes an active child, challenging limits and developing new skills every day. "Normal" parents allow their child to explore, but set reasonable limits. With every passing month, children venture farther and farther away from their parents. Psychologists have actually measured this in feet. The child frequently looks back, always needing to see that Mom or Dad is there watching. If they are not, the child panics.

Thinking about what such a child needs helped me to understand what Robbie had shown us and what he needed. A child who feels securely attached to his parent will look for them and run to them for comfort when they are frightened or hurt. The parent will usually run out to them, pick them up, and hug them. Then the child begins to cry.

Robbie didn't cry, didn't call for his mother in the hospital or the foster home, didn't run to her in our session, and was not easily comforted by her hug. He had learned not to expect comfort and relief from his mother. Something had interfered with her ability to provide Robbie with the attachment and parenting he needed. Karen would have to overcome this if she would ever be able to provide the security and love he needed.

Karen had also showed us a lot. The most striking thing for me in our work with Karen was her nightmare in which "no one heard me."

In fact, her family had never really heard her. I felt pulled to listen and feel the pain of this woman who seemed like a needy child herself. Karen grew up not being heard or protected. Her placements in institutions at a young age and her mother's grudging visits confirmed Karen's sense that she had no one she could trust. She still longed for love from her mother but was reminded time and again that her mother would not be there for her.

Karen attracted men to help her, presenting herself as a poor and dependent victim, but every relationship before Ralph had ended up with Karen beaten. I, too, had felt an urge to help her. This was part of her seductive stance with men. Sharon, however, heard Karen reject her comments and felt angrier as the session went on. Karen continued to defy and reject female adults. As Sharon and I discussed the session, we realized that both sides (the seduction and plea for help as a poor victim and the rage as a wronged mother) represented Karen's way of coping with her own past as a child who was rejected and struggled to survive, getting hurt along the way.

Now Karen's child was battered and showing that his screams had not been heard. Robbie had learned by age 3 that it was pointless or even dangerous to cry out or ask for help. His mute expression reflected his only way to survive: to shut down his feelings and expect little, just as Karen had learned growing up.

REFOCUSING

I always look for intense stories, actions, words, or feelings to help me focus on what's most important and to find a way to join with a family. I look for a metaphor that validates everyone's pain and central dilemmas, a metaphor with which we can engage family members to work on change. "No one heard" and the boy's mute and expressionless demeanor suggested to me a way that therapists could begin working with this family.

We needed to show Karen, Robbie, and Ralph that therapists would hear each of them and to affirm that Karen would have to hear her son and prove that she could keep him safe in her care. We started this process with Karen in our family session by showing that we would listen and had heard her pain. When we saw her again, we told her we supported her wish for visits and were glad that she had agreed to cooperate with CPS-mandated assessments and counseling.

Karen's work to reunite with Robbie would have to entail making it

possible for Robbie to always feel he would be kept safe when he
shared what bothered or scared him. He needed a parent he could
count on to protect him and show him his perceptions would be validated and his basic needs met. Karen would have to learn how to be
heard herself, how to protect herself, how to deal with her own experiences of sexual and physical abuse, and how to develop the resources (job skills, friends, and family connections, if possible) that
she would need to build a safe home for Robbie and herself. Rather
than confronting her on lying, her therapist could work with her on
convincing Robbie that she would always hear his cries and care for
him. If Karen couldn't do this, he would need another family to call
his own.

Returning Robbie to Karen's care without his being able to "be
heard" would have meant his growing up detached, suppressing his
own feelings, and learning that being hurt or hurting others was just
a part of life. Robbie, today's victim, could easily grow up to be tomorrow's abuser and reenact the traumas of his mother and himself.

From Karen's perspective, she was able in the family session to
voice her despair, to complain, and to state her desire to get her son
back. She thought someone was starting to hear her distress but was
angry about our recommending another delay before further visits
with her son. At the end of our session, she expressed a need to get
help for herself and a willingness to work with family and individual
therapists.

Sharon and I briefly shared the burden of CPS staff, felt the strain
of trying to protect yet another severely battered boy, worried with
them about implications of this type of assault for past (or future) sex
abuse, but we were not able to give them any clear proof about who
hurt the boy that they could present in court. Susan agreed to support
our recommendations for supervised visits as soon as Karen showed
she was cooperating with CPS by coming in for an individual evaluation. Our plan for work with Robbie was based on the recognition
that the longer this work was delayed, the longer Robbie likely would
remain without a lasting home and secure relationship to a parent he
could count on.

When I saw Robbie in an individual play evaluation, he repeatedly
played out explicit sexual acts with anatomical dolls representing his
mother, Diane, and Ralph. Robbie spontaneously took all of the dolls
and had them lie on top of each other with the doll representing himself buried under the other figures. He laid the doll representing himself on top of the Mommy doll several times and placed the head of

the Robbie doll between the Mommy doll's legs. He then took the clothes off all of the dolls and pushed the Mommy doll's face onto the Ralph doll's penis several times moving her head up and down. After this, Robbie placed the naked Robbie doll on top of the Mommy and Ralph dolls several times and again piled up all of the dolls making them giggle and roll around. Later, with different human figures, Robbie repeated scenes of his mother, Ralph, Diane, and himself going into a shower together and each time knocked the shower stall down on top of them.

Robbie's knowledge of sex shown in his play contradicted Karen's statements to us that he had never even seen any sexual acts and confirmed her involvement in sexually abusing Robbie. Several months after this play evaluation, he began telling his foster mother about sexual activity with Karen, Ralph, and Diane. The sexualized play he revealed seemed in many ways to be a reenactment of his mother's descriptions of growing up with physical and sexual abuse, which had left her feeling helpless and hopeless as a child.

Karen did not hear her own child's pain, just as she was never heard. Robbie had learned not to cry, to talk, or to share his distress. Karen did, to her credit, get Robbie to the hospital after he was hurt. And, after our session, she began working with a therapist and social services staff.

Our efforts in that first family session marked the beginning of the intensive work that needed to take place in order for Robbie to have a chance to live without serial traumas and placements. Regardless of who had battered Robbie, he needed to have a parent demonstrate that he or she would do whatever it took to provide a safe home and love him enough to put his needs first.

Karen was given the opportunity and challenge of working to be this parent and to take the responsibility for making sure that he was never left in the care of anyone who would hurt him. She needed to own her role in sexually abusing Robbie, deal with the triggers to her anger, and make sufficient changes in her life so that he would not be at risk in her care. Whether or not she had battered Robbie, she needed to accept her failure to protect him, her use of him in what appeared to be ritualized group sex, and would have to work hard over a long period of time to make him feel safe with her.

In the next two years, Robbie had an opportunity to become a child again in a foster home where he felt safe. I felt very frustrated, however, when I learned that the judge did not follow our recommendations for supervised visits and, instead, maintained his order barring any visitation. I worried about how our initial recommendation to hold off on visits had bolstered the judge's position that Karen must disclose what had happened in order to gain visits.

Robbie's case was transferred from the intake CPS unit to a social services worker who specialized in permanency work. She and her colleagues eventually won permission for supervised visits after Karen admitted to abuse "by known or unknown persons." The perpetrator was never identified.

Karen was never able to overcome the lack of bonding with her son, and demonstrated in visit after visit that she could not comfort or care for him. A year later, she surrendered Robbie.

Robbie got the chance to grow up with the loving and caring that his mother never had, to be a child instead of a crime victim living in temporary homes. Yet I remained troubled with my own role and the strain of the case. I wanted to find a way to have more impact with families like Robbie's without becoming constricted, constrained, and battered myself. I needed to protect myself and my work from unrealistic pressures and to maintain the focus of my assessments and interventions on each child's need for a safe, nurturing home and a bonded relationship to a parent he could trust. Robbie's case reminded me that our challenge in the long run was not to focus on "whodunit," but rather to get everyone working on who will protect and nurture each child now and into the future.

chapter 3

Do I ever go home?

Eight-year-old abandoned by her mother and placed after physical abuse by her father

writing to mom

"WHO ARE YOU?" DEMANDED A YOUNG GIRL WITH SHORT BLONDE HAIR, large brown eyes, and a few freckles sprinkled over her nose. She looked up at me with a sweet smile, speaking quietly but with a clear expectation of finding out what I was doing in her space. I was visiting our agency's emergency placement unit again and was looking for Kristen, a 10-year-old girl described as too dangerous to stay in her elementary school after threatening, hitting, kicking, and biting peers and teachers.

Kristen was placed by her mother because of defiant behavior at home and pressure from the school for something to be done. A day after being admitted to our crisis unit, Kristen provoked a fight with another girl, refused to stop, and began slugging and kicking as hard as she could. She was led away screaming. Later when she settled down, Kristen shared that her mother and her two siblings had been hit by her mother's boyfriend, Bill. She calmed down some more and called her mother later that night. Kristen hung up the phone with a smile on her face and told staff that her mother had promised to get Bill out of the house.

The next day Kristen's mother came for a visit and casually mentioned that Bill was home watching the other children and making dinner. "You fuckin' bitch," Kristen screamed. She threw a book at her mother and stormed out of the room. When child protective staff came the next day to interview Kristen about the hitting in her home, Kristen at first refused to see them. She was coaxed into meeting with them, sat down, and heard the child protective worker introduce herself. Kristen bolted out of her seat and screamed, "Nothing happened!" as she ran out the door.

In the next four days, Kristen became embroiled more frequently in arguments with other children. She lunged at them, pulled their hair, called the other girls "fuckin' bitches" and refused requests from child care staff to take a break with staff away from the group. She was physically restrained by staff four times to keep her from hitting and kicking the other children. Kristen struggled furiously with child care workers while being held, screamed more obscenities, and viciously bit her social worker and child care staff three times.

I was asked to see Kristen for a psychological evaluation to assist program staff in evaluating whether they could maintain her safely in this crisis residence or whether she needed a locked psychiatric facility with more staff available. Placement in a psychiatric hospital would mean moving her 100 miles away from her family's home.

I introduced myself not knowing if this was the girl I was looking for. Kristen was typing at the keyboard of a computer working on a "Clifford the Dog" word processing program. Although she typed slowly, searching for each letter, it was clear that she was very serious in her endeavor. Kristen wore a faded print T-shirt and looked like a typical fourth-grader in any elementary school

"What are you doing?" she asked with the same sweet but determined affect. I told her I came over about once a week to talk to kids and families and that I was a psychologist. I then asked what she was working on. "I'm writing a letter to my mother," she replied and turned back to her computer. Our little talk was over. She had told me what was most important.

SEPARATIONS AND LOSSES

A child entering placement feels alone, vulnerable, and often terrified. Toddlers experience separations as death. Infants and young children cannot survive without someone acting as their parent (Spitz, 1945).

For 1- to 2-year-olds, the grief process is apparent after two days of separation. For older children, the length of time before a child goes into typical patterns of grief is longer (see Bowlby, 1973; Steinhauer, 1991).

For children like Kristen, the world feels out of control. While she may have been temporarily safe from the hitting at home, her mother and siblings were still there. Her mother's boyfriend was still at home. Nothing was getting better. In fact, everything was worse. Now she could do nothing to help. She could only imagine what might be going on. Waking up, eating breakfast, having dinner, and going to bed were all reminders of what had happened before and what could be happening again in her home. Kristen tended to get into her worst fights after dinner and before bed.

Moving into a building with eight other children meant being on guard. Staff could only be seen as potential replicas of what Kristen had experienced from adults before—reprimands, yelling, disciplinary assignments, evictions from her classroom by her teacher, stern warnings and isolation by her school's principal, screaming and punching of her mother and Bill. Getting hit herself would have been far less frightening than watching a fight develop between her mother and Bill. At least when you get punished yourself, you feel a little control over what's happening. Watching your mother and siblings get hit leaves a child feeling that the world is out of control and that she will lose the most important people in her life.

Most children in placement will desperately try to take control of what appears to be an out-of-control and dangerous situation for them. They will reenact what they have experienced (rejection, violence, sex abuse, etc.) with anyone and everyone around them. With unnerving skill, children will pick out staff who are sensitive to their own issues and play out scripts from their family play.

Staff members working with abused children and adolescents may over time become so angry that they feel the urge to strike back at the child or at least send them away to another facility. They may become terrified of a youth carrying out verbal threats to maim or kill, especially if weapons are found in the youth's room. The youth is acting out what cannot be expressed aloud and, by so doing, brings the terror and rage of her family into a foster home or group care facility. The reactions of staff and foster parents can then easily replay the experiences of the child in her home with similar outcomes, for example, removal to another, more restrictive facility. Children in trouble can move from a temporary foster home to a crisis group home and on to a residential treatment program, psychiatric hospital, or youth corrections facility.

Kristen learned from her mother that giving up Bill was not an option. Kristen's mother was angered by the child protective investigation and bitterly accused staff of trying to hurt her and her family by calling in the hotline report. Kristen heard her mother's distress and the implicit threat to her own fragile tie to her mother. Placement away from home threatened Kristen's bond to her mother. We later learned that this was the second time Kristen was sent away from home. Kristen and her older brother had been sent to live with an aunt in another state two years before and returned to her mother six months later following reports by other relatives of neglect of the children in the aunt's home.

Kristen was furious at her mother's refusal to evict Bill, but her mother was all she really had. Like many children from violent homes, Kristen had learned to watch out and protect her mother at all costs. The risk of not doing so was something that could never be faced. Kristen had nothing to replace the fragile hope she placed with her mother.

"When a chicken separates itself from the rest, a hawk will get it" (Ashanti adage cited by Rattray, 1956).* Few adults can survive alone. Loyalty is part of survival for every group. Most children feel a tremendous loyalty to their parents. The less they have received, the more they yearn for their mother or father's love.

Placement means that it may not work out at home. But without another caring, nurturing parent to rely upon, the child in placement remains locked into a no-win position. The child is in effect placed on hold while the rest of the world moves on. This is the child in limbo (Finkelstein, 1980, 1991).

ENTRY, ORIENTATION, AND SERVICES

Each placement comes with a powerful message tied in with the referral and funding system used. With the advent of child protective statutes and increased enforcement in the 1970s, large numbers of children entered placement because of abuse and neglect. The number of children placed away from home has swelled in recent years with an increase in drug abuse, particularly cocaine and crack. In the United States, an estimated 450,000 children were living in foster homes, hospitals, residential treatment programs, and detention centers in 1993 (American Public Welfare Association, 1994). New York

---

*My thanks to Nathaniel Bracey for contributing this proverb.

state alone could fill Yankee Stadium with children living in state-funded foster care programs, thousands of "Kristens" who are frightened and frightening to those around them.

Family preservation programs launched in the last two decades have helped to keep together families whose children would have otherwise moved in and out of foster homes or residential treatment centers at a younger age (see Kaplan & Girard, 1994). When children still need placement despite outreach family work and the efforts of multiple counseling and family support programs, the family's problems are by definition severe and entrenched with elevated risks of someone being seriously hurt. Most of these children were placed into foster homes after repeated physical or sexual abuse or failure by their parents to provide sufficient food, medical care, or basic hygiene. Parents in such situations feel attacked and often view child and family services as a belligerent enemy stealing their child away.

If the child is placed for mental health reasons, the child must be labeled according to criteria listed in the Diagnostic and Statistical Manual, fourth edition (American Psychiatric Association, 1994). Neglect, abuse, parent-child relational problems, and stress factors are noted, but most diagnoses represent constellations of behaviors that constitute a disorder of the child.

Children and parents typically understand a psychiatric placement to mean that the child is mentally sick and in need of professional help, help that parents are unable to provide without an M.D., Ph.D., or M.S.W. after their name. Few parents understand the biological processes tied in with their child's behavior. Sensitive or irritible temperaments, biological depression, attention-deficit, hyperactive, and neurological disorders, learning disabilities, developmental disabilities, schizophrenia, and retardation are often found in children placed out of their homes. Too often, these factors are presented and/or accepted as a justification for placement away from home when children with all of these conditions can and do succeed in their natural families. The label of a child's biological condition makes it easy to ignore the family situation and how medications, supportive services, respite, psychoeducation, and often financial help could enable a child with a biological impairment to grow up at home. Many children in placement do have very real conditions that interfere with their functioning. Few, however, need long-term placement because of these conditions.

Most behavioral disorders represent how a child has learned to cope with the reality of life in her family. I am always reminded of the idiosyncracy of the zebra's stripes. We look at a zebra in a zoo and the black and white stripes make no sense. However, when viewed from the eyes of a predator trying to attack a herd of zebras, the mass of moving stripes suddenly takes on a new meaning: a way to confuse and to escape. When a child enters placement, our challenge is to discover how her behaviors make sense given both the biological and environmental forces in her life.

Many youths are placed in detention centers, institutions, and group homes because of their refusal to go to school or because of behaviors seen as dangerous to the community. These children and adolescents are often viewed as "bad" and in need of reform. A large percentage have experienced abuse and neglect that was never reported or sufficiently proven to warrant child protective intervention. As child protective caseloads have soared, social services departments have "indicated and closed" milder cases of abuse and neglect where interventions could have been very successful. The criteria for accepting and pursuing child protective cases has often centered on legal assessment of whether the social services department has enough evidence to win in court, even if abuse and neglect is strongly suspected. In many cases children learn that even with reports to child protective services, nothing happens, or worse, they get beaten for telling the family's business.

Conflicts that were manageable for a family with young children may lead to more dangerous behaviors when children become adolescents. Teenagers sense their growing stature, become more influenced by peers, and become fed up with dealing with the strife they feel at home, especially if feelings of attachment are weak. Adolescents and parents learn that truancy, fighting at school, vandalism, stealing, and especially violence directed at teachers or other adults in authority will lead to placement away from home.

If the underlying problems in the family have not been resolved by the time a child hits adolescence, family court often provides temporary relief from escalating conflicts for both parent and child. The child's refusal to follow rules or behave in school, along with her engaging in any destructive/antisocial behavior, leads to placement, which is defined as rehabilitation and almost uniformly experienced as punishment. The youth enters an institution or group home with the expectation of serving time and little hope that anything will change in her family before she returns home.

With each placement a child feels more vulnerable and less hopeful. A child in placement who feels things are not changing or will get worse is very likely to get in more trouble. This is like raising a red flag for the world to see that "it's not working!" The type of red flag will depend on what's happening at home and the severity of the situation.

Emotional abandonment is often experienced at the same level as death and destruction. The child will most likely repeat behaviors that led to the first separation from her family. Kristen bit, hit, and kicked. With each repetition, she became seen in another setting as a violent, seriously disturbed child who needed more staff and a more restrictive setting to control her (translation: GET HER OUT OF HERE!). No one wants to be bit, hit, or kicked.

For the child, each placement confirms the badness or craziness she must hold inside. Each separation from adults (teachers, foster parents, social workers, psychologists, etc.) who try to help teaches the child that she cannot trust grown-ups—even those who proclaim soothingly that they have come to help. No one seems to understand or be able to make things better. The child acts out a little more aggressively or destructively with each placement and in turn becomes labeled more seriously disturbed and in need of ever more restrictive placements. This is the "slippery slope" (Steinhauer, 1991) that leads to a youth's detachment, an "I don't care about anyone or anything" attitude, and long-term institutional placement.

PLACEMENT AS A TURNING POINT

Our challenge with Kristen was to use this placement as an opportunity for change, a turning point in her life and the life of her family. Moving Kristen off the "slippery slope" would mean confronting family members with the real traumas and dilemmas represented by Kristen's serial crises in school.

Working quickly to engage family members and address the underlying pain is, however, contrary to the emphasis in most placement programs on *stabilization* of the child. Kristen needed to learn not to bite, hit, and threaten. Behavior management of a youth in a placement setting typically becomes the paramount task undertaken by a new team of professionals (child care workers, nurses, teachers, psychiatrists, social workers, psychologists) attempting to do what parents, previous teachers, and former therapists had not succeeded in accomplishing. This can include medications to calm or sedate. Parents and previous workers are sometimes advised of a *projected stabi-*

lization date, that is, when they can expect that the child will have been calmed down following implementation of prescribed medications, counseling, and group living outside her family.

Family members see a new team trying to change and control their child. This puts family members in a paradoxical position where the child's defiance and refusal to change actually serves a function for the family. If the child improves in placement, parents can feel ashamed that they couldn't help their child themselves and that they must have a dysfunctional family. Failure to change can demonstrate that the child is so bad that not even highly trained professionals in an institutional setting could change her. By acting bad or crazy, the child becomes identified as the major problem and provides some relief for their parents. The child in placement can, in effect, stabilize the family as the bearer of everything the family cannot dare to look at. Children may come to see this as a crucial role and their primary role in the family.

The child/adolescent in placement is like an ambassador from their home government (Ausloos, 1985). No ambassador can dare change their position without permission from their country's leaders. To do so would be treason. Working to engage family members thus becomes essential for practitioners.

Beginning with the first contact, we need to give family members messages that we need their help to help their child. Parents sense from their first phone call and first visit to a program whether this is a "parent- and child-friendly facility" or a place where they can expect to be overtly or covertly shamed by practitioners. Do the staff sit behind partitions and formidable desks? What do parents have to do to arrange for visits? Are parents automatically greeted with suspicion? Are staff members seen as allying with the children in their care? Is there a comfortable area for families to meet or does involvement of parents and siblings appear to be an afterthought? The biggest questions for family members, of course, center on whether the staff they meet can be trusted enough not to demean them or be quickly scared away if some of the family's secrets are exposed.

At the same time, safety is essential for a group care or hospital program to function from day to day. The behaviors of children like Kristen can easily accelerate to a point where cottage staff can no longer handle them. No one wants to be bit; child care staff, teachers, and foster parents face the very real risk of infectious diseases such as hepatitis B, even without the blood-to-blood contact that could spread AIDS. Every placement program needs a carefully planned schedule with activities geared to helping children succeed, incentives for good behavior, opportunities to learn better ways to manage feelings, and staff who can understand and be available when a child is upset (see Klein, 1975; Trieschman, Whittaker, & Brendtro, 1969).

Children like Kristen have already learned to act out the distress in their families. Pain cannot be expressed, resolved, or sometimes even be allowed to be felt within families locked into chronic crisis. Kristen's mother was not calling up out of her own pain and anxiety. Nor was she calling primarily out of concern for what was troubling Kristen. With Kristen and most children like her, the referral for placement came from the pain of teachers and others in her community who said they could not handle her. Her mother wanted a break, some relief from Kristen's defiance at home, and, most of all, relief from the complaints of teachers demanding that she change Kristen's behavior.

With families in chronic crisis, it is often the community (teachers, neighbors, police, etc.) that acutely feels the pain of a child's dilemma. By the time a child is acting so badly as to pull outside intervention, she has learned, like her parents, to block out feeling and to act quickly. Shirley Schlosberg (Kagan & Schlosberg, 1989) called this the difference between real crisis and chronic crisis. Real crises include the traumas and challenges that everyone must face. The stress of a death, the devastation of an earthquake, the trauma of a murder puts people in predictable patterns of grief (see Lindemann, 1944). Denial, bargaining, idealization, and anger typically precede experiencing a loss and allowing oneself to feel depressed. Much later, acceptance, realistic views of the lost person or object, and rebuilding of attachments occurs. Real crises are experienced over a limited time. Survivors of real crises can eventually emerge feeling stronger with a sense of mastery: "I survived Hurricane Andrew."

Families in chronic crises appear stuck in denial, rage, and idealization. They seem unable to face what is happening because it is too risky. These are families that have typically experienced multiple separations and losses with an ongoing threat or experience of abandonment. Crises become a way of avoiding feeling (see Kagan & Schlosberg, 1989).

Children who grow up with ongoing violence in their homes become conditioned to survive in such environments. Infants and toddlers learn to be hypervigilant, always alert, easily aroused, and to move quickly without thinking. This helps the child to escape from dangers with quick perceptions of anyone or anything becoming threatening followed by fast and almost instinctive movements. At the sound of a car backfiring, most of us will look around. Children growing up in a war zone will already be on the ground or out the door. The child learns to be on guard and ready to fight or flee at the drop of a hat.

In later years, however, this orientation leads to great difficulties when the child is asked to sit still, listen, think things out before reacting, and generally *behave* in a six-hour school day, something many adults would have great difficulty doing. The hypervigilance that is necessary for protecting oneself from one's siblings, parents, or neighbors at home shows up as distractibility, impulsivity, irritability, and hyperactivity at school, especially in children with a biological temperament for short spans of attention and concentration.

THE NEED FOR PERMANENCY

Children cannot go through the grief process without a sense of safety and stability and a solid attachment. Often the less that the child has had from her parent, the more she needs to cling to an idealized fantasy of the missing parent.

All children need a bonded relationship with an adult who can be an ongoing resource to them in the future and who can provide a home with consistency, nurturance, and safety. Most of the children and families coming into crisis placements have not had this. The intensity, excitement, and risk of multiple crises provides a powerful distraction from memories of traumas and threats of abandonment. Denial of what happened and distortion of reality become ways to survive, ways to reaffirm loyalty to one's family, ways to protect everyone from the feared collapse of the family, and ways to avoid the anticipated deaths or loss of parent-figures. Chronic crises help family members to avoid facing what cannot be expressed and function like an addiction; crises provide a form of relief and a fleeting sense of control in a chaotic and dangerous world (see Kagan & Schlosberg, 1989).

Each child learns her own value and expectation of relationships from her parent's face, gestures, and actions. The parent's look when he or she picks a child up—pleasure and pride or anger and ridicule—and the parent's touch—cold and rough or warm and caressing—speaks worlds to a newborn about how she can expect to be treated by others. When a child cries out in pain, she learns whether she can trust her parent to ease her discomfort, who, if anyone, will care for her, and what she must do to survive. The child learns how much the parent values her. This in turn forms the child's own assessment of self-worth.

Primates need attachment in order to develop into socialized and functioning adults capable of caring for their own children (Harlow, Harlow, Dodsworth, & Arling, 1966). Assessments thus need to focus on attachments that the child may have had in the past and who could serve as the child's psychological parent now and into the future. For many children, attachments existed with people who do not have custody at the time of placement or who are no longer available to the child due to illness, death, or distance.

We ask children if they can remember feeling safe. Did anyone make you feel warm and comfortable when you felt bad? Who took care of you when you were sick? Who do you rely on now? Who can you count on to be there? Who listens to you when you're upset? Who will listen to you when you need someone to talk to? Who will help you?

Without a strong bond, children learn that no matter how hard they scream, no one will come to help. I have worked with children locked in closets for more than a day before someone found them. The shattering of attachment and a child's trust in her parent has become increasingly prevalent with the advent of cocaine, especially crack cocaine. Addicted parents focus all thought and energy on getting the drug and children learn that no one will relieve their pain.

Families of children going into placement have often experienced generations of separations, losses, and traumas. Children and parents have grown up with abandonment or threats of abandonment with placements from a young age in the care of different relatives, babysitters, or neighbors, as well as in foster care programs. Crises have become a way of life that seems to go on forever with no clear origin or conclusion. The family seems to be always on the move, running from what is too painful to be fixed.

Crises are also exciting. A family member in trouble can have teachers, principals, and police chasing them. This is like going on a roller coaster. Once it's started, there is no way that you can get off. You hold on, experience the thrill, and feel alive. If someone asks you to stop the ride, "There's nothing I can do."

To see, to hear, to feel much more than the thrill of the current crisis may be impossible. To speak of what happened (or is happening) may mean provoking Mom or Stepdad to leave, resulting in a financial crisis and loss of a parent. The family member who dares to speak up may be shunned as disloyal or risk death. I remember Maureen, a 16-year-old girl who, after five years in foster care, began disclosing her experiences as a young child. She remembered her father chasing her mother into her room during one of many terrifying battles between her parents in the middle of the night. Her father knocked her mother across Maureen's bed. "If she wakes up, I'll kill you!" he screamed at her mother with a voice full of menace and rage. Maureen kept her eyes shut. Maureen learned as a young child that she must limit what she saw and keep her mouth closed; her mother's life and her own life hung in the balance.

KRISTEN'S CHALLENGE

The need for permanence provides the framework for my work. Kristen was writing to her mother and I knew we must help her find out if her mother could provide the bonding and care she desperately needed. After reading the few notes available in the case record, I talked briefly with staff and asked to meet with Kristen. She had gone outside to play with the other children on the playground.

A male child care worker who knew Kristen approached her and asked her to come in to see me. Kristen flew into a rage, ran to her room, and screamed, "No boys touch me!" She kicked her bed, knocked over a chair and defiantly glared at the child care worker who had followed her into the building.

"Get out!" she screamed and began pulling at the door. I walked over to Kristen's room and into a battleground. Kristen was standing off two child care workers who were valiantly trying to coax her to come out of her room and at the same time trying to hold her door open. "Should we bring her out?" a tall male child care worker inquired. Kristen glared fiercely in response and shoved hard at the door. If there was to be a war, she was ready. Kristen was prepared to fight literally tooth and nail to maintain her position.

The child care workers had come to work this day, as every day, to help children in need and found themselves in the roles of persecutor and policeman. My hopes of a quiet talk with an easily engaged and studious fourth grader were quickly dashed. On the other hand, Kristen in a matter of minutes had again shown me what was most important in her life. Running to her room and barricading the door against male child care workers and a male psychologist while yelling

"No boys touch me!" was a strong message. For Kristen, men were invasive and threatening.

Kristen needed to protect herself and I silently appreciated her energy and spirit. She had laid down a gauntlet and challenged us to join her in a physical reenactment of her life. This was a test of our intentions and whether we could be trusted to respect her precarious position. If we failed this test, I knew that we certainly would not be trusted to talk respectfully with her mother and siblings.

I introduced myself again and asked the child care staff not to pull Kristen out of her room. "I don't force anybody to talk to me." I described my role as a psychologist and told Kristen that I had come to meet with her and her social worker, a female staff member. I had brought a few things I wanted to show her and would probably ask her to draw a picture or two, if she wanted, and to make up a few stories with me. No touching. No forcing. "You don't have to say anything."

"I'm not talking," Kristen muttered, but relaxed slightly in her struggle with the door. This was immediately reciprocated by the child care staff and a temporary ceasefire seemed to be taking hold. I noticed that Kristen had a large helium balloon floating in her room and I asked her about it. She grabbed the string and began bouncing it up and down. I asked her where she got it. "Yesterday on a trip," she mumbled bouncing it up and down even higher. I told her I liked balloons and she made a few thrusts with her balloon at me and the child care worker.

"Do you know what makes it float?" I challenged her. "Sure," she replied, giving me a "what do you think, I'm stupid?" glare. She kept bouncing the balloon higher and accidentally lost the string after a particularly strong thrust. The balloon sailed up toward a vent. I carefully pulled it down and handed it to Kristen asking her if she knew what the vent was for. This time I got a "no" with a questioning look. I told her about the vent.

Kristen was by this time out in the hallway, clutching her balloon and still glaring. I told her I was going to go to her social worker's office down the hall. She could come or not come. As I turned to walk away, Kristen darted ahead, running into the office and slamming the door behind her.

"You're a person who needs to say 'No!'" I told Kristen when I caught up to her in her social worker's office. I sat down across from where she was standing and was glad when she turned toward me momentarily. "I ask a lot of questions," I admitted and repeated that she didn't have to answer. "You don't have to talk to me."

"How do you say 'No'?" I asked. Kristen looked at her social worker who had joined us, sitting down in her desk chair near Kristen. "How will I know?" I continued.

"I go out. I say, 'Stop it!'" she replied with a stern look in my direction.

I told her that was fine. If I saw her get up to go or say "Stop," I'd know that I was asking about things she didn't want to talk about. I showed Kristen a few pictures of children and parents (Roberts, 1982) and asked her to tell me a short story about what she thought was happening in each picture.

Kristen stared at the first picture of a girl sitting up in her bed. "Nothing happened!" Kristen yelled and repeated this for every other picture I showed her. She climbed on to her social worker's lap and I saw again how this fourth-grader was looking for physical affection and protection. Despite her outward defiance and rage, she had not given up on people.

I asked Kristen who else she liked to hold her. Was there anyone else's lap she liked to sit in?

"Mom," she replied.

I asked Kristen to imagine some pretend situations with different people knocking on the door. "What would you do if you opened the door and it was your mom? What would you say?" Similarly, I asked what she would do and say if her siblings, her mother's boyfriend, her grandparents, and her biological father came to the door. I asked her what her mom would do and say if she was here with us in the room? What would her siblings and her mother's boyfriend do and say? Where would each one be sitting? Where would she be sitting? "With Mom!" Kristen affirmed and painted a concise picture through her answers of how her life centered on her mom with a lot of aggressive and competitive play shown toward her siblings. Outside of her mom, she was hostile or distant from people.

Children's stories and fantasies show what they've learned about people caring for each other. Do fathers provide caring? What do mothers do in stories? Who helps children who are upset? What can help children pictured as distressed? The child who responds "nothing" and tells repeated stories about children living alone has often given up hope. Asking fantasy questions about whether they would go alone or take anybody with them to a magical island, if they won a vacation trip, or if they won a car or a house in a contest also helps to discover who the child looks to as potential resources. Older and more cooperative children who feel safe with an interviewer can be asked directly "Who can you count on to listen to you? Who can you count on to be there for you if you have a problem? Who do you like the most?" Children who talk about going to "no one" and with "no one" have given up hope and learned to keep themselves detached from others. No one can be allowed to get close enough to hurt them again.

Kristen fortunately was still looking for someone. I pulled out my inkblots (see Beck, Beck, Levitt, & Molish, 1961) hoping to keep up our dialogue. "Mean face—it's blood—makes me sick—bloody face" she blurted out for the first card, with a wincing look that turned quickly into a glare. "Not my mother's face!" she yelled at me. "That never happened to my mom!"

Kristen jumped up and headed for the door. I told her that I had heard the "stop" message and would put away the inkblots. I had a game I wanted to show her. She busied herself looking at things in the room for a few minutes but eventually came over. I showed Kristen a puzzle with small foam rubber human figures representing family members (Lauri, 1984) and invited her to take them out. Kristen's emotional reactions suggested that this very tough fourth-grader was in fact feeling much more like a very young child, and often operating on a very primitive level.

Kristen hesitantly took out figures representing people in her family at my suggestion and added a figure representing me. She rejected my invitation to make up a story with the figures. I picked up the figure representing a girl Kristen's age and went up to the figure Kristen held representing her mother. I had the Kristen figure say what Kristen had already told me and staff members in the agency, using her words: "I love you, Mom. I want to be with you. I want to go home today! I don't want you to get hit again."

Kristen took all of the figures and one by one had them hit the figure representing me. I repeated the same message again and she reenacted every family member yelling "Shut up!" and beating the figure representing me, this time twice as hard. I must have seemed like a pretty dense person to Kristen and needed a repeated warning of what should have been obvious. If you speak up, you get beat up. It was too risky to talk. Kristen then had the mother figure take the Kristen figure home, placed the figures representing her siblings on top of her and her mother and threw the figure representing her mother's boyfriend on the floor.

Kristen's resolution of the problem was simple—just get rid of her mother's boyfriend. Instead, Kristen had ended up in placement. Her mother adamantly denied that there was any violence at home and accused Kristen of fabricating stories. Her mother also blamed Kristen's school for not managing her properly and for repeatedly calling to complain about Kristen's hitting and cursing when they should just deal with it and punish her if she was a problem.

Kristen backed away from her statements to staff about her mother and the children being hit. "Nothing happened! Nothing happened! Nothing happened!" she shrieked to child protective workers. Later, Kristen begged her mother and staff to send her home.

Crisis placement programs have been aptly described as MASH units (R. Schimmer, personal communication, 1994) and the children and parents served by child and family services and mental health programs as the walking wounded (Schlosberg, 1990). Kristen showed us that her hope for stopping the fighting at home was gone. She just wanted to go home. If I or anyone else spoke of the beatings at home, that person would be stomped by everyone in the family. As she said in her play story, "Shut up!"

In the middle of a war, you don't betray orders from the commanders. You do whatever you must to get back to your family. Regardless of the wounds, you just keep walking. The fight against outside forces becomes a rallying cry for the family to demonstrate loyalty to one another against anyone who challenges the family's delicate balance. The more precarious and dangerous the situation, the more family members need to fight to keep their balance.

Kristen's balance was very fragile. Her outburst about blood ("Not my mother's face!") for the first black and white inkblot showed how easily she could lose control as well as her preoccupation with the horrors that she could not share. She quickly regressed to a primitive view of objects and people dominated by raw emotions of terror and rage. At 9 years old, Kristen could almost instantly transform into a screaming, kicking, and biting 18-month-old terror. Kristen struggled between wanting to tell what happened and feeling it imperative to keep the secrets of her life. This struggle kept her on edge and ready to explode at any time in response to anything resembling the rejection and violence that she had learned could never be addressed.

From a larger perspective, this was Kristen's call for help for her family and herself. She was both scared to death and desperately afraid for her mother. She wanted her mother to be a mother and protect them all. Kristen raged against her mother and yet desperately loved her mother. Her energy gave me hope that something could be done.

I believe in this work that we have to trust children, parents, and grandparents to have enough strength to make changes. If we buy into the fragility expressed, we give up any hope for change. Our challenge with Kristen's family was to validate the love *and* the terror. We needed to elicit the family's courage to move on. Kristen represented both the family's rage and the courage to strive for change.

MEETING THE FAMILY

The next step was to begin to pull in the important people in Kristen's life for a network session. This ideally would have included a representative from her school and her mental health therapist. Kristen and her mother had been going to a community mental health center off and on for a year and a half because of pressure from Kristen's school. Each of these critical players in Kristen's life was invited along with her mother, 13-year-old brother, 6-year-old sister, and her mother's boyfriend. If we were successful in engaging this portion of the family's network, other relatives and community supports could be invited to later sessions at our agency or preferably in the family's community.

I was very pleased to see Kristen's mother, Janet, her siblings, and her mother's boyfriend, Bill, arrive for our family session five days after my individual session with Kristen. Given the child protective investigation in progress, engaging the family to come in for a meeting was a major accomplishment and a tribute to the efforts of the center's social worker and the program's emphasis on our need for their help in order to help Kristen, our need to learn from the family, and our commitment to helping the family make things work out. Equally important was a demonstration through phone calls, during Kristen's admission to the program, and during visits between Kristen and her mother that we did not discount or shame families.

Unfortunately, Kristen's school social worker and mental health therapist phoned in to say they couldn't make this session. We begin with family members and service providers who can and will come in and then work outward to expand the network.

Kristen immediately sat on her mother's lap while her 6-year-old sister hovered close to Bill. I introduced myself and my role as a psychologist for the crisis center and thanked them for coming in to help us work with Kristen. "I tend to get nosey and ask a lot of nosey questions. Stop me if I ask too many questions or ask about things that are too sensitive to talk about."*

---

*Shirley Schlosberg taught me this along with many other engaging messages for families. Please see *Families in Perpetual Crisis* (Kagan & Schlosberg, 1989).

At my request, Kristen introduced her siblings. I asked each of them what it was like not having Kristen at home and was pleased to hear that they all thought it was "bad." Janet said it was hard for her to put Kristen into the crisis center.

I told the family that I had met Kristen just once but that I and other staff were impressed with how much she was devoted to her family and loved them. "The first thing Kristen showed me was that she needed to write to her mother. I'm not surprised at all to see where she's sitting."

"She's got to be with me 100% of the time," Janet complained. "If I don't pay attention to her for a minute, she goes wild. . . . She hits her brothers. I end up yelling and screaming."

I told the family that this reminded me of what Kristen had shown during placement: her agitation, especially in the evening and around bedtime, her hitting and kicking staff, and then running and hiding. "She loves you very much, more than anything. She's also got things that she cannot say, that she's too scared to say, and that she even warned me not to say."

Kristen glared at me and tensed in her mother's lap but relaxed some when I stressed that I could see in the way her mother held her why Kristen was so devoted to her family. "She keeps looking to you," I told Janet. "She both loves you and is terrified of you and others in the family getting hurt. She's afraid of Bill hitting you and the kids but told me when I saw her that she loved everyone in the family and saw Bill as part of the family." Kristen looked quickly at Bill. Her 13-year-old brother looked down and her 6-year-old brother climbed onto Bill's lap. No one ran for the door or jumped up, kicked, and beat me as Kristen had warned in her play story.

I also shared that the way Kristen acted, her hitting, running, biting, and responses to my test pictures told me that Kristen's fears went far back to a much younger age, long before the last four years when Bill became involved in the family. I asked Bill if he had noticed this. He nodded and said she had gotten much worse in the last year.

I wondered aloud about what it was like for Kristen, her mother, and her siblings when she was a baby and a toddler and asked Janet if it would be okay if I asked Kristen's older brother, Doug, what he remembered. "Fighting, always fighting," he mumbled. I asked him what he would do during the fights between his mother and father. Doug looked down again and said he started going into his room as soon as they would begin fighting. He shut the door and played with his GI Joes. "At first, I got in the middle and tried to stop them."

Janet remembered a time when Doug was 5 and Kristen about 1 1/2. Her husband had knocked her down, put his knee in her back and told Doug and Kristen to grab a knife and stab her. "Do it!" he had screamed in a drunken rage.

"Now he's been telling the children to kill Bill," she added. With prompting from her mental health therapist, Janet had petitioned family court for an order of protection but had not been able to restrict her husband's visits with the kids. She shared this with little affect but Kristen looked agitated.

I asked the children how visits with their father were going and Doug shared that recently Kristen had gotten between their father and Bill, trying to stop them from fighting. Bill had ended up with a black eye from that encounter. "Don't bother me," Bill had said. "If he comes around, I'll be ready."

I asked Janet if she remembered what Kristen used to do during the fights between her and her husband. She thought Kristen tried to protect her but couldn't really remember. I asked the children who was most worried about the fighting between their mother and father. Everyone agreed that Kristen seemed the most upset. She shrugged her shoulders but looked up at her mother. I asked Janet if it was okay to ask the children what they had remembered happening to her. Doug remembered his mother's arm being broken. Kristen remembered a black eye and her mother's hair pulled out.

We talked about the children living for all of Kristen's life with the everpresent threat of their mother being hurt or killed, with commands from their father to stab their mother, and now threats against Bill. They had been living in a war that continued to this day, with Bill like a warrior ready to battle the children's father. No one knew when or if he might carry out threats to kill Bill or Janet. Kristen in particular seemed caught between her parents and her mother's boyfriend.

Janet complained that after a visit with her father, Kristen had grabbed at her hair. She thought that Kristen may have inherited a tendency from her father to become violent. "He used to bite, too." I agreed that temperament is a big factor with any child and we discussed how temperament is strongly affected by experiences and especially traumas such as the incident when Kristen's father tried to get the children to stab their mother.

I also shared my worries about Doug. Doug had learned to shut the door, hide in his room, and keep silent. Holding all of his feelings inside could hurt him as he grew up. I wondered aloud if he would like to change this and what his mom thought.

Kristen had a special job in the family. She needed to jump in quickly and fight to protect her mother at all times. She was on 24-hour guard duty to keep her mother alive. I asked Bill if he agreed with this. He nodded.

"She's got to be especially on guard against any man drinking and any arguments between her mother and a man," I continued. "That's like a veteran of a war hearing shots or helicopters swooping in. She loves her mother and does what she learned to do long before Bill came into the family. She hits, kicks, and bites to protect her Mom. For Kristen, to do nothing could mean her Mom being killed."

Looking toward Bill again, I added, "She's got to see even the slightest argument between you and Janet as the start of a war, a war in which her Mom could get killed." Bill nodded again.

I asked if it was okay if we talked about any arguments and fighting that had been going on recently in the family. I reminded the family of what I had said to Kristen when I first met her and what I had said when they first came in the room. "Stop me if I ask too many questions or about things that are too sensitive to talk about." Kristen had remained in her mother's lap, which I took as a signal that she did not have to say "no" yet. It was okay to go on a little bit more. We had reframed Kristen's hypervigilance as a symbol of her loyalty to her mother and years of service as a child-guard.

"She's always afraid of losing you, of you being killed." I continued looking at Janet. "I need to ask if anything was happening that made it worse in the last year or in the last month when Kristen has been getting into so much trouble at school."

To my surprise, Janet affirmed this. "She saw Bill and me get into a fight about a month ago. I sent the kids over to a friend's house but she brought them back." I asked Bill and Janet if there had been any hitting, since Kristen was doing a lot of hitting in the crisis center. Janet shared that Bill had struck her on the face. "It happened when he was knocking the door open."

This was just one of many secrets in the family, but a breakthrough, nevertheless. Janet had said aloud what all of the kids knew but could not say. She had been hit by Bill. They had argued and fought. The children had grown up witnessing her life threatened with ongoing battles erupting at any time between her and her husband and later between her and Bill and between Bill and her husband.

We had begun to talk about how scared and angry Kristen got
when she sensed that her mother was threatened and once again not
available to care for her. Janet, Doug, Kristen, and even Bill had been
able to share a little about the fighting, past and present, without
anyone being hurt, running away, or being rejected. Janet remained
committed to taking Kristen back home within the next week.

We ended the session affirming Kristen's wish to get back in the
family and at the same time her need to see the fighting end so that
no one, especially her mother, was in danger of being hurt or killed
again. Triggers to Kristen's going wild, such as how Bill and Janet
handled arguments, any drinking that might be going on, and contacts with their father, would be addressed in further sessions at our
center and with their mental health therapist. We would, with the
family's permission, share everything that happened with their therapist and try to set up a follow-up session. I hoped that in the future
extended family members could be brought in to help the family keep
making things better and to relieve some of the stress on Janet and
Bill.

I thanked the family for sharing so much and especially for affirming some of Kristen's fears about fighting. I asked for Bill's help in
particular to show his commitment to the family by demonstrating
that no one was at risk of being hurt again. We recognized that this
was only a beginning of the work. I asked the family if anyone was
frightened about repercussions from sharing so much and was glad
to see that no one seemed too upset. If anyone did become upset, I
hoped they would call us, the family's therapist, or anyone else who
could help the family. The center's social worker reinforced this by
talking about the next visit between Kristen and her family.

This session was just a beginning and it could be predicted that the
family would close down again quickly and revert to old patterns.
Child protective services did not see sufficient risk to indicate the case
for monitoring. Kristen had recanted her statements and Janet and
Bill had expressed a commitment to work in counseling on their relationship and end the violence. Bill's probable drinking and the possibility of any sex abuse remained largely untouched except for my
brief statement in this session about alcohol as a trigger for fighting
and Kristen's need to be hypervigilant and the concern I expressed
about what Kristen's saying "No boys touch me" meant.

My biggest concern, however, centered on whether Janet would
work to win Kristen's trust that she would not abandon her. We had
learned in this session that Janet had placed Kristen and Doug with

their father several years earlier. Their father took them four states away and in turn placed them with their aunt.

Kristen lost her mother every time there was a fight in the house. There was a real basis for Kristen's rage at her mother and the fragility of her attachment. Kristen had grown up feeling loved, then hated and rejected. She modeled her own behavior after the hitting, kicking, and biting she witnessed in her father's terrifying and powerful rages. Kristen raged whenever she saw her mother pulling away and had learned like many children that it was much safer to act out your rage with teachers, child care workers, therapists, and other authority figures than with your mother, father, or mother's boyfriend.

Still, the change in Kristen's behavior after this session seemed close to miraculous. She calmed down, no longer appeared agitated, didn't provoke other children into fights, focused her attention on schoolwork, and bit no one. She listened to staff members in the crisis center and they were able to relax and enjoy her feisty spirit.

The family's mental health therapist was glad to hear what the family had shared. Sessions were scheduled for her and the family to continue to work on Janet and Bill's showing the children how they would stop the violence and that Janet would keep them safe without threats of placing the children outside of her home. Kristen and her siblings needed to work on sensing, understanding, and sharing their fears and their anger in more appropriate ways. The mental health therapist said she'd attempt again to do some mediation between Janet and her husband and would continue to support Janet in her attempts to get an order of protection.

Kristen was brought home by her mother a few days later and returned to her classroom behaving like a fourth grader. Two years later, I learned that she had continued to do well in school and that her mother and Bill had worked in marital counseling for several months. I was very pleased that Kristen and her family had trusted us enough to talk about how frightened the children were of their mother being killed and to make a committment to continue this work in counseling. We had helped Kristen send her letter in a way that Janet could accept. Kristen's message, in turn, spurred Janet to share what everyone had been too afraid to say out loud.

part two

practice strategies

chapter 4

I hope you misbehave here so they can see how
bad you are.

Mother to her 7-year-old son after he was
placed in a crisis residence

setting a course toward change

NO MAGIC TOOK PLACE IN OUR WORK WITH KRISTEN AND HER FAMILY.
The disclosures by Kristen and the limited validation by her mother
stemmed primarily from the day-to-day engagement of Kristen and
her family by the crisis residence staff. If I did anything right, it was
to remain focused on what Kristen showed me on her word pro-
cessor. She was writing to her Mom and needed to find out how her
Mom would answer.

Permanency work is not glamorous. It means working with what
most people would like to avoid: the shameful and painful side of
life. I'd love to present a cookbook recipe guaranteed to produce permanency but that's not how people (families and service providers)
really work. A therapist seen as following a regimented procedure
(fill in this chart, ask these questions, prescribe these tasks . . .) will
not be trusted with what really matters in a family. The family may
show up grudgingly but the real work will remain on hold. At the
same time, I have found that successful work follows a fairly predictable course based on the principles and practice strategies outlined in
Table 4.1. These interventions are discussed in Part Two (chapters 4–6).

TABLE 4.1
Permanency Interventions for Children in Placement

Pass the family's test

- Introduce ourselves—who we are, what we do.
- Create safety and basic respect in our sessions and programs; we need the family's help.
- Talk about what's real without shaming.

Make placement a catalyst for change

- Recognize how a child's placement and behaviors reflect deep-seated wounds in many family members, wounds to their core sense of self and family.
- Frame placement as a family crisis with children and parents at risk.
- Focus on permanency; children can't wait!
- Work with time limits for change.

Map family resources

- Help the family develop their own map.
- What's working?
- Who can help?
- Search for the child's attachment.
- Who can be the parent now and into the future?
- Perform psychological evaluations of attachment.

Trace the roots of a family's struggle

- Why now? Help the family to share their experience over time and their hopes (past, present, and future).
- What happened leading up to placement?
- Learn from the child's behavior and development.
    √ What does the child's behavior tell us? Where is he/she stuck?
    √ Are other family members struggling with similar dilemmas and developmental impasses?

Work with metaphor, the key to the door

- Use our images, feelings, and fantasies.
- Where have I felt like this? What does this remind me of?
- What are parents and children telling us through their first words, body language, family stories, dreams, and crises?
- What is our dominant impression?
- How can I frame this as a metaphor which captures family behaviors and offers hope for change?
- How does the child in placement represent the family's struggle and experience (basic needs, abandonment messages, traumas, and hopes)?

TABLE 4.1 Continued

Develop centering messages for stormy waters

- Identify split messages to the child (or double binds) which drive dangerous behaviors.
- Understand the child's struggle and message.
- Does the child's behavior reflect unresolved traumas in the family?
- Open up lost dimensions of time.
- Move beyond "bad" and "good."
- Frame dual centering messages which link both sides of a child's response to splitting messages.
    - √ Tie in loyalty/love and the struggle to end threats of abandonment or violence.
    - √ Use metaphors to link messages and the child's struggle.
- Make placement a turning point.
    - √ Challenge parents to make choices that show they can care for themselves and define who will parent a child.
    - √ Challenge children to make choices that earn age-appropriate rights and rewards.
    - √ Work with family members to build enduring attachments.

Mobilize a supportive network

- Start with the child acting out distress.
- Move progressively outward to bring in parents, siblings, extended family, and community resources.
- Work with respect for ethnicity, heritage, and economics.
- Coordinate work with other service providers and family court.
- Help family arrange for positive school or job training programs.

Set a course toward permanency

- Set goals with parents and children as partners.
- Set a time frame for reuniting or making another plan for who will raise a child to maturity.
- Work one step at a time.
- Build skills for relationships, parenting, and conflict management.
- Coordinate substance abuse treatment when needed.
- Predict problems based on past crisis cycles and develop safety plans: Who will do what? What will signal that a crisis cycle is starting again? Who can serve as protectors against any further abuse or neglect? How can they be contacted? Who will help to maintain change?

Work for the long run

- Keep goals realistic and focused on what's needed to foster attachments and safe, nurturing homes.

TABLE 4.1 Continued

- Show children that staff and foster parents can see and respect their pain and divided loyalty.
- Use group care, when necessary, to maximize the best possible relationships a youth can have with extended family members and provide opportunities to build new attachments.
- Make visits with family members the time to do the work and demonstrate how things will be different.
- Coordinate review conferences every four to six weeks and keep to the time limits allowed for permanency work.
- Double-check plans. Who will do what and by when?
- Maintain back-up plans for adoption or a child growing up with an extended family member to maturity.
- Work with the messages. Help children face what their parents do and don't do.
- Help children grieve if their parents fail.
- Build long-term connections if a youth cannot live in a family. Where will a youth spend holidays?
- Arrange for follow-up services to be available.

CHANGE DOESN'T MEAN SHAMING

My intent from the first contact with families is to show that this placement can be different. Families come into hospitals, residential treatment centers, emergency shelters, and foster home programs expecting to be blamed and shamed. Professionals, community authorities, agencies, clinics, and schools referring children for placement often have similar expectations for how they will be treated by the new therapists called in to resolve a desperate situation that developed during their watch. Our first challenge is to show parents, children, relatives, and other service providers that we work to help families overcome problems without disparaging or shaming anyone.

"We need your help to help your child" (Ausloos, 1985). Our role is not to find out who's to blame for a child's troubled and troubling behaviors. We want to know what is working well in a family as well as what has led to placement. Our role is to mobilize the network of family, extended family, community, and treatment providers to help a family move past the dilemmas that have blocked change and growth. We search for the competence needed to care for and raise children that is shown by family members within their cultural, religious, and ethnic communities. Recognizing signs of loyalty, concern, understanding, and caring are keys to engaging families to deal with old wounds and the traumas in their lives.

Much of our work has to do with longstanding feelings of shame and worthlessness. More than one parent has told me their own experience as young children of being literally thrown out the window or into the garbage by their parents. Now, their children fight against feelings of being thrown away, of being disposable, unwanted, and needing to go into a strange home or institution.

Shame fuels the crisis cycle as a way to avoid what appears to be overwhelming stress. Parents and children demonstrate a desperate need to deny, minimize, and distort in order to protect against hopelessness and despair (Nace, 1987), to hold a fragile sense of self and family together, and to prevent the unbearable from occurring. Denial serves a protective function; yet, at the same time, it takes away the ability to overcome and master a crisis. Distortions of what happens and mandates to not see, hear, or feel (Wegscheider, 1981) feed the crisis cycle.

Shame is about the self. "With guilt I make a mistake; with shame I am a mistake" (Mason, 1993). Change in shame-bound families requires building safe relationships to protect each individual from feeling he is being backed into a corner with no escape. The therapeutic relationship provides a way out of what appears hopeless and overwhelming.

We need to demonstrate a competence-based approach from the first contacts. My respect for family members is based on a recognition that I could be in the same predicament as the parents and children coming into our programs (Madanes, 1995a). Receptionists and staff receiving referrals show respect for parents, children, and other professionals, and welcome them to the program. The structure of buildings needs to be open and inviting to families with staff accessible and not hidden behind walls, desks, or rigid appointment times. Group activities should frequently involve families. Visits are a critical time. Family-centered programs have playgrounds, picnic areas, comfortable child-centered waiting rooms, and large, child-friendly meeting rooms with sturdy moveable chairs and toys, such as stuffed animals, paper, washable markers, toy houses, and human figures that children can use to express themselves.

Work begins with messages to families that introduce a program, our commitment to helping families work out problems, and how we work to help parents to help their children. We tell parents and children that they can share as little or as much as they want. Our work includes meetings of different staff members (for example, psychologists, psychiatrists, social workers, child care staff, foster parents) with family members. We ask parents for permission to invite others involved in working with them to our sessions with the premise that we need to work with everyone involved in order to help families. This can naturally lead to questions to family members about what they found helpful in previous counseling or placement programs and what was not helpful.

Our intent is to learn from the family and to empower family members to tell us when they feel we are doing something unhelpful. It's also a good time to remind families who have already worked with multiple agencies, therapists, hospitals, etc., that there is no reason for anyone to assume that we can do anything better.* At the same time, the family may be in a different position now. Working in sessions demonstrates a renewed commitment to make things better.

PASS THE FAMILY'S TEST

I want to learn about multigenerational patterns (rules, beliefs, and experiences) and biological factors that shape a child's potential within a family. Assessment needs to be done without encapsulating a family's turmoil into diagnostic labels and psychological terminology that imply that they are certifiably bad or hopelessly sick. Rather, I want to look at the cluster of behaviors expressed by each individual as a message about their experience and expectations.

My objective in the early stages of work with family members is to establish trust that we will not push them too fast or allow ourselves to be pushed so fast that people become overwhelmed and reenact the family's patterns of crisis.† For example, a family's social worker began a review conference with 12-year-old Mandy and her father, Doug, by launching into the treatment team's concerns about Doug's behavior. These were very real concerns—Doug had abandoned Mandy and two other children, leaving them in the care of foster parents and later their mother with multiple placements of all the children over the last nine years. Doug had only recently begun to work to reunite with Mandy. During this latest placement, Mandy's mother had failed to show up for visits at the agency and cancelled visits at her home, showing Mandy that she would not do anything to work on getting her daughter back home.

Mandy asked to live with her father even though she had disclosed

---

*Based on interventions from S. Schlosberg; see Kagan & Schlosberg (1989).
†Specific strategies for working with common patterns of resistance are detailed in chapter 4 of *Families in Perpetual Crisis* (Kagan & Schlosberg, 1989).

several times in previous foster care placements that her father had sexually abused her when she lived with him as a preschooler. Child protective services could not find enough evidence to validate the sexual abuse charges and Mandy now denied they were true. By stressing these concerns in the first minute of the conference, the family's social worker heightened what Mandy and her father perceived as an adversarial proceeding, blocking their shared wish to forget the past and start a new life. Doug stiffened, glared, and rebuked all of the social services people in the room for falsely accusing him of sex abuse and ruining his life over the past decade. Mandy leaned toward her father and buried her head behind his shoulder; he was her only hope.

I believe we have to be straight in addressing real concerns, but our first step in every session must be to show respect and to establish a sense of safety. I like to begin by thanking family members for coming in to an assessment, review conference, or initial session and asking what they expect we'd be doing and what they would like to do in this session. This can then lead into a review of the purpose of the meeting and my hope that we can use the time to work with the family on achieving their permanency goals. Setting a time frame for the meeting and inviting everyone to feel free to talk or not talk helps set a positive climate.

Some sessions, of course, will almost inevitably be adversarial given the pressure on family members to attend, their longstanding negative experience with service providers, and the deep concerns of service providers for the safety of a child in their care. In the review conference noted above, I quickly interjected that I too wanted to be very "straight" and certainly believed reports by two of Doug's children about sex abuse. At the same time, I added that I was most impressed by Mandy's nuzzling into her father's back with tears in her eyes. Mandy looked to him as someone who had cared for her in the past and her only hope now for someone to care for her in the future—someone she could not afford to upset.

I asked for Doug to work with us to help his daughter understand and deal with what had happened over the last eight years when he and his children lost each other. He lambasted Mandy's mother for scheming and taking everything he had. I asked what had helped him survive and he described how he had overcome his "disease" (alcoholism) through rehab programs and AA.

With this very minimal recognition of his importance and competence, I was then able to ask him what he thought Mandy's tears meant as she nuzzled into his back. By the end of our session, he agreed to work in counseling sessions on helping his daughter to understand what had happened and to deal with her fears about reuniting and being alone with him. He was still angry, distrustful, and on guard. Nevertheless, both he and his daughter saw that we were willing to work with him.

We had respected Doug's role and rights as Mandy's father and yet had not been afraid to say out loud our concerns about his abandoning his daughter. We accepted the childrens' past reports of sex abuse as a given, and, at the same time, showed our respect for the caring this father had shown to Mandy in the past and the steps he had taken to improve his life in the last eight years.

Doug was Mandy's only hope of regaining a family. She needed to see that we were working with her. Only then could she find out if her father would really provide her with the safety, validation, and honesty she would need to deal with the abandonment and sex abuse and provide a home she could count on in the future. After a few visits and family sessions, Mandy shared how she could never feel safe or comfortable in her father's home. Rather than fighting Mandy and her father's hopes, we had worked with them to see what was real.

Move the Family Away from the Wall

I remember one mother who abruptly stood up in a conference session with child protective staff and walked backward until her back was literally up against the wall. That's how many parents feel when outside authorities become involved. And, like any animal, humans pressed up against a wall are dangerous. They yell, bite, throw, and sue. Our challenge is to help everyone (parents, children, and other service providers) move away from the wall.

When someone is up against the wall, we need to validate their position and recognize if they are being court-ordered or otherwise pressured to come to our session. We can then move to join and empower parents with messages such as: "I believe parents have rights. Do you feel like you're being pushed against a wall, that your back is to the wall? What would help you feel like you could take a step away? Who else feels that way? How can we help you and other family members to get away from the wall?" Such questions can lead naturally into a discussion of what it will take to get child protective services, school officials, etc. "off their backs." This in turn can lead to a common goal for family work and a way for therapists to join with a family.

We begin working by collecting information about how the family functions and trying to understand the meaning of what is being shown. We respect family members' need for loyalty, work to build up the safety each individual will need to face what may be seen as painful or shameful, and try to locate and unlock natural forces of health in each family member.

Our task is to slowly move toward family members' pain without going so fast that individuals freeze or run. Most families of children going into placement have long histories of trauma, multiple stressors, and, often, physical impairments. We are confronted with the challenge of working with children who are living day to day with threats of abandonment and all forms of abuse, trauma, and neglect of their core needs. At the same time, we must work with many parents who are survivors of abuse and neglect from their own childhoods and have come to reenact the abuse and neglect with their own children.

This means helping family members feel safe enough to share secrets at their own pace. With each family, we expect to be tested to see if we can be trusted enough for family members to begin to share what drives family crises and to experiment with risky changes. We need to demonstrate that we can hear their rage, terrors, and shame without running away, sending them away, or adding to their shame with disparaging comments or neglect of an individual's loyalty to his family.

Families test us by not showing up for sessions (Ausloos, 1985) or they may try to scare practitioners into not raising important questions or addressing critical issues. Thus, if a parent routinely fails to show up for scheduled sessions, I believe we must stress our need for Mom's or Dad's participation in order to help his or her child and talk about the parent's message to the child. With every missed visit, family session, or phone call, a child hears a message about his parent's commitment. It's up the parent to choose what message he or she wants to send.

Showing families that my colleagues and I can talk about what's painful is necessary to engage family members and to keep the work moving. I expect to have to confront families with difficult issues and to be confronted by families with the challenges they are struggling with themselves.* Passing the family's test means showing family members that we can hear what's happened and respond to the family's pain without demeaning parents or children.

Working with Wounded People

Change means working with pain. Placement usually happens when one person in the family system is bearing too much stress and pressure. This person could be a child, a parent, or someone outside the nuclear family who has helped to hold the family together but now feels overwhelmed. A child acting up in school may in many ways be the strongest member of a family.

Getting into trouble often serves to bring in help for other family members. As tensions and the threat of a parent's collapse or running away grows, acting-out behaviors may increase. Placement outside the home typically works to temporarily stabilize a family system that has grown dependent upon chronic and accelerating crises (including placements) as a way of avoiding what is seen as unbearable. Placements of children (or adults) with caring and supportive professionals often decreases pain and thus inadvertently diminishes the healthy motivation to make needed changes.

Engaging families means showing them that I can talk about what is painful. I want family members to hear at the onset of our work that a child's separation from his family is a wound in itself and indicates that the child, other family members, and the family itself is at great risk. I share my belief that placement of a child usually means that many family members have been hurt and feel ripped apart with deep-seated wounds to their core sense of self and family. Roots and connections to extended family have often been torn or cut off. With many families it helps to describe these as spiritual wounds (after Madanes, 1990b, 1995) that everyone in the family has suffered, not just the child in placement. I invite family members to work with us on healing torn connections and spiritual wounds and to rebuild hope that children and parents can make their lives better.

Louise momentarily glared at the supervisor of her children's foster care program and then stared off into the distance. Her back stiffened and she raised her voice to a threatening pitch, "You want me to give

---

*Confrontation has been described as a precondition for building a therapeutic alliance with borderline clients (Klein, 1989).

up my (second) job so I can meet with Beth (her social worker)! I need that job to pay the rent. Is Beth going to pay my rent? I can't do everything. Give me a break!"

Louise had missed visits and family sessions for the last three weeks after taking on a second job for added income. She had arranged for Samantha, her 13-year-old daughter, to be involved in afterschool activities and thought Samantha would be okay even though Louise was gone from 8:00 in the morning until 12:00 at night with only a brief time between jobs. A few months earlier, she had dropped out of a relapse prevention and anger management program and said she was unaware that Samantha's probation worker had ended informal probation services because of Louise and Samantha's failure to attend meetings. Louise's two youngest children remained in a foster home, 16 months after being placed because of Louise's drinking and fighting with her boyfriend.

In this session, my colleagues and I validated the financial strain Louise felt; her main job did pay for the rent and basics but didn't leave her with the money she wanted to give to Samantha to go to the mall and buy what other teenagers had. This was also a way for Louise to gain Samantha's respect and boost Louise's respect for herself. Beth offered to meet with Louise and her children in the evening between her jobs but Louise continued to complain about taking time for family counseling.

Louise had told me that she went to church when she could. "Are you a spiritual person?" I asked. Louise looked sternly at me and nodded her head. "I think what Eddie and Dedie (her children in foster care) are showing us are like wounds, spiritual wounds. And, when I see children act so hurt and scared, I have to wonder who else has been hurt so bad."

Louise nodded again and seemed to relax a bit in her chair. "Placement is like a wound. It means the family is threatened and everyone is at risk. Samantha, Eddie, and Dedie are looking to see if you can do it. You're telling us that there's no one else and you know the children have waited too long."

Louise agreed with this and I added, "I think children at Eddie and Dedie's age look at every visit with their Mom like a message. Is Mom going to get us or not?"

"I know," Louise said. "Eddie just doesn't click with me."

Louise ended our session saying that she knew we were talking straight to her. I asked her to show the children in the next four weeks what her message was. What was her priority? Would she show them that they could count on her, overcome their fears of her anger, and get them home? Would she work with us on repairing some of the torn connections to relatives and help negotiate relationships for the children and herself with their father? Voicing the deeper wounds to Louise, her children, and her family helped all of us to focus on what each of them needed for the future.

MAKE PLACEMENT A CATALYST FOR CHANGE

Placement can become a catalyst for change by using the current crisis to generate pressure for family members to make choices and take necessary steps to help their child and themselves (Kagan & Schlosberg, 1989). Crisis-oriented families are often spinning in time and driven by events (Ausloos, 1986). The crisis of placement can be used to set a time frame for change. Louise in the case mentioned above needed to hear how long she had to work to reunite with her children. She wanted and respected straight messages—what had to be done and by when. The pressure of time serves to keep the pain alive and to provide a framework in weeks and months for the work needed to get a child home.

The child's crisis provides a focal point for efforts to engage and build a supportive family network of family members, service providers, and community resources who can work to get the child back into a family. This is facilitated in cases of abuse of neglect when child protective services advocates strongly for a child's safety and need for permanence. With a clearly delineated permanency approach, placement begins with a stress on what needs to change and the maximum time period allowed by law. Parents are responsible for working to make needed changes to provide the safety and care their children need or they risk termination of parental rights.

Under the Federal Adoption Assistance and Child Welfare Act of 1980 (Public Law 96-272), parents of children placed due to abuse or neglect have 18 months to accomplish what is necessary to implement a permanency plan (return home or adoption). In New York state, under the Child Welfare Reform Act of 1979, parents have one year in which to work and the Department of Social Services is mandated to provide "diligent efforts" during this time period to help parents accomplish permanency goals. Social services departments share responsibility for working to help families reunite. Setting a time frame creates the pressure needed to keep parents and helping systems on track and working for change.

For mental health, probation, and educational placements, we work to develop a time frame for change based on the developmental needs of the child. Families are engaged to work on the pain and dilemmas behind behaviors before it's too late. We try to tap into parents' and children's natural motivation toward health with a message that "this can't go on" if they want to keep the family together. The cycle of accelerating crises is framed as leading to the current placement and in the future to even more restrictive placements if underlying problems are not addressed. Family members need to make choices about what they are willing to do to keep their child out of jail or locked hospitals.

The length of placement is determined largely by how long it takes to engage and mobilize a support network that can develop and implement a plan for safety, nurture, and lasting attachments. By stressing that "children can't wait" and setting time frames for placement, networks are kept engaged to work on what needs to change. Time becomes a critical part of the intervention.

I focus on family attachments and permanency plans in every contact, assessment, and intervention. Each behavior and crisis is viewed and dealt with in terms of the child's permanency needs and the family's plan for who will be working with the child to give them the support and guidance they need as they grow up.

MAP FAMILY RESOURCES

With scary families and children at acute risk of injury, abuse, and long-term neglect, this work requires a team approach with supports for staff. The program needs to have a clear mission and focus shared by supervisors, consultants, family workers, foster parents, child care workers, teachers, and medical staff (see chapter 9).

Our understanding of family members' strengths, distress, and triggers to crises provides us with a map of where a children and parents need to go, who's out there to help, and what obstacles will predictably block any efforts toward change. Recognizing the children's and parents' core needs to build or renew attachments and to heal from longstanding wounds provides us with a sense of direction for weathering the storms to come.

Like a canoeist on rough waters, we need to put our bow into the waves and stay close to the shoreline. If we allow the waves to hit us broadside, we will wallow and sink. Sometimes, the best you can do is to hold your position, trusting that the storm will blow on. Safety comes from planning and engaging partners for the voyage ahead. We watch the sky for clues of what is to come. We cannot control the future but we can work together to stay on course, map out short, do-able legs of a longer trip, move from one land base to another, wear life preservers, and carry some basic provisions. We also have to keep our expectations realistic.

When children are placed away from home, we become guides to family members making their own trip. Rather than a rescue service, our role is to engage family members in successfully journeying through a risky passage. Children like Kristen will often clearly share their fantasies and hopes about who will take care of them. Parents sometimes verbalize their own wishes to gain the trust they never had as children and to give their children a better life than they had growing up. Yet, the placement of a child marks a sense of failure and loss. The family feels shipwrecked and desperate. The would-be res-cuers are often seen by family members as pirates who caused the shipwreck by interfering and now threaten to steal their children.

Family members will test us from the first encounter to find out if we can offer enough safety for them to try to move through stormy seas and past their personal monsters of the deep. We develop maps together with families using information, behaviors, and emotional clues elicited from the family members themselves. Children, parents, and grandparents hold their family's maps inside, maps that chart both their dreams and the obstacles (currents, shoals, and sea mon-sters) that block any movement.

Our challenge is to uncover the drives toward health that every individual carries inside and to help family members discover signs of their own competence that can be used as landmarks to inspire renewed hope. We can then use the crisis of a child's placement to mobilize supportive family members and other helpers to join in the challenge of charting and powering change.

What's Working? Who Can Help?

We start by working to build and rebuild connections to other family members and outside support groups who can provide the safety net individuals will need in order to deal with longstanding secrets. We need to know who's involved and who should be involved. I assume that the family members who come into a crisis session when a child is in placement are feeling stuck and lack significant supports for themselves. The people needed for multigenerational change, the people with the most power, are very likely not in the room.

I begin by exploring what is working in a family. How do they have fun? Who does what with whom? Who do family members go to for help? Who are the most likely resources for the family? Who has the power to make decisions? Who helps to calm things down? Who does an angry adolescent go to for support? If children are running away, we need to know to whom and to where they run (to relatives, family friends, peers, or to be by themselves). Can these relationships help a child in the long run?

Isolated children have often given up on finding people who care. Who goes to look for them? Who worries the most when they are gone? Who would worry if they knew what the child was doing? For suicidal individuals, it's helpful to find out who would be affected if they killed themselves and to develop a list of those who would be especially hurt.

I use projective questions about nuclear and extended family members to explore positive connections that could help a child and a family in crisis. Who is most hopeful that a child or parent can change (Combs & Freedman, 1990)? Who would a parent want to invite to their wedding? Who would come to visit a parent or child in the hospital?

If Grandma (Grandpa, Dad, Aunt June, etc.) was here, where would she be sitting? What does she look like? Who would she be looking at? What would her eyes and face be showing? If I asked her what she liked best about you, what would she say? If I asked her what she thought would be the best thing that could help you, what would she say? What would give her hope that things could get better? Would she be willing to help? How does she help you? Such questions can be used to paint a picture of who should and could be in a family session. Who would be sitting where? Whose arm would be around whom? Who would be sitting between combative family members? Who would be keeping the peace? Who would be angry? Who would cry? These perceptions provide a map of possible resources.

The placement genogram and timeline (McMillen & Groze, 1994) are very useful in highlighting possible attachments and losses of children who have moved through multiple foster homes and treatment centers. In this model, the genogram format (see Hartman, 1978;

McGoldrick & Gerson, 1985) is extended with a line drawn down from each child who has experienced placements. Under each child, genograms of parents and children in foster families or relative's homes and boxes for psychiatric hospitals and group care facilities are diagramed to show the child's position in a succession of placements. To the right, a time chart can be included, vertically listing the dates, location, and important data about each placement. The placement genogram captures the separations and potential attachments of each youth in a family.

Assessing who's feeling pain, who's motivated to change, and who has the power to change is critical. These questions help to determine who needs to be invited to sessions. We begin with the key family members at the time of placement and the service providers and authorities making the placement. From a network perspective,* one person in the family may have particular power as a "gatekeeper," deciding who does or does not gain access to the family. This person may or may not be part of the initial group of family members involved in a placement. We work to engage missing people and especially gatekeepers with permission from family members. Phone calls, letters, and visits by both family members and family workers may be needed to bring together the fractured parts of a family in distress.

This means involving grandmothers, older siblings, aunts, neighbors, clergy, and anyone else who can offer long-term commitment and help for children and parents. At the same time, we need to keep expectations of change realistic and recognize that some relationships are too toxic (after Madanes, 1990b) to maintain or to bring into our sessions. Anyone arriving intoxicated can be asked to leave and join us at another time when they are sober. Family members who cannot stay peacefully in the same room with one another can be met at different times. I would not invite family members who would likely become violent in a session, threaten others, or promote others to be violent or suicidal. This, however, is rarely a problem when three generations are involved (Landau-Stanton, 1994). Problems that have been acted out by siblings and in-laws can often be managed when grandparents demand respect.

Fathers can easily be overlooked in this process, especially when presented as nonentities or scum by the mother's side of the family. The "diligent efforts" requirement in many states mandates work with both parents. Delaying work with a father until after a mother

---

*For references on network therapy, please see Kliman & Trimble, 1983.

works for a year often means doubling the length of time a child will have to remain in temporary placement(s). If the mother fails to re-unite with her child, workers would then have to first begin search-ing for and then working to engage the father, who also has legal rights to work and get assistance during a year or 18 month's effort to reunite.

Search for the Child's Attachment

Often, we begin at the start of placement with family members who lack emotional ties, a history of attachments, or an expectation that parents will care for each other and their children. A child may be currently living with a biological mother who appears to be at her wit's end. The child may actually have been raised in his early years by a grandparent, aunt, etc., until something happened to that person (e.g., an illness, a job change, a need to care for another grandchild, a need to care for an ailing parent of their own). Or, the biological par-ent may have gotten a job, a new boyfriend, girlfriend, or spouse, and better housing, leading the adults to feel it is time for the biological parent to take over the responsibilities of child care. The child may then be blamed for not abruptly shifting his trust and affection to a parent who had abandoned him in the past or who acted more like a sibling, aunt, or uncle than a mother or father.

With a focus on permanency, I look carefully for past and potential attachments. The child may need to go back to a previous caretaker or at least deal with his grief at losing his primary parent-figure. Who will work to provide a child with the bonded relationships and safe, nurturing, and consistent home he needs?

I want to know who children go to when they are hurt or upset. Who calms them down? Who do they go to in our sessions and dur-ing visits? Whose lap do they want to sit on? Who do they embrace? Who do they talk about with foster parents or staff during the day and especially at night? Who did they go to as a young child when they scraped a knee, fell off their tricycle, had a bad day at school, or felt sick? If different family members were present (for example, an aunt, a mother, and father in the same home), who did the child go to first?

Who had the time to care for a child in his early years? Who re-members the child when he was 1, 2, and 3 years old? What was the child like as a baby, toddler, and preschooler? I'm especially inter-ested in hearing about age periods when a child was doing well. Who was there for the child and what did those people do that helped the child to succeed, feel better when sick, and learn to cope with problems?

A child who can relate to teachers, child care staff, or foster parents reflects some previous attachment. The child who is appealing and well-liked has most likely received nurture and was bonded with someone. Like a detective, we trace threads of attachments and search to discover who was and could in the future be the primary parent-figure for a child.

I want to know how a child relates to adults or other children. Are they clingy, suggesting an anxious fragile attachment, or detached, suggesting that they have given up on getting what they need from relationships? Do they show caring about someone, an animal, plant, anything? How do they respond to affection from foster parents, staff, teachers, and their family? When they're physically or emotionally hurting, do they look for someone to care for them; and if so, what kind of person (older, male, female, a relative, a peer)? Can they be comforted when upset and, if so, by whom? Such questions and observations of what the child does with people in sessions can help to assess the child's history and capacity for attachments.*

I ask parents to share some of the things they like best about their son or daughter. What did they enjoy doing with them in the past and what do they do for fun now? Were things different in their relationship when the child was younger? Was there a time when they felt closer? What changed? What would they like to do for fun with their child in the future?

I also want to know how sensitive they are to their child's needs. How do they know if their child is upset? What do they think works best to calm him? How do they understand what has led to a child's behavior? What would they think would help?

This ties into the parent's own experience of being cared for. Who was there to care for and raise each parent when they were children? Could they trust their own parents to be there when they needed them? Parents who complain about the burden of caring for their children are not likely to be willing to provide the nurture, time, and attention a child needs. Parents who grew up without feeling cared for by their own parents (or a parent substitute) may not recognize the attachment their child needs and will likely be unable on their own to

---

*See Carson and Goodfield's "The Children's Garden Attachment Model" (1988) for a valuable guide to assessing capacity for attachment.

build an attachment with their child. Humans, like other primates, learn to parent from their own parents (see Harlow et al., 1966).

I ask parents for their own goals to assess their motivation to provide the parenting the child needs now and into the future. Celene, a 21-year-old mother of 4 children under age 6 answered: a car, a better job, and a new boyfriend, with no mention of improving things with her children. Celene's children had been placed for neglect after she left them overnight in the care of a heroin addict who in turn had left them alone for the night to get his fix. The children were not present for our session due to a scheduling mix-up and when I asked about the children, Celene complained about the time of day when she had to be available for her weekly two-hour visit. Otherwise, she didn't want to talk about the children. The judge in this case unexpectedly sent the children home despite child protective requests for extended placement and before we could schedule another family assessment with the children involved. Within a few days of the children's return, the second oldest (age 4) was severely burned in what Celene described as a bathtub accident.

In graduate school I was taught to carry out comprehensive assessments and as a rule of thumb to ascertain three supporting facts before accepting a hypothesis. In child and family services, I learned the necessity of speaking to judges, child protective workers, children's services directors, and agency directors before it's too late. That often means tentative hypotheses and cautionary statements before assessments are completed or even initiated. This case strengthened my resolve to focus on a parent's devotion to a child and a child's trust and comfort with his parent as the most crucial predictors of how well a child will do back in the parent's home.

Who Can Be the Parent?

Parents need to know that they have choices. Not everyone can raise a child. Parents may lack the cognitive ability to understand what a child needs, to set up and maintain a home, to care for a child when ill, to play with a child at different developmental levels, to help him or her with schoolwork and to face the challenges of growing up. Parental rights may be terminated in many states when a parent shows an incapacity to care for a child and has an IQ below a certain level, for example, 67; but many borderline retarded parents are above this level. Some may be able to provide food and basic care for an infant or toddler with daily help from parent aides and public health nurses, but lose control when the child goes off to school and begins to develop greater skills and awareness than his parent. Such parents may need another full-time adult to act as a co-parent in the home (for example their own mother or father) in order to successfully raise a child. Frequently, our job is to say out loud what a child needs and help parents find out in a limited time period whether they can do what is necessary.

In other cases, parents may cognitively be able to understand what is needed and yet show over time that they cannot make the emotional commitment or demonstrate the sensitivity needed to care for their child. A child may remind a parent of a cruel lover or a traumatic time that he or she desperately wants to forget. If parents were absent in the child's first years, they may never be able to develop the trust, security, and empathy that could lead to attachment. A child's temperament (shy, active, demanding, impulsive, etc.) may not be tolerable for parents. This does not mean that parents don't care about a child, and yet, the best they may be able to do may be to love the child from a distance, like an aunt or older sibling.

In some cases, a parent may be so disabled by his or her own biological depression, schizophrenia, or a manic condition that he or she cannot parent a child now or in the foreseeable future. Although many states allow a judge to terminate a parent's rights with two statements from psychiatrists to this effect, this rarely happens because of the difficulty predicting how a parent will act in the future and the hope that the parent may some day respond to a new medication or another attempt at psychotherapy. Similarly, alcohol and drug addiction blocks a parent from being able to care for and raise children. The parent may go in and out of rehabilitation programs for years without his or her parental rights taken away or permanent custody of a child given to a substitute parent.

Children who are not attached to their mother or father may have grown up unable in their early years to look to anyone as a primary and consistent parent. They may have temporarily bonded to an aunt, then to a grandmother, and then to other relatives as they were passed around. After several moves, children learn that parent-figures are only transitory figures. Take what you can from people and expect them to leave or send you away at any moment.

A 16-year-old veteran of 10 foster placements told me that he felt "like a ping pong ball" bouncing from home to home. An angrier youth described his experience as more "like a pinball," slammed from side to side of the machine and kept in play by "the system."

This youth was determined to break out at any cost. He moved fast and hit hard.

A crisis placement of a child means that family members and current service providers are stuck. A crisis placement gives us an opportunity to get to know parents and children and to help them search for a passageway out of impossible situations.

I want to acknowledge the real challenges facing parents and children. The task of building or rebuilding a positive bond will be arduous when a child has grown up with separations, developmental problems, and expectations of violence or abandonment. The task may seem impossible when the parent grew up the same way.

It helps to stress at the beginning of our work that parents have rights to make choices. If they want to work on bringing their child home, they need to be able to provide all the care, love, and guidance that a child will need to grow up. If parents are ambivalent or have shown that they have not been able to provide what a child has needed, I ask them where they would want the child to live if they are not able to do what it takes to bring their child back into their home. We will not rush them to make any decision in the first sessions, but they need to know that helping their child and themselves will mean exploring options and making difficult choices as adults.

We stress both the rights of parents and their need as adults to make difficult decisions. Helping family members find more than one option reduces their sense of desperation and exhaustion. Hope for change comes out of the search for key people who can help both a child and his parent.

Psychological Evaluations of Attachment

Survival for a young child literally means finding a nurturing parent. For older children, memories and fantasies of being cared for will lead to desperate efforts to regain that relationship. We need to find out who a child sees as a potential parent and how we can help them to find out if this is a viable relationship.

Psychological evaluations with children are very helpful in assessing who a child looks to for safety, affection, and comfort and how much they can trust that person to be there for them. With young children, I use a simple foam rubber family puzzle (Lauri, 1984) and ask the child to pick out figures representing people in their family. I then give them a chance to make up spontaneous stories and will play any parts assigned to me by the child. I limit what my figures say to the language and words that I have heard directly from the child and his family or through reports by staff of conversations with family members.

I will then introduce some set situations, taking on the role of the child. I often ask the child to play his parents and I have the figure representing the child start a story by saying "I'm hungry" to the parents. I will start other stories with "I'm bored," "I'm not feeling good," or "I'm having trouble with my homework." Children reenact what they've come to expect their parents to do in these situations and show whether they can get what they need from their parents and what happens if they ask.

After several stories, I usually try to introduce a situation from the child's history tied in with his need for placement, for example, a mother going into a psychiatric hospital, a father and a mother getting into fights. Young children (and older children functioning socially, emotionally, or cognitively at a young age) use play much better than words to show their perspective of what has happened.

Children can often be engaged to show their hopes for closeness with people through stories about pictures of children and families showing different feelings. Standard psychological tests such as the Roberts Apperception Test (Roberts, 1982), Thematic Apperception Test (Murray, 1971), and Projective Storytelling Cards (Casebeer Art Productions, 1988) are very useful to assess what they have learned to expect to happen with parents and whether they see themselves on their own or getting help from parent-figures. Children are asked to make up stories with a beginning, middle, and end about pictures of children alone or with parent-figures in different situations. For younger or immature children, asking them, "If this were a picture from a book, what would be happening?" often helps to generate a story. I find it helpful not only to ask the traditional prompts about "What is happening?" "What happened before?" and "What is going to happen?" but also to ask children and adolescents "What would help?" when a child is described as distressed in some way. Children show in their responses who they typically look to for help (mothers, fathers, peers, teachers, grandparents) or whether they see themselves on their own.

Traditional projective questions such as "What would you do if you had Aladdin's lamp, the genie popped out, and gave you three magic wishes?" and "What would you do if you won a million dollars in the lottery (or for younger children: What would you do if you found three bags full of money outside the door with your name on it)?" are very helpful. If the child mentions buying a house or a car, I always want to know who they would have living in their house or who they would take with them in their car.

I also ask children what they would do if they won a vacation trip and $2000. Where would they go? Would they take anyone with them? This is similar to the traditional desert or magical island question with the same basic question: "Imagine that a magician took you to a magical island with all the food, clothes, toys you'd need and a place to live. But before the magician sends you, he (she) wants to know, 'Do you want to go by yourself or take anyone else with you?'"

I also ask children a series of pretend questions about important people in their family. "What would you do if, just pretend, you heard a knock on the door (dramatized with knocks for young children), you opened the door (dramatized with door squeak) and you saw your _____? What would you say? What if he said 'Hello'? What would you do? Would you let him in? What would you do with him?" I start with family members who are not too threatening and then work toward those that the child may become more anxious to see.

From a network and permanency perspective, I want to include in these pretend situations anyone who has been or could be a strong parenting figure for the child, for example, grandparents, aunts, uncles, foster parents, babysitters, and other people with long-term relationships to the child. With young children these questions may have to begin with some discussion about what *pretend* means. I would not use such questions with children who quickly regress into a fantasy world in which they cannot separate *pretend from real life*.

I have also used the same questions with feeling thermometers (see Walk, 1956) in a test booklet with the question "Imagine that you walk into a room and see your _____(mother, father, stepfather, grandmother, grandfather, etc.)." Children are asked to shade in the mercury to indicate how they'd feel. Four thermometers are used with 0 to 100 scales showing "How happy?" "How scared?" "How sad?" and "How angry?" The interviewer can then use the situation presented to lead into questions such as: "What would you say? What would your (mother, etc.) say? What would you do? What would your (mother, etc.) say then? What would happen?"

Drawings of a person, a combined drawing of a house, a tree, and a person (Buck, 1948), and a drawing of their family with everyone doing something (Burns & Kaufman, 1970) can be used in many ways (see Di Leo, 1983). I ask children to make up a story for each drawing and indicate what everyone is doing in their family drawing. Some children will spontaneously draw memories of traumatic situations or pictures of their nightmares.

I am interested in how each story plays out, who might be represented by the monsters and victims portrayed, and especially what positive forces and characters are involved to help resolve a crisis. We can then work in family and individual therapy to help the child develop ways to master their nightmares by finding strengths within themselves and connections to positive forces and people in real life.

Sentence completion items are also very helpful in assessing attachment. In addition to traditional items such as "Today I feel _____," I use several questions focusing on other family members (see Lazarus, 1971). With blank spaces on the sentence completion form, I will insert the most relevant names for each child: "I wish my _____ (mother, father, brother, grandparent, etc.) would _____." "I wish (mother, etc.) knew _____." "My _____ (mother, etc.) would say I am _____." "I think I am _____." "If I could I'd tell my _____ (mother, etc.) _____." "The people I like the most are: _____." "Who will really listen to you when you need to talk to someone?" and "Who can you count on to help you in a crisis?" Questions adapted from depression inventories (see Beck, 1978; Reynolds, 1986) can also be helpful in assessing attachments. Children can be asked to circle "Not True," "Sometimes True," or "Often True" for questions such as: "Nobody really loves me," "I feel alone," and "I would like to hide from everyone."

In the course of such an evaluation, most children and adolescents will spontaneously share who they want to live with after placement and where they see their home. Some children will draw their foster family's home when asked to draw a house, tree, and person. Others will remember a home shared in past years with their parents before things got bad. Many children will include a wish to reunite with a parent or relative as one of their "three wishes." And in play stories with human figures, I will sometimes introduce a story in which the child meets with a judge who asks the child, "Where would you want to live?"

Adolescents can be asked more direct questions to assess attachments (see Fruchtman, 1995). "Who did you feel closest to as a young child?" "Who took care of you the most?" "What would you do when you felt upset about something?" "How would you describe your _____(mother, father, etc.)?" "Are there any stories (songs, movies) that remind you of that person?" "If something terrible happened to you, who could you talk to?" "Has anything ever happened to you that you couldn't tell anyone about?" "What words would you use to describe how you and your mother (father) got along?"

After building up sufficient rapport, I will ask older children directly who they would want to live with after placement. I also want to know who they would want to live with as a back-up plan. I often remind children of how generals think. You always need a couple of back-up plans. "If Mom or Dad cannot stop drinking and stay out of jail, who would you want to live with?" These are painful questions but necessary to ask so that practitioners can develop permanency plans that can offer some hope.

Finding someone who will treat a child as special and love him unconditionally is a crucial part of any assessment. Extended family members, previous foster parents, and community resources who could validate and support children and parents form the basis for mapping a course toward permanency. Individuals mentioned as possible resources can be contacted with the permission of parents or guardians. These are typically aunts, uncles, grandparents, or close family friends who could be invited to help in the work to reunite the child with his biological parents and, if necessary, to work themselves to provide a home in which the child can grow up to maturity.

TRACE THE ROOTS OF A FAMILY'S STRUGGLE

I ask each family member to share his perception of what happened and to tell as much of the story as he feels comfortable doing. I want to focus on what led up to the crisis leading to the current placement (or crisis in placement). The days and weeks before a crisis include the stressors, often overlooked, which repeatedly lead to major blow-ups and people giving up (see Kagan & Schlosberg, 1989).

What was happening in the family? Who was there? Who was missing? What developmental changes were transpiring, for example, adolescents moving out of the family, a grandfather becoming ill and needing help? What obstacles prevented the family and network from coping this time? What was different in this crisis—a new boyfriend, a new baby, an older sibling leaving home?

Who did what before, during, and after the crisis? Crises demonstrate how the family works to manage critical conflicts, their rules, roles, and patterns of interaction with outside people and agencies.

If previous placements occurred, what happened then? The first placement usually reflects most clearly the foremost developmental hurdle and family crisis which could not be overcome. Later placements and crises may repeat these themes but often add the impact of past separations and traumas experienced during previous placements. I remember working in an intensive residential treatment program where 4 out of 20 adolescents had been sexually abused during years of placement in a previous group care facility. With each placement, layers of problems and behavioral shields amass, covering the original trauma.

Learn from a Child's Behavior and Development

Kristen's biting reflected how she had never been able to move past the life-or-death crises and the dread of being abandoned that began in her first years. What a youth does for fun, for example, playing with toy figures, watching cartoons, playing with Barbie dolls, playing kickball, etc., helps denote social and emotional age levels.

Tony, a 14-year-old who frequently skipped school and consistently defied his mother and stepfather, lived in a nicely furnished apartment with multiple pictures of his siblings on the living room wall, but none of Tony. Tony's mother said that he would not allow any pictures to be taken of him after age 8. This was the year when his stepfather moved in, his baby brother was born, and his grandfather died. His mother became consumed with her own losses, her new husband, and her youngest baby. From that point on, Tony began seeing himself on his own. The third-grade honor student became a ninth-grade drop-out who spent his time with a group of similar youths—his substitute family on the streets.

The words, expressions, and speech patterns used by a child and parents often reflect preoccupation with normal challenges of a certain age level, for example, breaking away from parents in adolescence or establishing intimate relationships in young adulthood. Clues abound in a family's home. Each family member's likes, dislikes, favorite activities, mannerisms, social relationships, skills, and independence reflect levels of social, emotional, and cognitive development and the developmental challenges they are struggling to master. Posters, pictures, and stuffed animals in a child's room reveal what may be most important.

The child in placement is often acting out the primary unresolved struggles of their own parents. By focusing on the developmental age of the child in placement, we can often discern critical dilemmas that other family members have not been able to overcome. An adolescent's rebellion may represent his own parent's submerged anger at feeling trapped with adult-like responsibilities as a young teenager or child of alcoholic parents. A child's terror may reflect his parent's traumatic memories from a young age of being battered, someone being killed, or witnessing his mother (the child's grandmother) being savagely beaten, nightmares which the parent has never been able to overcome or even talk about.

I want to focus on the developmental transition (Landau-Stanton, 1994) that the family is struggling to achieve. We can then work to pull together family members and service providers to overcome the current crisis and the longstanding developmental hurdle it represents.

Asking parents and children what they remember when things were going well can lead to valuable information about competence and how far the family was able to move along a developmental continuum. Erikson's stages (Erikson, 1986) of social and emotional development often mark the challenges family members are struggling to overcome. Clients who repeatedly act in ways typical of very young children often seem unable to move past "trust versus mistrust," "autonomy versus shame," or "industry versus inferiority."

Helping the child in placement to move from one stage to the next will mean helping his parents negotiate the same conflicts. We can use the developmental challenges of a youth at risk to help older family members to remember their own struggles, what helped, what was difficult, what they would do now in hindsight, and how they could help the next generation surmount these challenges. This will mean finding ways to help an older youth experience the support and security needed to master an earlier stage, for example, "autonomy versus shame." Parents and other adults can work at the youth's social and emotional level to provide recognition, guidance, and support for acting independently, while at the same time involving the youth in age-appropriate activities that he can master, for example, after-school sports, Boy Scout projects, choir, etc.

It's helpful to ask family members how old they actually feel (Waters & Lawrence, 1993), to ask other family members how old a child often acts, and to look at children's behavior in terms of roles played in the family. A child may see himself as Grandma's nurse or as an army guard ready to defend the family if someone feared comes to the door.

Often, children show behaviors typical of two or three ages: a young age where they were not able to get their needs met, a much older age in which they tried to parent others in the family, and some of the competence and striving of their current age. I ask children, "What age would you like to be?" This helps in framing goals that a youth is willing to work toward with his family.

Age-appropriate privileges can be earned with age-appropriate behavior. A 15-year-old who screams, hits, bites, and throws tantrums like a 2-year-old will be treated like a 2-year-old. Two-year-olds need constant supervision, very strict limits, and restrictions from anything conceivably dangerous. For an older youth acting like a 2-year-old, this often means hospitalization or highly supervised detention centers.

At the other end of the continuum, youths will have tremendous difficulty giving up longstanding roles as the family member who watched over, cared for, and protected their siblings, parents, or grandparents. For these youths, childhood is unknown, often unattractive, and typically seen as impossible to regain. Who else can be trusted to maintain the family? How else will they feel so needed?

An adolescent in a parenting role needs to see over time that someone else is picking up the parenting responsibilities and that he will be valued by family members if he begins to act in age-appropriate ways. He will need the courage to experiment with and eventually to develop an equally important role that fits his cognitive age, age-appropriate striving for independence, and need to be part of the family. Involvement in sports, arts, drama, adventure programs, community organizations, mentoring programs, etc. can provide avenues for transforming a youth's dedication and energy into skill development and leadership.

WORK WITH METAPHOR: THE KEY TO THE DOOR

The crisis leading to placement reflects family struggles that cannot be faced directly. Metaphors represent what cannot be said and what cannot be resolved. I try to focus on the most poignant metaphors expressed in the behaviors leading to placement and to use these metaphors to engage family members and work toward change.

Children and parents who have lived with trauma often feel and act like a fractured mirror (Gil, 1991). In order to survive serial crises with an ongoing threat of abandonment or annihilation, pieces of experience are broken away and separated. Like a cracked mirror, feelings of panic may be placed in one area and visual memories of an attacker locked in a distant corner. Rage and sadness may be locked into other fragments. Putting them together may represent an unbearable reminder of incest, rapes, beatings, murder, etc.

This is the process of dissociation, which helps a child to survive but leaves him broken apart. The child depends on denial and often becomes preoccupied with multiple crises that symbolically reenact parts of old memories while helping the child avoid thinking about what really happened.

Metaphors provide a way to focus and clarify the blurred images and shattered pieces of family members' experiences. Bringing out the metaphor in a nonshaming manner can tap into a family's sense of truth, show that we are not afraid of dealing with powerful emotions, and provide a framework in which to work slowly and carefully in therapy on putting the pieces back together into a meaningful whole.

Metaphors are symbolic keys that can unlock doors for change and reintegrate shattered pieces of experience. We find these keys by using ourselves as finely-tuned diagnostic instruments to trace patterns of emotional energy and center our attention on what is most gripping. Beginning when I hear or read referral information about a family, I try to remain aware of what I am feeling about becoming involved with the family.* Our feelings (scared, angry, detached, shaming, tense) resonate from the inherent messages of a family's lifestyle and living environment. How do I feel about visiting them in their neighborhood, their apartment? What am I expecting will happen? What would it be like to live with them? How would I like to be the worker who visits them every week?

I want to gently touch on each of the problem areas a family presents and assess which is the most intense. This is the area most tied to the family's primary struggle and reflects losses, gaps, and terrors that have left them stymied.

I remember a 17-year-old girl who complained incessantly about her mother and stepfather. Cheryl clashed in loud, verbal battles with her stepfather, who tried to protect his wife from what he saw as

---

*My thanks to Shirley Schlosberg for this and many other tools for understanding metaphor and transference.

verbal abuse. Cheryl had been placed in a shelter and desperately wanted to return home. However, she only seemed able to elicit acrimony and rejection from her mother and stepfather. My feeling in the session was predominantly one of mourning; it felt like a funeral— heavy, cold, desperate, doomed.

Cheryl had been very close to her father until he died when she was 6. She then became very close to her maternal grandmother, until she died when Cheryl turned 11. Since then, she had struggled in vain to get the same level of intimacy and nurture from her mother. Her mother's remarriage brought in someone to protect her mother from Cheryl's intense demands. The more Cheryl demanded closeness, the more her mother needed to pull away. A vicious cycle ensued, leading to eviction from the home and nowhere for Cheryl to live.

We needed to address Cheryl's unfinished mourning for her father, her grandmother, and the mother that she wanted but could never have. In family sessions, we helped Cheryl and her mother to begin to grieve and to find a way for Cheryl to maintain the best parts of her relationship with her mother, even though they could not live together. At the same time, she needed to build connections to a substitute family that could support her as she moved into adulthood.

A colleague shared with me how he was working during a home visit to engage a single mother to provide safety in her home. He found himself ignoring the entry and exit of the mother's crack-addicted uncle who was barred in a court order from being in the home because of his past violent behaviors. My colleague felt he was "walking on eggshells" and was afraid to talk about what was really going on. He was focused so much on not upsetting this mother that he found himself buying into the family rule: "Don't talk about Uncle Rodney."

I ask myself what strikes me or intrigues me the most about a family (Andersen, 1991). Kristen was desperate to hold on to her mother. Rebecca was initially hospitalized because she described a monster at the foot of her bed.

Several authors have described valuable techniques for assessing and working with metaphors (see Bergman, 1985; Combs & Freedman, 1990; Duhl, 1993; Imber-Black, Roberts, & Whiting, 1992; Lankton & Lankton, 1989; Madanes, 1990a; Roberts, 1994; Waters & Lawrence, 1993). It's helpful for me to look at what is being shown and to ask myself, "Where have I experienced this before? When have I felt like this? Who does this person remind me of from books, movies, family, friends, relatives, and past therapy sessions? I look at body posture and repeated or dramatic actions in a session or by description from referral material about the crisis leading to placement. I try to pull images from appearances and postures or repetitive movements—a father who looks like a pioneer guarding his home against assault, a boy who acts like Huck Finn escaping down the local stream, a couple fighting over their car to see who gets to escape.

First words are valuable clues. "I'm dried up, I'm exhausted," said a grandmother. She was accused of neglecting her 6-year-old grandson who was placed in her custody after his mother died of AIDS. "I want this over with," said a mother during her intake session with her fourteenth assigned service provider in 8 years. "Don't talk about my drinking; I'm sick of it and I throw things," ordered another mother looking ominously at some Tonka trucks close to her feet in our family meeting room. I noticed to my dismay that the agency had brought in the heavy metal version. Words and phrases repeated in a session often reflect key elements, for example, references to "monsters" or "volcanoes erupting." Dreams, of course, provide rich clues.

Sessions with clients are loaded with rich metaphors that are available to practitioners who are listening carefully to their own feelings and reactions. We are pulled to repeat the family's story, to feel their unspoken anguish, and to reenact lessons from the past. Family members can quickly sense our own triggers and issues. My sarcastic comments and hard-edged looks betray simmering anger at passive, depressed mothers and a grimace and abrupt move backward reveals a fear of agitated and bellicose fathers. We can quickly become part of the family script. Our challenge is to use our understanding, skill, and supports to understand our reactions and what this reveals about the metaphor of the family's struggle.

A small, waif-like girl keeps looking up at me for a lap to sit on. I feel an urge to hold and protect her, but my role in the family is to encourage the real parents to carry out this function or, if necessary, to decide to assign this responsibility to someone else who can raise the child. I can use the pull to be a father for this girl to help me understand what is missing in her life and most likely the parents' lives.

With another family, I feel scared, disgusted, or angry. I may find myself simply thinking of getting away. Each feeling is a valuable clue to a family's message: "Care for me," "People get hurt here," "I'm ready to explode," "No one's really here. No one really cares." Images and feelings that come to my mind can then be tested out. "I get the feeling you're like a bomb ready to explode. What helps you hold yourself together? What would trigger you to explode?"

Before I can express these metaphors, I want to make sure no one feels pressed up against the wall in an adversarial interrogation. When someone tells me to stop or gives me a signal that indicates their way of saying "stop," I thank them. They are exercising their power to protect themselves, a key to any change. This is a therapy about the use of time. I am not going to push for any miracles in our session or rush family members into another crisis.

A family's stories about key events in their history often provide invaluable clues to what has blocked change, hidden strengths, how family members see themselves, and the rules family members maintain as a way of coping and demonstrating loyalty to their family. I elicit stories by asking parents if it is okay to ask their children what they remember or think happened at critical times in a family's history. "It helps me to understand what the kids have learned or remember." Stories about what led up to parents separating, a mother no longer speaking to her mother, an absent father who suddenly stopped visits and "disappeared," or other key family events and changes often contain powerful messages and may reveal in a nutshell central dilemmas that have left family members feeling trapped and powerless.

Stories often reflect past traumas, who children and parents sought for support, developmental transitions that family members are attempting to master, who in the past provided some help, and who acted like a parent to today's children and their parents. Jackie, a separated mother of three children, shared with me a story of how she remembered being in a boat on Burden's pond with her parents and another man when she was 5 years old. Her father threw her into the pond, yelling, "You drown or you swim"; she felt that neither of her parents would have cared if she had drowned. The other man in the boat rescued her; however, he ended up killing himself after his wife moved in with Jackie's father. Jackie felt more attached to this man than to either of her parents.

Jackie lived with reenactments of near-fatal violence throughout her life. She was referred for family counseling after her 10-year-old son established a reputation for getting into repeated fights with older children in which he would end up bloodied and severely hurt. Jackie had left the children's father, an alcoholic and cocaine addict, after repeated incidents in which she was beaten and he threatened to kill her. Jackie took her two daughters away with her but left her son with his father for a year and a half. During that time, she never spoke to her son. She was now enraged at his defiance of her commands and felt like killing him.

Jackie's son had heard the same message that she had learned as a child: "You drown or you swim." Both repeatedly put themselves in situations where one or the other could end up killed. At the same time, both were still looking for someone who could save them, but always with the expectation that this hero would in the end be lost too.

The message of the Burden's pond story was that safety and a trusting bonded relationship were impossible. A change in Jackie's relationship with her son would mean finding a way out of the tragedy of her own childhood, a way in which Jackie could help her son get the caring, valuing, and protection that she never received as a child. She would have to learn how to swim herself, teach her son how to swim, and convince him that she would not abandon him again or let him drown. This would mean filling her life with supportive people she and her son could trust.

Storytelling and game therapy are very effective ways of helping children gain the courage to deal with painful situations (see Gardner, 1975; James, 1989; Roberts, 1994). Together with the child, we can create a story tied to the metaphor and explore different ways to master the dilemma expressed in a metaphor. A child's affect, actions, and perspectives are matched to a character in a story. Stories can address the challenge of mastering problems and resolving a child's impasse at a developmental stage, for example, feeling shame versus developing autonomy. Using a typical framework (beginning, middle, and end), we can help a child develop his own resources for managing overwhelming and terrifying situations and dealing with his needs for support, safety, and hope. We can also help a child to create his own game (see Kagan, 1986) to represent how he copes with family crises and to explore use of different beliefs, perspectives, and actions, leading to different outcomes.

Often, children (and parents) can use poetry, music, artwork, and sculpture to represent symbolically what they can't say in words, or even bear to face directly, about what's happening in their families. Linesch (1993) and James (1989) describe many innovative techniques, including representing family members in clay or drawings as objects, shapes, etc. Parents and children can be asked to draw the family in the best times remembered, in the worst times, in the time just before placement, and how they'd like the family to appear in the future.

Children can draw how they feel or felt inside, how they think they look to others in the family, and how the family would look/act if, by magic, their problems went away. Drawing what could help a family move from pictures of the current crisis to pictures of the family with problems resolved (Mills & Crowley, 1986) can help family members to identify the resources available to make changes.

STARTING THE VOYAGE

Permanency work is difficult and painful. It often seems like a treacherous voyage with storms raging from day to day. Metaphors help me to center my efforts and maintain a focus in the midst of multiple problems. With prominent metaphors and developmental challenges in mind, we can help family members develop their own map, locate and understand their personal monsters, reaffirm meaning, and set a direction for strengthening attachments and resolving the crises which led to placement.

Metaphors can be used to identify family landmarks that mark progress and symbolize the strengths and resources (extended family, friends, practitioners, community organizations) that will make the journey possible. Like any canoe guide, I would never want to embark on a voyage without a map in hand.

chapter 5

Help my father.

*Ten-year-old placed after trying to drown
herself in a tub of hot water*

centering in the storm

TIMMY LUNGED AT HIS GRANDMOTHER, SYLVIA, WITH A SEWING SCIS-
SORS. "Fuck you!" he screamed. "I hate you!" Moments before, Timmy
had resisted Sylvia's demand to stop whining for candy and her voice
exploded, "Get in your room! I don't want to see you!" Sylvia
shrieked when Timmy grabbed the scissors, rousing her husband
from his football game.

"I can't take any more," she ranted. "That's it! He's got to go!"
Sylvia saw the menacing look on her husband's face and ran out of
the house screaming, "I'll kill myself if that kid comes back!" Like so
many other children entering a crisis group care facility, 8-year-old
Timmy felt scared of losing the only home he knew, begged to go
back to Grandpa, and was enraged at everyone around him.

Children can be removed from their homes for abuse and neglect
but are often placed, like Timmy, after trying to hurt or kill themselves or someone else. Taking things from others, putting toxic sub-
stances in one's mouth, hitting, shoving, screaming, and running
away are common problems. "Fix her," demand some parents. "Keep
her safe," demand referral sources. "Keep us safe," demand others.

Professionals are brought in to control a youth's behaviors, teach the youth to behave better, manage neurological problems, reduce emotional disturbance, and send a child back home as soon as possible.

Placement for older children and adolescents often begins when a school or the parents file a PINS petition, which cites the youth as a person in need of supervision. During placement, the youth's behaviors become the responsibility of the service agency. Distance, detachment, and isolation are increased. When the youth is about to go home, or soon after returning home, the underlying fears of abandonment or violence are often acted out by this child (or in some cases by a sibling), leading to further interventions by practitioners and another placement, often in a more restrictive facility.

Over time, the family and service providers may revolve in crises (see figure 5.1) in a manner typical of addicted families, moving from "wet" to "dry," from shame to rigidity (see Berenson, 1976; Fossum & Mason, 1986). Practitioners and agencies begin to play an ongoing role in the family's crises, often providing temporary periods of control.

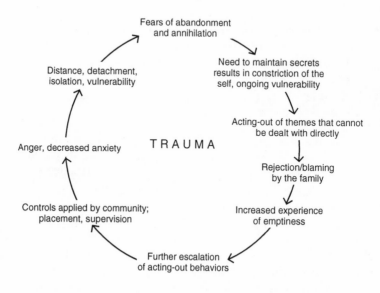

Figure 5.1. Dancing around the pit of despair
(from Kagan & Schlosberg, 1989; based on Ausloos, 1981a)

"I want to go back to Grandpa!" Timmy demanded every day. Yet when I saw Timmy, he shared dreams of pedaling furiously on his bike as he tried to get away from his grandpa. Timmy made up story after story of men yelling, cursing, and attacking children and women. Women in his stories did nothing for children and screamed in exasperation when children asked for food. Boys needed to be tough and gain super powers to destroy the attackers.

MOVE BEYOND BEHAVIOR CONTROL

Every organization and practitioner need to decide what their primary objective will be in working with families in crisis. Pressure to serve as behavior control agents, especially with children and youths displaying risky behaviors, will be intense. Taking on this role, however, sets practitioners up as enforcers who replicate the parent-figures youths have learned to defy. In a battle over who's in control, no one usually wins.

Youths who see placement as offering no hope of change in their family typically act out, leading to highly supervised and restrictive placements. The youth and her underlying problems are locked up for a defined period of time. Practitioners who take on behavior control as their priority feel overburdened, always on guard, and often end up like Timmy's grandmother, demanding that a troublesome youth be expelled.

To move from being control agents to therapists who help family members change, we need to look at the child's behavior as a message. The actions and beliefs of the child show where the child became stuck developmentally (see chapter 4), what family dilemmas are being acted out, and often the greatest fears of family members. From a multigenerational perspective, the behaviors of parents and often grandparents appear very similar. Timmy's struggles with violent men and abandonment were also the struggles of his mother and grandparents.

Lessons from Two-Year-Olds

Behaviors leading to placement are typical of children in the "terrible two's," a challenging and delightful age when children naturally strive to develop a sense of independence and mastery, "autonomy versus shame" (Erickson, 1986). Defiance, tantrums, magical thinking, and running away are normal behaviors. Month by month, the child ventures a few steps further away from her parent but always turns to look back and make sure Mom or Dad is still there.

This pattern of development continues through latency and adolescence, with 18-year-olds charging off to work, their own apartments, or college. Parents are expected to remain behind, scorned for being middle-aged but counted on to remain stable and entrusted with the responsibility for maintaining their daughter's or son's room as a sanctuary, a shrine to the child of the past.

Change for children and parents in crisis-oriented families requires mastering the struggles of the 1- to 3-year-old. Schlosberg (1990) challenged practitioners to think of what "good parents" do with 2-year-olds in a normal day. From breakfast in the morning to a good-night ritual (bath, pajamas, bedtime story, kiss good-night), "good parents" provide a safe world for the preschooler to explore and grow. Safety comes through a regular schedule. "We get up, eat breakfast, brush our teeth, go to day care, and eat lunch. Then Mom or Dad comes. We go back home, play, eat dinner, watch TV, then time for bed," a child will tell you. Safety also comes through limits on what the child can and can't do.

What happens when the 3-year-old hops on her tricycle, heads down the driveway or sidewalk, races past the tree or pole that Mom or Dad warned never to go past, turns the corner, flips over and skins her knee? Her knee stings with pain as if she's been stabbed with a hundred needles. Blood oozes out under the dirt. The preschooler looks at her wound and feels like she may die. Her insides are coming out. This is where the 2- to 3-year-old learns how to deal with pain. She runs back to where Mom or Dad is supposed to be. Tears stream down her face. Her mouth is drawn and her eyes downcast, a wounded soul searching for salvation.

What do good parents do with their hurt child? Mom or Dad reaches out, picks her up, gives her a hug and shows how we make it "all better" by gently washing the cut, putting on a protective cream, and adding the bandaid. Not just any bandaid, of course—super hero, dinosaur, or cartoon characters work best. And don't forget Mom or Dad's magic kiss. But Mom or Dad isn't finished. "Remember what I said. Don't go past the tree!" the 3-year-old is admonished. Losing the tricycle for a time may be a consequence.

The child goes back out to play, equipped with the magic bandaid and the magic kiss. Her pain has been validated. She told her story and was believed. Hugs release endorphins, chemicals that calm and soothe. The child learns she can survive feeling pain and she learns how she will stay safe in the future.

IDENTIFY SPLIT MESSAGES AND DOUBLE BINDS

Of course, it's not like this for many children. Children growing up with abuse and neglect learn that crying over a scraped knee may mean getting a whack with a hand, belt, or board and hearing their parent scream, "Don't be a sissy!" "Don't bother me right now!" "Can't you see I'm busy with your brother?" "You kids are driving me nuts. One more problem and I'm outa here. . . . Now get back outside and play. . . . If I don't get some peace, I'm putting you all in a home."

The child's head goes down. Her eyes narrow and the tears stop. She has learned a vital lesson for survival in her family: Don't upset Mom or Dad at all costs. The child learns to ignore the pain in her leg and to keep her mouth shut. It's best not even to look at it. She learns to carry on, pretending nothing happened.

Later in the day, she may hear or remember a very different message. "Come here baby," coos the same parent who shunned her hours before. "Rub Mommy's back. . . . You're my sweetie. . . . You're Mama's special one. . . . None of the others are worth a damn. . . . I could never make it without you." The girl is drawn into a special role: a companion who watches over and cares for her parent. The memories of the scraped knee and her mother's rejection are blocked. "I love my Mommy!" she'd tell anyone who asks about her mother. "It's the two of us against the world."

The child grows up hearing two conflicting and powerful messages from her primary parent: "I love you; you're a part of me" *and* "Get out! I hate you." Living day to day with both messages leads the child to split her own identity into two parts (Masterson, 1976). The "good" daughter is always there for her parent, ready night and day to hold, serve, and care for (see figure 5.2). The "bad" daughter acts out the fear and rage, often repeating what she has heard but cannot dare say at home. She calls her teacher a "fucking bitch," smacks the girl in front of her in the lunch line, and takes what she needs from another child's locker.

In the double bind theory, Bateson, Jackson, Haley, and Weakland, (1956) posited that psychotic behavior resulted from an individual's learning to live with repeated communications that conflicted at dif-

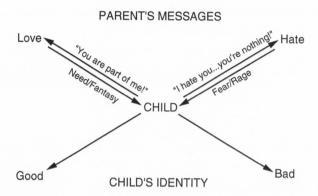

Figure 5.2. Splitting messages and a child's identity
(after Masterson, 1976)

ferent levels. The individual had to respond to punitive and conflicting injunctions from parents, spouses, or other primary people in
their lives without being able to talk about these conflicting messages
or to escape. For instance, a girl may be ordered to give her mother
(or father) a hug, but when she puts her arm around her parent, she
feels her mother stiffen and the girl pulls back. Her mother then says,
"Don't you want to hug your mother anymore? What's the matter
with you?" The daughter can never win, no matter what she does,
and at the same time can never leave the relationship. Any move
away elicits dire threats. "I'd never be able to live without you," a
mother may sob. Regression to infantile behavior and idiosyncratic
thinking may serve as the child's only refuge and at the same time
symbolize the only developmental level where parents and a child
feel safe.

In contrast to families with rather rigid, repeated, and often psychotic behaviors, families revolving in crises are continually on the edge
of falling apart and dissolving. The critical element in these families is
symbolized by the child in placement or at risk of placement. Abandonment and eviction from the system are real threats established over generations, with siblings, cousins, parents, grandparents, aunts, and uncles
ending up outside the family in residential treatment, foster homes,
drug/alcohol rehabilitation, criminal justice programs, or scattered across
the country growing up with different people "on the streets."

Temporary living arrangements may be the norm in the family for
everyone by age 14. Children may spend their first years with grandma

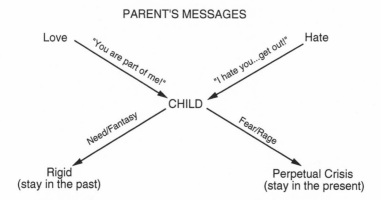

Figure 5.3. Splitting messages and time orientation

before moving in with their "real" Mom at age 6 when grandma gets too tired, becomes sick, or needs to care for a younger grandchild. By 13 or 14, they may be looking for any means to get away from their "home."

Families of children in crisis placements often revolve from a rigid "walking on eggshells" orientation to an intense crisis stage. This shift corresponds to the split messages given and received by generations of family members (see figure 5.3). "You are part of me!" and other all-encompassing messages of love renew a child's desperate wish and need to cling to the parent she has become so terrifed of losing. Because the parent-child attachment is so weak and often threatened, the child acts in a very constricted and immature manner, trying to recapture the bond she may have had as a toddler. She climbs onto her mother's lap, sucks her thumb, and asks to be rocked like a baby. This is the rigid side of the split.

A few hours or moments later, the child may once again hear a hate/rejection message from her parent. This generates an almost immediate and often overpowering sense of fear. The child may react with rage and begin to get into trouble outside of the family.

Peers provide excitement, escape, and brief moments of intimacy. Gangs provide substitute families. Pregnancy is often seen as a second chance to create the intimacy and attachment that a teenage girl lost (or never had) with her own parents. Pregnancy can also lead to temporary respite from one's family, a sudden swelling of attention (positive and negative) from family members, and support from teen pregnancy programs.

Practitioners worry about a teenager's ability to provide the caring her infant needs and the probability of another generation growing up with neglect and poverty. Taxpayers increasingly resent the financial burden of teen pregnancies and government subsidy of unwed mothers. Yet, for a youth fleeing a life of abuse and neglect, pregnancy may appear to be her best chance to feel successful and to be validated as someone important.

Counter Split Messages

Haley (1977) described "perverse triangles" between two parents and a child in which parents detour conflicts through an acting-out adolescent. Systems messages and paradoxical injunctions have been used in family therapy (see Nichols, 1984; Watzlawick, Beavin, & Jackson, 1967) to counter the paradoxes experienced by family members. For instance, therapists may give a message stressing *both* how a family maintains its balance with a cycle of interactive behaviors *and* the necessity for a child to continue enacting a problematic behavior in order to protect the family (Papp, 1983).

Ferreira (1960) described delinquent behavior evolving from the "split double bind," in which a youth hears conflicting messages from *two* parents. Ausloos (1981a) found that giving chaotic families paradoxical injunctions led to more crises. Instead, he developed an intervention that group care staff could employ during family sessions to counter split double binds experienced by a delinquent youth. Ausloos suggested that the family therapist stress how the youth's behavior (running away, stealing, etc.) plays a critical and competent role in maintaining her parents' and family's homeostasis. The youth's primary child care worker would then stress that this was true but, at the same time, the child care worker saw the positive potential shown by the youth and would work with the youth to make small changes to *avoid* going back to court.

In this approach, the therapeutic messages from the family therapist and the child care worker are presented in a united manner to counter the conflicting messages received by the youth from her parents (Ausloos, 1978, 1981a). The youth and her family hear how her delinquent behaviors help maintain the family system and at the same time the youth is given a positive message validating her potential. The covert processes of the family are made overt (see Papp, 1983). The group care worker serves as the youth's advocate, providing a message of hope based on recognition of the healthy drives and successes of the youth.

UNDERSTAND THE CHILD'S MESSAGE

Children growing up with toxic secrets and threats of abandonment lack the stability and security needed to successfully manage traumatic events. The onset of sexual abuse, the burning of a home, or the death of a nurturing grandmother can end a child's development. Major traumas in the family's life cycle may not be discussed without risking total abandonment, someone dying, or dissolution of the only family the child knows. Repeated crises reflect these unresolved traumas and become a way of life.

Traumas endured without stable, nurturing attachments create wounds that cannot heal. Traumatic events often encapsulate the ripping apart of a child's fragile sense of trust. After the trauma, the child enhances any memory of love she received in the past. Out of her desperate need for someone to care for her, the child creates a fantasy of magically getting love from her parent.

When the same child experiences hate and rejection from Mom or Dad, she may deny or minimize that anything happened. Yet, the child's fantasy remains threatened by her own fear and rage. These feelings cannot be directed at her parent because this would mean facing both her parent's wrath and the reality of her mother or father's neglect. Instead, the fear and rage are acted out with tantrums, crying, demands, stealing, and aggressive acts toward siblings, peers, teachers, and neighbors.

The child's behavior shows what she cannot dare express to her parents without facing permanent eviction and losing the hope (even if it's just a fantasy) of gaining (or regaining) her parent's love. Unable to assert her needs without abandonment, the child feels split apart, leading to a fractured sense of herself. She oscillates between good and bad—a "no-win" situation. The child feels unbalanced with no foundation. She learns to move impulsively and becomes part of the crisis cycle. The original traumas become lost in the midst of swirling crises but the child's behaviors replay the same themes in a desperate effort to cope with the underlying threat of abandonment.

Heed the Child's Call for Help

Children are drawn to the wounds of their parents: the tense lines on a mother's face when her father is mentioned, the sudden and insistent change of topic when drinking is mentioned. Children have an uncanny sense for what remains unresolved in a family's past.

Adults busy themselves in the details and struggles of daily life, leaving the past buried, hoping for time to heal. For a child, the ghosts of the past take on a real form in the unconscious gestures, the averted looks, the drawn eyes, the angry glares, and the shrill screams of their parents.

The worst thing in the world is to see one's primary (or only) parent severely and repeatedly hurt or threatening to abandon by running away, taking drugs, or committing suicide. Children learn to distract their parents from old wounds. The child learns to be hypervigilant and on guard "24-7" (24 hours a day, 7 days a week). Getting into trouble diverts a fragile parent from facing an old trauma and provides a sense of control in a perilous world.

I visited a family reported to child protective services following the father's leaving a mark on his 10-year-old daughter's face. He smacked her with the back of his hand when she lied to him about having completed her homework. This was the second hotline call and, according to the parents and the child, the second time that the father had struck her hard enough to leave a mark.

The session had begun stiffly with Alice, the girl's mother, standing angrily in the living room of the family's home. She accused child protective services of harassing the family over nothing. Ed, an immigrant from a northern European country, saw nothing wrong with what he had done and appeared to be trying earnestly to teach his daughter to "think double" before she said something untrue again.

I was able to validate Ed's concern over getting his daughter to do her homework and his attempt to teach her to be honest. Rather than harp on how hitting his daughter was wrong—a shame-based message—I focused on how his intentions to teach his daughter had certainly been important but simply didn't work. And, in this country, slapping a child and leaving a mark was not allowed.

"I don't like the truth," Maria, his daughter, said in our session. I talked with Ed about how his effort to teach his daughter to "think double" had not achieved what he wanted and instead his daughter was "thinking double" all the time, leading to a series of lies that made him and his wife increasingly angry at Maria.

I was interested to learn what had happened leading up to the first hotline call and whether the same issue had resurfaced again. Maria had been 4 years old when she and her older sister were sent to a babysitter while her mother began working. After the first day, her sister, Erin, told their parents that the babysitter had made Maria kiss and embrace the babysitter's older sons. Alice said she feared losing her job and had no other day care available, so the children were sent back the next day. Ed warned Maria to not do any kissing or anything else with the babysitter's sons again.

Erin reported that Maria was again made to do things with the babysitter's sons the next day and Ed slapped his daughter on her face, leading to the first hotline report. Ed said this was when he began to teach Maria to "think double." Alice found another sitter and told us she blamed herself for sending the children back a second day.

As we talked about these incidents, I noticed that Alice tensed up, her expression changing from belligerent to a distant gaze. She physically stepped back, almost withdrawing from our session. Alice and Ed had worried about Maria being sexually molested but she had never taken her daughter for a medical evaluation and never reported the incident. Alice seemed to move into a trance when we talked about the possibility of sex abuse; it was almost like she drifted away, becoming unreachable.

Alice began the session incensed at being "indicated" by child protective services for neglect following the latest hotline call. She had failed to do anything about her husband's hitting and supported his right to smack Maria. I acknowledged her anger; this was a family, I said, that obviously cared about their children, fed them, clothed them, gave them a well-furnished home, and wanted them to do well in school. At the same time, something had happened leading Maria to become locked into the role of a chronic liar who provoked her parents' and older sister's anger.

I asked Alice if we could talk about how things had changed so that Maria ended up getting in so much trouble. "Do you remember a time when no one worried about Maria lying or getting in trouble?" Alice shared that, when Maria was 2-1/2, Alice had become ill with a life-threatening illness. Despite the risk of her dying, she and Ed told no one about it.

"Maria had a different experience as a toddler than her sister," I pointed out. It was no one's fault but she experienced her mother becoming unavailable, which would have been extremely frightening to any normal child. Maria had learned as a 2-1/2-year-old that really scary things could not be talked about. This was like Ed's teaching Maria to "think double," which was not something malicious or bad but, rather, Alice and Ed's effort to manage a truly frightening situation.

Ed confirmed his concerns about his wife's health when Maria was a young child and his continued concern about a recurrence. Alice agreed that Maria had a different experience growing up than Erin had and expressed a willingness to work in counseling on finding a way to help Maria to be able tell the truth.

Several weeks later, I saw the family again at an initial meeting to begin counseling at my agency. Alice was still angry at child protective services and was glad they had stopped monitoring the family. Maria had been doing much better in school. Alice reported that after our previous session she had taken Maria into her bedroom and shared with her how she had been sexually abused as a young child. Alice, like so many other sexually abused children, had learned that she could never talk about what happened. Alice and Ed wanted to use this counseling to help Maria and Erin become comfortable telling their parents what troubled them, something that Alice was not able to do as a child.

Born under a Bad Sign

A child can become the focal point of a family's struggle by picking up on festering emotional wounds and her parent's traumas. The child learns to act out what cannot be said, and, from this perspective, is acting in a competent way in her family system (Ausloos, 1981b; Waters & Lawrence, 1993). Her bad or crazy behavior helps to balance a system in crisis.

A child born at a time of terrible crisis or otherwise tied in with traumas in a family may learn over time to carry on the tension, the stress, and the fighting of the past. The child and other family members remain imbalanced with conflicting pressures reflecting the split messages: love/hate, loyalty/defiance. As pressure moves too far in one direction, the crisis cycle is engaged (see figure 5.1). The family revolves from wet to dry, shame to rigid perfectionism (see Berenson, 1976; Fossum & Mason, 1986).

Toxic secrets lead to splitting and fractures of each family member. A child cannot deal with what has happened when she sees her father on the verge of exploding in rage or abandoning the family and her mother hiding in fear or threatening to hit again or kill herself. What cannot be said often represents the terrors and fears of abandonment (Ausloos, 1986). These are snag points (Pittman, 1987), which lock a family into revolving patterns of crises and block change. The broken pieces of the child's life cannot be put together because this would mean facing the threat of abandonment and the break-up of the family.

OPEN UP LOST DIMENSIONS OF TIME

Ausloos (1986) described how crisis-oriented families move from event to event in a seemingly chaotic manner, while rigid and psychotic families act as if time had been arrested, with few changes taking place over long periods of time. Families embroiled in one crisis after another appear to be dealing only with the present. Stress is dealt with by creating and responding to events of the moment. Family crises escalate directly in response to pressures from inside or outside the family. Outsiders usually see these families as chaotic and crisis-ridden. Practitioners quickly become immersed in crises and feel pressured to act immediately to rescue or protect.

Another way of dealing with enormous stress is to take on a "no-change" position in which time appears to have stopped. The past equals the present equals the future. Stress is dealt with by stopping time and all development. Such families are characterized by belongings, furnishings, and clothes from an earlier period. A mother may keep her 5-year-old in diapers. Things should stay just the way they were when Mom or Dad or Grandma was a child. Escalations are covert but powerful. Family members appear rigid and work hard to keep to what they have.

A third way of dealing with time revolves around families who focus almost entirely on the future, with no present and no past. These families are marked by obsessions, a driven quality, and overt anxiety about what could happen in the future.

Time can become fixated in one primary dimension or families may rock abruptly from one pattern to another. Different family members may appear locked into one or another time dimension.* For instance, a teenage daughter may serve as the family's memory of the past, a grandmother may fret over the future, and a mother and father may live from one day to the next, striving to keep themselves high.

Each dimension has its own rules. Painful dilemmas are avoided but family members become restricted within a predominant time zone of awareness and action. This, in turn, constrains how they see the world and how they act (see figure 5.4). The challenge for families is to regain the lost dimensions of time and thus open up and maintain previously blocked perspectives and possibilities for resolving traumas.

The repeated dangerous behaviors of parents or children leading to emergency or court-ordered placements often reflect a longstanding

---

*My thanks to Charles Frank for describing this pattern in a family he worked with.

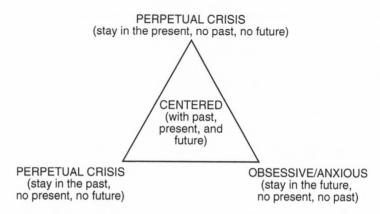

Figure 5.4. Time orientation

crisis orientation that has provoked action by police, schools, child protective services, mental health clinics, or probation departments. When children are in the midst of chronic crises, I want to engage family and network members to summon their courage and resources to face the past and make choices for the future.

With crisis-oriented families, Ausloos (1986) asked youths to learn and share family histories in order to help family members to regain a sense of the past and slow down time. Timelines of key family events, photo albums, genograms, family stories, and visits with relatives to find out about the past are useful assignments. The power of these assignments lies in family members becoming safe enough and feeling strong enough to share what happened before.

MOVE PAST "BAD" AND "GOOD" LABELS

Will, another boy I saw at the crisis residence, had a reputation for defying teachers and stealing. I asked his mother what she liked about him, what good things he did, and what they did for fun together. We talked about his defiance and stealing as his way to show what he could not say, and that he could be a very caring and likeable boy. Will's mother warmed up in our session, dropped her animosity toward therapists, and participated in counseling with her son. At the end of our session, she said that after years of work with school officials and several previous therapists, "you're the first person who told me that he's not a bad boy."

In mainstream American culture, "bad" boys are often assumed to come from "bad" parents and "bad" mothers in particular. Labels of "bad" and "sick" can perpetuate perceptions that change is impossible and foster continued hunts for someone to blame. Our task is to get beyond a blaming orientation without neglecting real problems.

I assume that each parent and child has his or her own "both/and" dilemma. If a child feels torn in two directions, for example, the boy pulled between his mother and grandmother, I would ask if others felt the same way. I encourage each family member to express his or her own dilemma and look for common themes. In this way, I can validate the dilemmas experienced by each family member.

FRAME DUAL CENTERING MESSAGES

I have found dual messages very effective for dealing with splits experienced by a child who is facing the very real threat of abandonment by her *primary* parent (see figure 5.5). Children in crisis-addicted families have often experienced the loss of one parent and are desperate to keep the fragile threads that connect them to their remaining Mom or Dad. Therapeutic messages can stress *both* the child's loyalty

Figure 5.5. Countering the split

and dedication to her parent and the child's struggle to change what's terrifying and too painful to talk about in the family.

A boy in a crisis residence told his father he wanted to go home, but also to "just stop the sex." Timmy (described above) demanded to go back to his Grandpa but showed everyone that he was scared to be alone with him. In chapter 3, Kristen fought to return to her mother and at the same time desperately wanted the hitting to stop. In each case, we needed to focus on *both* messages.

This is contrary to what is generally expected of therapists in child and family services. Parents often expect that we will advocate for the child and cast blame on the parent for a child's problems. Such parents come in prepared to fight for their self-esteem and to see practitioners as the enemy. Or conversely, we may be expected by many parents and most children to fix a "bad" or "sick" child before she can return home. We become locked into a "no-win" struggle if we advocate for one position or the other and soon find ourselves immersed in a family's serial crises.

For instance, we could have stressed Kristen's need for the hitting to stop at home and pushed her mother to move her boyfriend out in order to stop the violence at home. This would have been a legitimate position reflecting the probability that battering would continue. On the other hand, a one-sided message would have invalidated Kristen's mother's position that she was unable to manage without her boyfriend and that he helped her. In our family session, Kristen's younger brother appeared to go to this man for comfort much more than to his mother. Kristen probably would have seen us as enemies of her family and accelerated her biting and hitting in the crisis residence, resulting in a longer placement or transfer to a more secure facility. Or, her mother may have chosen to extend Kristen's placement by saying she could not take her back at that time.

We often feel pressured or compelled to push one side of a dilemma or another. This would be like pushing on one side of a canoe in the middle of a storm. The canoe would tip and someone in the family system (perhaps the grandparents or other professionals) would be propelled to quickly apply an equally powerful (or more powerful) counterforce on the other side of the canoe. The resulting battle would in effect keep the canoe afloat, though tipping from side to side in a cycle of crises, with the family always in jeopardy of sinking. Working with "both/and" messages (see Auerswald, 1983) allows us to center our work on the family's need for balance with powerful forces impinging from different sides.

Mending the Split

Joan placed her 9-year-old son in a crisis residence after he set a fire in her kitchen. The affection she and her son once shared had evolved over the last five years into an escalating pattern of taunting by her son and rebukes and slaps by Joan. After two weeks of placement, Joan confided that she often felt like killing her son. In a family session involving Joan, her mother, and her son, Joan's mother shared how she had felt like killing Joan when Joan was a child.

If a child feels torn between love and hate toward a parent, it is very likely that a parent grew up feeling the same way toward their parent. This split becomes the focus of our interventions. Our challenge is to help family members to reweave the torn fragments of their lives.

The child in placement is torn between her need to love and care for her parent and her fears and anger. The child struggles to maintain the image of a loving parent while suppressing memories of being hurt, rejected, or abandoned. The fragility of parents (their depression, threats of suicide or violence, or likelihood of their running away, hospitalization, or incarceration) make it impossible to voice the fear and hate side of the split.

A child needs a secure attachment in order to heal from trauma (Bettelheim, 1960; Bowlby, 1969, 1973; Erikson, 1963). The child growing up with mixed messages learns to numb her own pain, withdraw, and dissociate in order to manage her distress. She cannot let go of her parent but she feels a drive to escape, which grows as she enters adolescence.

The child absorbs the split by incorporating both sides—the good child who is loving and loyal to her parent and the bad child who rebels, defies, and becomes the "bitch," provoking more of her parent's wrath (see figure 5.2). When it is too dangerous to rebel against one's own parent, the child learns to defy and resist other adults who act as authority figures, provoking the child's fears and anger.

Dual centering messages can be used to link a child's split responses to the conflicting messages they have received from their primary parent. In this way, we can frame a "both/and" message that directly counters and relinks the split message received by the child over time. Such a message focuses the family's struggle for change on the primary dilemmas that have threatened the family's collapse while at the same time validating the family's experience in a balanced way. The canoe does not have to tip.

A dual centering message reflects every family member's need for enduring attachments and provides a frame for making choices to continue old behaviors or develop new approaches to problems (see figure 5.5). Each choice offers a challenge for family members to utilize healthy drives to make things better and define who they will be: a parent or more like a visiting uncle, a 14-year-old or a 5-year-old.

By accentuating both Kristen's (chapter 3) devotion to her mother and her terror of her mother getting hit, Kristen's rages and cuddling were reframed as a desperate effort to save her mother by a girl stuck emotionally at a point in time when her mother's life was very much at risk. Challenges for Kristen, her siblings, her mother, and her mother's boyfriend were centered on the need to help everyone manage the impasses created by the split messages symbolized by Kristen's behavior. Kristen experienced her father's demands that she and her siblings help him kill their mother and she grew up feeling a desperate need to save her mother. Kristen desperately wanted to gain her mother's love but raged against her mother's repeated rejections and allegiance to her boyfriend over Kristen.

Validation of Kristen's love and loyalty for her mother was also a validation of the nurturance that her mother wanted to provide. Empowerment of her mother and stepfather to help the family was tied to their responsibility to make choices to stop the hitting and care for the children if they wanted to maintain their family. Kristen was challenged to act at her chronological age and leave her mother and stepfather in charge of providing safety for themselves and the children. Working within a network approach by bringing in other service providers served to offer the family the support and back-up they would need to begin and maintain changes.

The child in placement provides a focus for reframing the splits experienced. At the onset of placement, family members and service providers are temporarily united by the dangers shown by the youth in placement, or in cases of abuse/neglect referrals, by the dangers the child is seen as living with. We can utilize the crisis of placement of a child (or children) to engage a network of family members, community resources, and service providers to work on the critical issues reflected in a child's predicament.

Use Metaphors to Link Messages and the Child's Crisis

When working with families in crisis, I try to find a metaphor that can link both sides of a split message and frame the struggle embodied by the child in placement. I tell parents and siblings that when I see one family member feeling such a desperate struggle between the need to love and protect their family and their fears or rage at what's happened, I have to expect that other people in the family feel the same way.

I ask parents for permission to ask their children what they learned about key events in the family's history and how they understand what happened to family members at critical times in a family's history. Why did Mom and Dad separate? What helped Mom get by in the terrible year when her parents died, the children's father left, and she was hurt in a car accident? What was it like for Mom or Dad when they were the same age as the child in placement?

I usually learn about a traumatic event that symbolizes the primary splits and dilemmas represented by the child in placement or at risk of placement. For Maria's family, this was the necessity of "thinking double" to avoid dealing with sex abuse. Kristen, in chapter 3, needed to find out if her mother would protect Kristen and herself from the death threats dating back to when Kristen was a toddler. This approach also allows me to validate the healthy strivings and yearnings for love and attachment of all family members, not just the child in placement.

Metaphors help parents to move away from shame-based thinking—good versus bad. Parents and children can use a metaphor to validate the split messages coming down over generations. By owning a metaphor, the parent can take charge. For example, Kristen's mother needed to decide what she was "writing back" to her daughter.

Taking charge means moving away from the good/bad splits and slowing down the spin of events. It means learning to recognize triggers and developing a safety system—who will do what when anyone in the family once again perceives the early warning signs of a return to the old patterns of crisis. Who can a child or parent go to for help? How can family members signal each other? What is the agreed-upon plan for dealing with the threat of Mom's relapse into alcoholism, Dad's losing his temper, or Billy's running off with his old crew.

Family members can be challenged to move from dissociation to reality, from incompetence to skills and achievements, from depression (anger directed inward) to self-care, from violence (anger directed out) to a series of safety steps, and from depersonalization to respect for self and others.

Centering on the metaphor and need for permanence also provides a way for different practitioners, community resources, and family members to join together and provide a consistent message. Consistency is necessary in order to help clients to slow down time and move out of battles and crises. Without a united approach and common goal, we will be quickly drawn in to reenact the different messages and battles that have kept family members in crisis.

Validate Positive Striving

Dual centering messages allow me to validate the positive striving of a child or parent, for example, a child's yearning for her Mom or Dad or a father's efforts to give his child more than he received growing up. "Bobby keeps asking when he can go home. I can see how he loves it when you hold him." Validation of the positive and accentuation of *real* signs of competence allow family members to avoid feeling they are being shamed and symbolically pushed up against a brick wall with no escape. I can then add, "At the same time, Bobby keeps struggling to manage his terror that the beatings will happen again and that no one is safe."

The dual message leaves a way out. We demonstrate that we're not afraid to hear or talk about the frightening or harmful things that have happened and that we respect the loyalty of family members and their need to maintain the family's balance. This is an implicitly empowering message. We are telling family members that we are not afraid to validate what is real but will do so in a nonshaming manner. This understanding allows us to engage family members to begin working on what is not being said directly.

Dual centering messages play an integral part in this effort to empower family members and work toward reintegration. The focus on every child's need for attachments and a consistent, safe, nurturing home provide the framework for therapeutic messages and setting a direction for work. Healing splits means countering the threats of abandonment that lie below the family's serial traumas.

A child's defiant behavior can be reframed as a desperate and often misdirected call for help for everyone in the family based on the child's loyalty *and* rage. The "bad" and "good" responses of the child are pulled together with a stress on everyone's need for enduring bonds and permanency.

Opening up perspectives of the past and future changes the context of what happens in the present. Parents and children can learn to recognize the beginning stages of renewed crisis cycles and are challenged to make choices. Each choice by a parent is a message about whether Mom or Dad is making changes in their home so that the family can be reunited without returning to the crises of the past. Each choice by a child demonstrates whether she feels it is safe enough to change and whether she has the courage to try another way to get what she needs.

Choosing goals based on positive aspirations for love and success can fuel the difficult work needed and regain a future. Family members can be challenged to decide whether they will repeat the old ways or focus on their goals and their children's need for lasting attachments.

Dual centering messages allow the practitioner to validate both sides of a dilemma that the family has not been able to resolve. Centering messages help to give families a reframe in which they are both empowered and challenged to own what they do (the present) and what will happen (the future). Rather than the therapist taking over and trying to rescue, family members are asked to decide what they will do.

Stating the duality of a child's perspective opens up previously hidden forces that drive a child's acting-out behavior. Each family member, including children, is challenged to recognize what leads up to crises and to make choices about continuing typical responses in escalating crises or slowing down the crisis by experimenting with a different stance or response. For instance, angry outbursts can be replaced by walking away, vigorous exercise, writing everything down on paper, or punching a pillow or mattress. Yelling, screaming, hitting, running away, or evicting become choices that tell everyone whether the same old crisis cycle will go on. The dual centering message provides a way for family members to reintegrate conflicting pressures and asks them to decide whether they will replace cycles of crises with day-by-day, hour-by-hour choices to provide consistency, safety, nurturance, and trust.

Tie in Loyalty and the Revolving Cycle of Crises

The child in placement symbolizes the family's struggle and serves as a focal point for family pressures to both remain the same and change. The child shows the splitting in the family and how family members have learned that they can only be half-good or half-bad, half-right or half-wrong. Pushing to any one side triggers the crisis cycle.

If the child is an "angel" today, her sisters and brothers may be "devils" getting into trouble. And today's angel knows that tomorrow she, too, may be castigated as "the bad one." Today's good feeling of being wanted is precarious. Family members balance themselves with a multistep dance (see Minuchin, 1974) around the pit of abandonment.

Crises become addicting in the family, as they provide both thrills, intimacy, and relief from greater threats. It is safer and easier to battle a teacher, fight off the police or defy warnings of child protective workers than to directly face unspoken traumas in the family or the prospect of Dad or Mom leaving for good. With crises, one can remain loyal to one's family (see Boszormenyi-Nagy, 1972). Crises provide a break from feeling, thinking about, or doing something about the greater threats.

Masterson (1976) described how the child cannot individuate for fear of her mother's withdrawal of affection and availability. The child, over time, learns that she cannot tolerate intimacy because intimacy is tied in with rejection. At the same time, the child cannot develop autonomy or individuation because she has learned over and over that to do this means threats and experiences of abandonment and often an overwhelming sense of responsibility for her parent's rage and depression.

The child learns that to grow and achieve means to lose her parents' love and to feel alone in a barren world. The only way to get attention is to regress, to cling, to have tantrums. The child, in effect, learns she must remain emotionally like a toddler.

The child learns to be hypervigilant and hyperactive, to act before the wound can be touched. She must remain on guard, paying attention to the signs of a dreaded event and then move quickly becoming a major part of the crisis "dance" of the family.

Revolving through the cycle of crisis generates thrills and intimate encounters and provides a sense of balance, like a teeter-totter moving up and down. The family's dance mirrors their struggle with unresolved conflicts: enmeshment versus isolation; avoidance versus traumatization; shame versus rigidity.

MAKE PLACEMENT A TURNING POINT

Choice by choice, hour by hour, parents and children have the opportunity to mend the splits that have torn them apart. Each choice provides a new, albeit tentative, link that pulls together the traumatic splits from the past. Like a seamstress reknitting a torn garment, parents are helped and challenged to sew together the split parts of themselves and their children. The first stitches are tentative but mark the beginning of a new chance for the family to heal and grow.

Rebuilding Attachments

The child in placement is like the 2-year-old with the scraped knee, hurting and bleeding. The child needs a parent who can validate the physical pain and the emotional hurt. Safe hugs and warm embraces help a child to be able to feel again, to cry, and move past her anger. Attachment means being attuned to a child, recognizing her thoughts, what she sees, how she responds, and working with a sense of time that includes the past, present, and future.

Parents bonding to an infant respond to every gesture. The infant's smile elicits a smile in return from her parent. A cry, a wave of the hand, a look of surprise are all reciprocated. The child learns that her parent is attuned to her feelings and perceptions and acts in sync with her needs. The child is not alone.

Some parents of children in placement never had an attachment to parents of their own, have little motivation to learn how to give this to their own child, and simply want a child to serve them. Others had enough bonding with someone that they will commit themselves to giving their child the same and more.

Just as therapists can use an understanding of how people operate in visual, auditory, and kinesthetic dimensions to engage clients (Bandler & Grinder, 1976), parents can learn to recognize how a child is thinking, feeling, and seeing the world. By tuning into the child, parents can help both the child and themselves to expand their capacities.

When a mother or father hugs their hurt 2-year-old, they are saying, "I will not abandon you. I will help you survive the pain. You are not alone." When a parent from a violent home becomes strong enough to say, "I know you were scared I'd be killed (kill someone or kill myself)," the child can begin to see and hear a little more. When a little girl sees day by day that her parent is working to end the violence, stop an addiction, and care for his or her children, the girl can start to feel safe enough to trust again.

With a child in a crisis placement, the first step is to validate the conflicting messages—love and hate, loyalty and fear, affection and rejection—that drive the crisis cycle and that have led to placement. Focusing on the child's struggle with these conflicts presents parents and children with both the challenge and the opportunity to face what could not be said out loud, with support for their efforts to make things better. Family members can begin to relink the torn fragments that make up each person's identity and open up possibilities to see, hear, feel, think, and talk about the past, the present, and the future.

The safety and trust established in a nonshaming relationship with a therapist provides the context within which parents can show their children that it is safe enough to share their experiences of trauma, the terror of abandonment, and their hopes for a better future. The child can then move beyond split messages and develop positive relationships with peers, teachers, and other adults without having to be disloyal and risk the break-up of a family. This allows the child to move on with her own development.

Real World Therapy

Without a magic wand, change comes slowly, one step at a time, with a mixture of courage, pain, risk, and hope. Timmy, who lunged at his grandmother, showed us that the turmoil in his family reflected pains so dreadful that someone could die.

Sylvia had reason to hate what Timmy represented, a reason she didn't want to know and had struggled throughout his lifetime to avoid. In the course of Timmy's brief placement, I helped Sylvia, her husband (Grandpa), and her daughter look at what drove Timmy to become so angry that he would want to kill someone and his grandmother to become so upset that she threatened suicide. Why was Timmy, in his story, pedaling furiously to get away from his grandfather and yet demanding in the crisis residence to go back to his grandfather's home?

Angie, Timmy's mother, had left Timmy to her mother, Sylvia, and stepfather to raise. Angie was only 16 when he was born and went on to have two other children before she was 20. Timmy had grown up thinking of her as his sister. With family members, I stressed the love *and* hate that led to Sylvia and Timmy's death threats. Angie felt her mother and son's desperation and in our second session she shared the bitter truth she had locked inside for 9 years: Timmy's grandpa was also his father.

Timmy's grandpa was also the only one who consistently said he wanted to keep Timmy and raise him. Our focus had to remain on who could parent Timmy now and into the future. Would Timmy's grandfather stop the hitting and sex abuse and together with Sylvia make it safe enough at home that no one needed to pedal furiously away? Could Sylvia develop the affection and trust needed to parent the son of her daughter and husband?

Timmy calmed down somewhat after seeing his grandparents and mother survive this disclosure. Timmy's grandpa stopped denying he was Timmy's father, although he never apologized or really admitted what he had done. After he agreed to work in counseling, Sylvia said she wanted to take Timmy back and raise him with her husband.

Timmy's placement was voluntary and his legal guardians, Sylvia and Timmy's grandfather/father, took him home after just a few weeks without making further progress on resolving the years of incest, marital battles, and probable spouse abuse. It wasn't surprising that Timmy returned to placement a few months later. This time Sylvia disclosed how her husband continued to threaten her. After a few weeks of Timmy's second placement, she decided to separate from her husband and told Timmy that she could not raise him.

Timmy was able to share a little more about how Grandpa was fun to play with and then without warning would get into a fight with Grandma. Timmy looked to his grandfather/father as the only one who had consistently cared about him and the only one in the family who wanted to raise him. His grandfather had custody and there were no reports of Timmy being abused by his grandfather. Staff in the crisis residence could only encourage Timmy's grandfather to implement a safety plan with outside resources for Timmy and himself. He refused to go into sex abuse counseling but did participate in family counseling at a community mental health center. Timmy's placements had opened up the family secrets behind Timmy's rage and he returned to his grandfather's home to find out if his grandpa/father would keep his promises to raise Timmy without the secrets, the fighting, and any physical or sexual abuse.

Not all parents or assigned legal guardians can raise a child. Each placement of a child marks a time for family members to look at the split messages that tear children apart and propel cycles of crises. The crisis of placement can be used to catalyze a crisis-addicted family to rebuild attachments or face the inability of parents and children to create the lasting bonding that would allow a child to safely return home. No magic words exist to heal the traumas of children facing abandonment. But, I believe children and parents can face the realities of their lives. Facing the reality of who cares enough and is strong enough to parent a child is painful work but also sends a message of hope. The answer to threats of abandonment is the struggle of family members and practitioners to help each child gain a safe, secure home and a bonded relationship to someone the child can count on now and into the future.

chapter 6

It feels like a hundred years. I'll be a skeleton.

Ten-year-old boy who was asked when he
thought he'd be able to return to his
mother's home

staying the course

DOROTHY INTRODUCED HERSELF AS AN ALCOHOLIC AND APOLOGIZED for being so tired; she hadn't slept well the night before. Her face was prematurely wrinkled and her hair somewhat disheveled. Dorothy appeared weary but her eyes flared at any suggestion that she would not do what was necessary to get her children back from placement. She had been resistant to court-mandated family counseling but now declared, "I'll do whatever it takes to get my kids back!"

Dorothy was intelligent, well-dressed, and had the support of her two siblings despite 20 years of heavy drinking and 6 unsuccessful rehab programs. She wanted to work with our staff on getting her two children back from their most recent placements; she had heard good things about our program to reunite families. She had successfully completed the initial phase of an inpatient alcohol program earning praise from her counselors. With a smile, Dorothy shared how she liked the social worker my agency assigned to work with her far more than any other family therapist she had ever had before.

Dorothy's 4-year-old son, Billy, put his arms around his mother and his head on her lap. Those of us in the room were drawn to help her, moved by her determination, and struck by her warm embrace of her son. I saw her firey eyes as a welcome sign of strength. She looked ready and determined to change, an excellent client—bright, verbal, motivated, honest about her drinking, and appealing with a sense of humor. . . . Suddenly, Lisa, her 11-year-old, darted from the room and ran out the door. The mirage was broken. I knew we had to look at what Lisa was showing us.

I assumed that I and my colleagues were only the latest in a long line of people who had tried to help Lisa's family in the past. There was no reason for Lisa or her mother to expect that we could be more effective than the last 2 or 22 professionals. Most likely, we would be drawn to repeat what had happened before, become locked into problem-maintaining roles as rescuers, enablers, or bad guys, and eventually give up, run away, attack, or otherwise reject a family.

With the mirage broken, my colleagues and I began to explore where the power and resources lay in Lisa's family and to enlist these people in the work that lay ahead. We needed to map out who was involved, understand each of their roles, their power, and contributions, and work to involve them in an effort to help the family.* It would have been futile to attempt this voyage alone. To pretend we had all the power needed to help Lisa's family would have set up unrealistic expectations and provoked those with real power to sabotage our efforts. Instead, I wanted to recognize and learn from the family's history of working with service providers.

Understanding that Lisa's family had a map inside them, I could free myself from the burden of providing directives and solutions and instead focus on using my feelings, perceptions, and experience to help family members understand what they have been showing everyone about life in their family. This meant pulling out of the often expected role that I would become the new pseudo-father (or mother) who would try to take over and with whom parents and children would reenact age-old battles. Instead, I worked to validate real efforts by family members and service providers to make things better and stressed the importance of everyone pulling together.† The crisis of Lisa

---

*The impact of adding network interventions to short-term home-based family work with families in crisis was demonstrated in a comparison study by Rowland, Taplin, and Holt (1983).

†Hartman's ecogram (Hartman, 1978) can be used to visually map out family member–outside system interactions. A small genogram of the family (three generations) can be drawn in the center and then family members connected to nonfamily groups, for example, school, sports teams, mental health therapist, religious organizations, etc.

and Billy's placement offered a chance for the network to come to-gether, build on what had been tried before, and move a step further.

MOBILIZE A SUPPORTIVE NETWORK

Parents, stepparents, siblings, aunts, uncles, grandparents, child pro-tective services, foster parents, child care workers, mental health pro-fessionals, educators, probation officers, physicians, lawyers, judges, and administrators are typically key stakeholders in a family's ex-tended network. Who can family members call for help? How can they be contacted? How can family members signal their distress and get support?

I ask family members to tell me what they expect to happen in counseling, what their hopes are for their family, and what they liked in previous counseling. If a parent (or child) describes how much he hated a previous therapist telling them what to do, I validate this concern and work to take a different position. "I am going to count on you to tell me if I start to tell you to do anything. That's not what I am here for. I think parents have rights. Will you tell me if I start to sound like your boss?" Statements like these do more than show re-spect. With these messages, we are sharing the responsibility for the relationship and the work to be done. Meaning, direction, and em-powerment come from the family as they define their future and make choices.

Network interventions can start small, with whoever is present. We work quickly to bring in key members, including referral sources, child protective workers, and current practitioners working with the family. Initial sessions need to be scheduled as soon as possible, ide-ally within the first two days of placement. These meetings are essen-tial to show a child that his parents and siblings are all right, that everyone is working together, and that our staff will work to help a family solve problems and reunite. Meeting soon after placement al-lows us to use the crisis of this placement as a focal point for change.

Subsequent sessions can include other important relatives, service

---

Connecting lines can symbolize the intensity of the relationship and whether it is sup-portive or conflictual or primarily powered by a one-way interaction, for example, a parent going repeatedly to a neighbor for help, or whether it is a two-way process with energy coming from both sides. Arrows can symbolize the direction of energy repeated in typical interactions, with the thickness of lines showing intensity. Jagged lines can symbolize conflict and smooth connections can show support. Dotted lines can show tenuous connections. Slashes can show cut-offs.

providers, and family friends. Invitations are optimally made by the parents, but this can be done conjointly with family therapists through letters and phone calls, with the permission of the parents or legal guardians.

With each invitation, I stress our need for that person's help. Long distances can be overcome with teleconferences. Each network session takes multiple calls, letters, and sessions with family members to arrange. For Dorothy's family, I wanted to bring in her alcohol rehabilitation counselor, her sister and brother, Billy's foster parents, and group care workers from Lisa's residential program.

Building or rebuilding a network (see Bronfenbrenner, 1979; Galanter, 1993; Garrison, 1974; Imber-Black, 1988; Kliman & Trimble, 1983; Landau-Stanton, 1990; Landau-Stanton et al., 1993; Speck, 1967; Speck & Attneave, 1973; Trimble, 1980, 1981; Trimble & Kliman, 1981) is time-consuming and hard work by everyone involved. It's not a magical approach, but it does pay off with real change and far fewer sessions than traditional individual or family therapy that is limited to working with the family members who are most in trouble or feeling the most pain. We are providing a therapy for abandonment; this means working with family members to build (or repair) positive and enduring connections.

Work with Respect

Engaging network members requires respect and sensitivity to ethnicity, spirituality, and gender. I want to learn how a family is strengthened by its heritage and culture, how people are expected to heal and overcome dilemmas, and their expectations of service providers such as ourselves. Respect for others begins by respecting our own roots and the values taught in our families, ethnic groups, and communities.

An openness and desire to learn about cultural, historic, and religious factors can be shown through "I statements" that recognize our own ignorance of another's experience and our wish to learn what helps in the daily lives of family members.* I want to let prospective clients know that they can ask for a therapist from their own ethnic

---

*Please see Fong (1994), Giordano (1994), McGoldrick, Pearce, & Giordano (1982), and Pinderhughes (1989). Reading books by authors such as Maya Angelou, Marion Edelman, Barbara Kingsolver, Sarah Lawrence Lightfoot, Toni Morrison, and Amy Tan has helped me to understand the experience of other ethnic groups.

background, even if that means switching to another agency, and how we could work on arranging this. I tell family members that I cannot fully understand what it's like to be a parent suffering from a seizure disorder, to be a single mother with eight children under the age of 10, or to be a father who grew up experiencing racism and discrimination because of the color of his skin. By asking how it is for a black father to work with a white psychologist or for a Greek grandmother to work with someone with little knowledge of the role of women in Greek culture, I am inviting family members to talk about their experiences of prejudice, their fears about what will happen if they work with my agency, and the strengths they want to preserve from their family's history.

I have felt the sting of prejudice and exclusion based on religion and the hate of those who search for scapegoats to give meaning to their lives. I want to give each prospective client the same kind of message that would show me that a therapist of another race, religion, or community respected my heritage.

My agency developed a list of consultants on staff willing to assist practitioners working with families from a wide range of religious and ethnic backgrounds. Respect for the sexual orientation shown by parents and youths is being augmented by workshops for staff and revision of client rights and policy statements.

Work with other Service Providers

I've learned the hard way how missing or secret therapists working with one family member's needs and goals can sabotage efforts to pull family members together. It's important to recognize who's out there, what they are working on, and make an effort to pull them into a common approach. This, of course, is no easy task, especially with therapists who cannot or will not come in for network sessions or refuse to answer phone calls. The effort, successful or unsuccessful, pays off by earning the respect of family members who see that we are taking a comprehensive view and not excluding anyone. Going to another therapist's office shows family members we will go the distance, deal with missing pieces, and are unwilling to work in a vacuum.

We can move past the initial resistance of busy practitioners and model the courage and commitment that family members will need to deal with conflicts and cut-offs in their lives. Everyone needs to hear what's happening and what needs to happen. This is a major intervention in itself as it breaks down the isolation of individuals, shares responsibility and pain, and promotes new ways of coping that can take the place of old rules of not talking, not feeling, and not seeing.

Respect for family members' relationships with other practitioners does not mean giving up my role, voice, and whatever power I have to help a family. I need to keep my focus on the child's need for a consistent, nurturing home and a secure relationship with a parent who will care for and guide the child into the future. This is a therapy for parents to work on ending multigenerational abandonments and traumas that are now damaging their own children.

I remember Maggie, an alcoholic mother of three children who had been in and out of placements for five years. Maggie resisted meeting with my agency's family worker and emphasized the importance of her current alcohol counselor who she saw in a private, for profit clinic. When our attempts to engage this counselor to come to sessions at our agency or the woman's home failed, we stressed the importance of including her in the permanency work and offered to hold the next session at the counselor's clinic.

At the agreed-upon hour, my colleagues from our agency's home-based prevention of placement program and I were present, along with two other service providers and Maggie. Maggie's counselor failed to show up but sent a message that we should use her clinic's conference room and go ahead. Maggie's eyes watered. She was left alone again. I wanted to show Maggie that I understood her isolation, not as a sign of shame, but as a choice point on the road to helping her children and herself. She did not have to work with my colleagues and myself just because we showed up for this meeting. If anything, her feeling let down would be another lesson not to trust any professional.

Maggie dropped her outward defiance and shared a little bit of her experience of losses and rejections. She accepted the offer of a family worker in my program to meet a few times to decide whether she wanted to work on giving her children the stability and consistency that she never had.

Family workers must be able to speak intelligently and strongly with lawyers and judges as well as with psychiatrists, psychologists, social workers, nurses, probation officers, and teachers from hospitals, agencies, probation departments, schools, and clinics. This means understanding and using their language and the mandates of their funding sources and accrediting bodies to engage them in work on a common goal. For example, practitioners in child and family services must be able to use the DSM-IV (American Psychiatric Association, 1994) in order to speak to practitioners from mental health systems. Family practitioners need to respect what their colleagues have learned, take the behavior clusters shown by a child or parent, and work with everyone involved to understand how a child or parent's behavior fits with their family's relationships, economic situation, history, and biological factors as a way to cope and often literally to survive.

Sometimes, too many therapists are involved for family members to do any serious work with any one therapist. The myriad of relationships, appointments, and advice promotes confusion, exhaustion, and stalemate. It's important for the practitioners involved to delineate roles and to consider who can work on a long-term basis with the family and who could help the family most by terminating at this point so family members could focus their efforts. Staff from a short-term placement program can work with everyone involved to get unstuck and center the family and their network of service providers on crucial work that needs to happen for a child to go home. Children in placement will usually calm down when they see that critical issues are being addressed and with the understanding that home-based or outpatient clinic staff will continue this work when the child returns home.

It helps to engage other service providers by asking them to share their objectives, understanding of their client, perspective on the family, and plans for helping family members. Each practitioner involved has a particular perspective, language, goals, and way of working. A father's individual therapist will most likely be focused on helping the father move carefully toward change without risking further harm to himself or others. A parent's mental health therapist may fear bringing up serious issues, for example, suspected child abuse, for fear of losing the fragile relationship established with a client and with the assumption that someone else is addressing those thorny issues. Typically, mental health and substance abuse funding is limited to work with an individual's problems and any additional efforts to address family crises mean extra work for the practitioner outside of their primary contract and funding, and extra hours in a long day. Treatment plans must remain focused on the identified patient, for example, a father seeing a mental health therapist.

If differences in orientations, assessments, or agendas exist, it's useful to recognize that each reflects one point of view and most likely a part of the truth for a family. Practitioners can easily get caught up in an "I'm right, you're wrong" battle that mimics longstanding conflicts within families and blocks any change in the system.

"Dr. G told me not to deal with my own history right now . . . I'm supposed to repress it," Kelly told me. I had asked to meet with her privately after a family session including her 7-year-old daughter, Amy, her 10-year-old daughter, Gina, and her 13-year-old daughter, Ellen. Kelly had custody of all three girls. Ellen's father never visited or contacted the family; Gina and Amy's father had court-ordered visitation every weekend.

Gina had been placed in our crisis residence after several incidents, including hanging from a third floor window, placing a plastic bag over her head, and trying to hit her mother with a broomstick. Several months earlier she had threatened to kill herself with a knife.

In our family session, none of the children wanted to talk about anything. Gina, however, acted out a story with puppets in which a large spider came and knocked down the walls of her house, grabbed her mother, and took her mother, sisters, and herself away. Gina called the spider her "father's evil villain." In a previous individual session with Gina, I had asked her to draw everyone in her family doing something. She drew each person on a separate sheet of paper and I was concerned with how remote she felt from her mother. Gina pictured her father as an alien. Huge menacing arms and hands extended from his chest and his body was covered with slime and warts. Gina also shared a nightmare with one of my colleagues in which her mother was lying dead on the floor and her father was standing over her laughing, after killing her.

Eight years earlier, Ellen, Gina's older half-sister, had told her kindergarden teacher, "Daddy fucked me," referring to Gina and Amy's father and leading to a CPS call. Kelly had also called CPS a year ago when Amy confided that her father insisted on helping her put creams on her genitals for a rash; neither case, however, was substantiated sufficiently for CPS to "indicate" it as neglect or abuse.

Kelly had tried to stop the children's unsupervised visits with her ex-husband; Gina's suicide attempts followed soon after she lost in court. Gina's latest suicide attempt followed the return of Amy from a weekend visit with her father.

Kelly had urged her children to share with her any concerns, but during the sessions she sat shaking. She had kept her own history of sex abuse a secret and became agitated and depressed whenever her children talked about any concerns with Gina and Amy's father. She described her husband's violent temper and his battering her before she left him six years earlier and she believed they all remained at very high risk.

I had asked Kelly to consider telling the children that she was starting to deal with her own history of sexual abuse. This would model for the children that sex abuse could be talked about in the family, which in turn would renew the children's hope that their own experiences could be managed. Dr. G, however, saw Kelly as too weak and told her she couldn't handle uncovering anything related to her own experience "right now." Dr. G also said she was too busy to join us for a meeting of service providers working with the family.

When radically different recommendations are offered by service providers, I try to present the reality of both perspectives to family members. By validating differences in perspectives of the practitioners involved, I can advocate for family members to test out what is real and what is the best way for them to achieve their goals. In this way, I can highlight family strengths and empower family members to choose what is best for them.

I wanted Kelly to know that my colleagues and I believed that there was an important message in what Dr. G was saying. Dr. G had worked with her on and off for stress relief for almost five years and knew how painful it would be to even begin talking about her sex abuse. At the same time, Kelly was telling my colleague at the crisis residence about increasing flashbacks, dreams, and memories that she had not shared with Dr. G. I wanted Kelly to see this as a healthy sign, part of her drive to recover. I also wanted her to know that her willingness to begin dealing with her own history of sex abuse would be a powerful message to the children that they could share whatever made them so terrified of their father or anything else.

It was up to Kelly to decide what message the children would get. Would she work in a slow and safe way to deal with scary feelings and memories? Or, were some things too scary to tell anyone? It was unlikely that the children would feel safe enough to share anything about their father if they saw their mother as too afraid to talk at all about what had happened to her long ago. Gina would most likely keep on acting out her fears of Mom being killed or killing herself.

While Kelly could not control her husband, I challenged her to decide what message she wanted to give her children about facing traumas. Above all, the children needed to see that she had the courage to face whatever happened in their lives without killing herself.

SET A COURSE TOWARD PERMANENCY

I wanted to believe that Dorothy (cited at the beginning of this chapter) had the capacity to give Lisa and Billy the safe, nurturing home and secure relationship they needed. When Lisa bolted from the room, we had to face Dorothy's repeated history of failing to maintain a home, despite wonderful promises and periods of sobriety in which she appeared to be a model parent.

Lisa had been left in charge when their mother went out drinking, often with little food in the apartment. When Dorothy came back from a binge, she often blamed Lisa for pushing her to drink or, in one incident, to take an overdose of painkillers. Billy taunted Lisa, and Lisa in turn slugged Billy, leading Dorothy to scream at Lisa, smack her, and send her to stay with one of her aunts for weeks or months at a time. Lisa had been accused of stealing by neighbors and frequently provoked fights at school and in the neighborhood, which led to her being badly beaten up. The children had been removed twice before by child protective services for inadequate care and temporarily placed with their aunt.

Both children had been placed in a foster home after Lisa called one of her aunts when Dorothy failed to return home after a weekend of drinking with a new boyfriend. This time, neither aunt was willing to care for the children and they were placed in a foster home. In the foster home, Lisa fought with Billy, threw him into a window, and threatened to kill herself. Lisa was placed into our crisis residence.

When Lisa ran out the door at our initial meeting, she showed us how desperate she was to get away from the old pattern. Lisa wanted to believe her mother and had always needed to help her mother, but couldn't tolerate the false promises. Lisa needed to stuff down her anger at what happened before and what she expected to happen again. Billy's face appeared blank. He shrugged his shoulders when asked any questions and showed almost no feeling, which concerned me even more than Lisa's behavior. Lisa, at least, showed an attempt to make things better by acting out her fears about her mother. I assumed Lisa's behaviors (threatening to kill herself and repeatedly provoking larger girls and boys to beat her) reflected how bad things were at home with her mother and her mother's boyfriends—experiences Lisa couldn't talk about. Clearly, neither child could afford to keep moving in and out of placement with no real change in their mother's home.

Set Goals

I want to use the first network meeting with a family to focus on permanency and to address what has to happen for a child to return home. Billy and Lisa needed to hear that Dorothy would be provided with all possible help to overcome the isolation and depression that led to her addiction and to help her provide a stable home where the children would not have to fear for their mother's or their own safety. At the same time, the children needed to hear that we understood their wishes for their mother to care for them as well as their fears and anger that they would once again end up disappointed.

The county worker, probation officer, case manager from the mental health system, or family therapist needs to review laws and regulations governing placements. If the child has been placed because of abuse and neglect and the parent makes no significant progress on providing a safe, stable home in the course of a year (eighteen months under federal law), the county (children's services department) is required to file a petition citing permanent neglect and to seek termination of the parent's rights.

Our primary goal is to help families focus on permanency and slow down time (see Ausloos, 1986). Schlosberg (Kagan and Schlosberg, 1989) called this "holding the crisis." The goals selected can be framed to focus on the metaphors and developmental transitions that family members need to resolve. Learning to slow down time and crises will mean beginning to feel again and an opportunity to master the impasses that blocked family members from coping in the past.

Goals need to be addressed within the language and understanding of clients. For children, this means concrete actions that symbolize changes. Lisa and Billy needed to see that Dorothy could sustain her sobriety, maintain a home, keep out violent boyfriends, and show them they could share with her their fears and anger without her turning back to the bottle, screaming, or leaving them alone. In other families, children need to hear that Mom and Dad will be working on cleaning out a bedroom to make space for their return, that Mom and Dad will be working to stop any more violence, that Grandma will be visiting every other day to help Mom take care of the kids, or that Dad has a plan for handling the stress of his job. Most important, they need to hear that it is up to Mom and Dad to make the choice whether or not they can and will be the parents who raise them to maturity.

Kids have work to do, too. It's not possible to simply give up roles as caretakers or troublemakers. These roles gave them power, a function, and an identity within the family. I encourage children and adolescents to try out other roles and ask parents to help them find other ways to succeed in school, sports, jobs, and the arts. It is important to help the family secure an educational or job training program in which the youth can succeed.

I look for areas in which students excel and encourage pursuit of their own goals. This may mean sticking it out day by day on the football team, with practice in self-talk on dealing with the coach. For another youth, this could mean using money earned in an afterschool vocational program to pay for karate classes or forming a rap group and auditioning for a local talent show. We all need to find ways to succeed by doing something that involves pride in one's efforts, learning new skills, and helping others. At the same time, I expect and predict that everyone, including the kids, will be pulled and pushed back to old roles as "the troublemaker," "the jerk," "the problem." We can identify, plan, and practice responses that say "No" to covert or overt messages by friends, authority figures, and family members to go back to the old ways.

I challenge youths to go beyond the limits of the past—to learn and use different ways of dealing with their anger and frustration, to summon the courage to show feelings through words, drawing, sculpture, or music, and to succeed in school and activities. It means mustering the guts to say to a parent or guardian, "I want to run away . . . hit the wall . . . cry in my pillow" or "I've got to walk around the block before I explode. I'll be back." Working on goals means experimenting with ways to manage the dilemmas of real life and the traumas of the past. It means giving Mom or Dad and themselves a chance to do something different, small steps that interrupt old patterns and that can lead to big changes over time.

Goal setting also defines the roles and efforts of network members. Group care workers and foster parents need to affirm their support for the efforts of family members to make reunification work. This needs to be shown in the day-to-day practices of foster parents or group care workers. Respect is shown for parents working to reunite by asking how to fix a little girl's hair, how to dress a young child, and what kind of religious worship is appropriate. I want parental input in a psychological evaluation. Parents show they are taking responsibility by advocating for their children in school conferences and appointments with physicians, dentists, psychologists, and other specialists.

Even when reuniting looks doubtful, children need to see that everyone involved is giving their parents help and opportunities to succeed. Keeping the time frame of a year of "diligent efforts" is essential to mobilize change and to show everyone that this will not go on forever.

Working with Substance Abuse

Addictive behaviors present a common obstacle to lasting changes. Substance abuse has been a factor in over 70% of families referred to child protective services (American Public Welfare Association, 1989). Often, parents have gone in and out of rehabilitation programs, achieving temporary sobriety, and relapsing when stress resurfaces. With each relapse, family members become more desperate and stuck. Children feel that a parent is too fragile to change. Less and less can be said about the addiction while family members' fears, shame, and anger grow. Billy had already learned to say nothing that could in any way upset his mother.

Therapy takes courage and often pressure from family members and the community to face the addiction. We need to talk about how the addiction began, how self-medication helps a person cope day by day, biological effects of past substance abuse, what is needed to risk changes, and what can take the place of drugs or alcohol. We can learn from relapses about unmet needs and unresolved problems, the subtle triggers for relapse, and what needs to happen for a parent to achieve his or her goals.

Parents who have abused alcohol or drugs can be expected to keep using whenever the permanency work becomes difficult. Children typically expect that a parent will relapse again and only begin to develop more trust after a parent has remained alcohol- or drug-free longer than any other previous period of sobriety. Children need to see that their parent has been able to manage holidays and anniversaries of traumatic events without alcohol or drugs.

Relapses block any change. For parents who minimize or deny the extent of substance abuse, a court order mandating participation in a treatment program and frequent urine testing* will be needed before any change can be expected. The addiction must stop within the time frame of the permanency work if adults want to take back their roles

---

*Since cocaine use will not be detected by standard urine tests after just a few days (one day for alcohol), urine testing needs to be conducted on a random and at least weekly basis.

as parents. We support both parents' efforts toward recovery and their choice to work on becoming sober *or* to show everyone that they cannot raise their children.

DEVELOP SAFETY PLANS

Clues to what is likely to happen in a family can be gleaned from past crises. Family sessions can be used to plan and rehearse different ways to handle potential problems: sensing when problems are beginning; signaling family and designated network members through calls, letters, or actions; getting help; taking steps to calm oneself down; and carrying out a plan of action. In a family where a single mother periodically goes on alcohol binges, a plan may begin with ways that each family member first senses that tension is mounting and another binge cycle is starting. This may mean a tightening in the 6-year-old's stomach, a 13-year-old's staying away from home, or a mother's finding herself too tired to prepare dinner.

Family members need to work out their own map of who needs to talk to whom, for example a child calling grandpa or an AA sponsor. As in trauma therapy (see Figley, 1989), the need for action could be signaled anonymously by moving a previously agreed upon symbolic object, for example, turning a photo upside down, or a child mailing a post card to her therapist. This would then be a prompt for the family's plan of action, which should include family members taking responsibility for calling or bringing in different network members and, most of all, doing something different that breaks the usual binge cycle, for example, going out for dinner, a parent taking a day off from work, visiting supportive relatives or friends, or calling for a counseling session.

Parents who have been abusive need to rehearse and share a safety plan if they feel any impulse to repeat physical or sexual abuse (Madanes, 1995b). This could include immediately leaving the room, going to an AA sponsor, calling their own parent, going to church, or calling their therapist.

Children need to know who they can call for help when they fear that their parent is about to relapse or that violence or neglect could resume in the family. This should be a strong person outside of the nuclear family (see Madanes, 1990b, 1995b) who children and parents can count on to protect the children from further harm. The protector needs to be willing to check regularly for signs of renewed neglect, secrets, threats, or abuse. Whenever possible, an aunt, uncle, grand-parent, or older cousin from the extended family can serve in this role.* If finding a protector within the extended family is not possible, a member of the family's community, for example, a religous leader, a mentor, or a Big Sister could take this role.

WORK FOR THE LONG RUN

Use Group Care to Foster Attachments

Lisa calmed down after she saw that group care staff, my colleagues in a prevention of placement program, and I, a consultant to both programs, had heard her request to live with Aunt Becky and how torn she was between raging at her mother and feeling she should go back to help her. Becky offered to take Lisa and we were able to get Lisa out of group care and into her aunt's home in just a few weeks.

Group care provides a critical service for youths who cannot toler-ate the closeness of family life. Time-limited programs offer a chance for a family to regroup. Network interventions can focus efforts on the permanency issues underlying a youth's acting-out behavior. The effectiveness of a treatment center's services corresponds with the program's ability and commitment to engage family members, ad-dress painful issues that have led up to placement, work with family and community resources to support a home where the youth can grow up, help a youth to master vital skills for succeeding in school and the community, and assess, with parents, extended family, and other network members, the reality of whether a youth can successfully return home or needs to find another home before discharge.

Some youths have been so scarred by repeated abandonments, family traumas, and prolonged institutionalization that they cannot tolerate returning to their biological families or living in a foster or adoptive family. The only viable long-term placement may be in group care programs. These young people need facilities that promote long-term connections to staff, volunteers, or foster families and offer placement to at least age 21 followed by opportunities for active in-volvement in organizational activities and special functions as an

---

*In later work with a family, supportive relatives can be encouraged to organize peri-odic reunions around holidays, birthdays, etc. Such reunions may have been lost in a family and reflect the loss of support and increased vulnerability of family members. Extended family events provide a natural time for children (and parents) to renew connections with extended family members who can support the safety plan.

alumni or volunteer. We need funding for agencies that can provide youths with a place where they can return to visit, where their services are needed to help others, and where they can find support in times of stress and a place they can count on to welcome them for Thanksgiving and other holidays.

Group care programs can work to build the best possible links between these youths and their extended families, recognizing that in some cases a youth may need an order of protection barring contact from an abusive parent who feels no remorse and makes no effort to protect the youth. We need to look at long-term connections to relatives, a mentor, or a former foster family who wants to maintain contact, assist them with getting a job, apartment, etc., and involve the youth in holidays.

While many older adolescents have given up on family living and say they just want to get an apartment and make it entirely on their own, I have never seen this work. I do not believe that any child should simply have the goal of "independent living." Every one needs to have a place to go on holidays and people who will care enough to come to graduations, sports events, etc.

Group care gave Lisa a chance to share her rage with staff who were not scared away by how angry she felt and who could validate her need to find out if her mother would change. In group care programs, I think it is essential to keep the focus of work on a child's need for permanency and to take a competency approach. Phase or level systems should emphasize developing competence and life skills rather than focusing on taking away points and privileges for negative behaviors. To make this possible, programs should offer small home-like living units of four to six children and avoid the stresses and contagion of putting large numbers of traumatized children or adolescents together. Very few of us could manage as parents, children, or adolescents in a group home with 10 to 14 youths.

For adolescents, learning practical skills such as how to get a job, manage a bank account, set up a budget, cook meals, get the best buys on clothes, etc., are important ways to expand their perspectives and build self-esteem through accomplishments. They also need to learn to be assertive rather than aggressive or repeatedly victimized. Life skills include recognizing frustrations and managing conflicts with peers, parents, and authority figures in a safe way throughout the week and during home visits without running away, hurting oneself or someone else, taking drugs, or resorting to the types of behavior that brought them into placement.

A good way to assess how a program is actually working is to ask youths in placement what messages they have received from staff. If phone calls are limited to once a week and visits with parents are based on the number of points a youth earns during a week, it is not surprising that youths get the message that any change is up to them. They have the power through their behavior to control contacts with their parents and thus to control the pace and pressure of work on reuniting.

This is a power that many youths in placement have become accustomed to in their roles as emotional caretakers for parents or younger children in neglectful or substance abusing homes. Their escalating infractions of rules and dangerous behaviors reflect their sense of danger, their inability to find a way out, and the pressures of feeling responsible and to blame for family crises (see Haley, 1976).

Programs that center efforts on changing a youth's behavior apart from her family reinforce a youth's sense that nothing can change the threats, violence, neglect, or tension at home. Children and adolescents in placement often feel they have no way back and no options for another home. This in turn contributes to a sense of "No one really cares. Nothing is going to change. So why should I give a shit?" A treatment plan may list "return home" as the goal but a youth may see no hope for reuniting in a positive way with her family. When this happens, the youth will likely end up feeling invalidated by the treatment program's neglect of her core problem, homelessness.

Make Visits a Time for Change

Visits are a time for parents to work on making changes in how they care for and manage their children and for children and adolescents to try out new behaviors and to negotiate conflicts together with their parents. Visits are not something that should be earned by children in placement for good behavior. Rather, visits are part of the work youths *and* their parents must carry out in order to make things better.

This does not mean sending children home for lengthy visits before it is safe. The length and timing of visits need to be based on the progress of both youths and their parents in addressing the conflicts and impasses which led up to placement. Progress will be shown by youths and family members meeting together in family therapy sessions, feeling safe and strong enough to voice goals, needs, and feelings, honestly sharing perspectives about what happened leading to placement, learning why individuals did what they did, testing out new ways of coping with critical conflicts, identifying triggers to a recurrence of traumatic incidents, demonstrating new ways of managing problems and dilemmas, and implementing safety plans involving protective network members.

In cases of physical or sexual abuse, it is important for the perpetrator to own responsibility for what was done, apologize to the victim and the family, make a meaningful reparation, and show genuine repentance. The steps outlined by Madanes (1990b, 1995b) for sex offenders can be adapted for different types of abuse. Secrets need to be revealed and forbidden in the future. Every family member needs to have ongoing access to individuals outside the nuclear family who are committed to helping the family and protecting against further abuse. Consequences for renewed abuse need to be established and understood by everyone with a clear safety plan involving the perpetrator leaving the family. If a child has to fear that her mother or father will keep a perpetrator in the home, she can never feel truly safe or validated.

When neglect or abuse has been present, visits need to start out supervised for short periods of time. The frequency of visits needs to match the developmental age of a child. For toddlers, visits need to be scheduled several times a week in order to maintain or develop a bond. For older children, visits could be scheduled weekly at first, beginning with one-hour visits and working up to two-hour, half-day, all-day, overnight, weekend, and multiple-day visits home.

These are times for family workers to help parents show their children that they are making things different at home. The absentee parent who simply wasn't there for his children, needs to step in and learn to change diapers, read stories, play games, cook, feed, meet with teachers and carry out the day to day tasks of being a parent. Parents need to learn to manage their children's conflicts and show everyone that the violence of the past will not be tolerated for anyone.

Visits are times for parents to work on building or rebuilding a sense of attachment through activities that involve working or playing together with their child: touching, holding, looking into their child's eyes, laughing or crying together, planning events, reading stories, drawing, crafts, talking about extended family members, sharing photo albums, listening to what each family member has done in the last few days, etc. Rebuilding an attachment can be fostered by encouraging a parent to share memories of when they felt a warm and strong bond to their child and what kind of relationship they would like for the future. We expect children to test whether or not their parent can hear and validate their experience. Parents working on reuniting need to show that they are able to hear, see, and feel what it is like for their child and to demonstrate how things will be different.

Use Review Conferences to Keep Time Moving

Increasing the length of visits keeps everyone focused on the shared goal of returning a child home. In Dorothy's family, as in most permanency cases, I wanted to hold network review conferences every four to six weeks. This kept the work on track and reminded everyone of the time frame to achieve family goals and get Lisa and Billy home.

Review conferences remind everyone that time is slipping by and that the children cannot wait. This helps to generate the anxiety needed to drive change and maintain the focus of work on what is needed to deal with the metaphors behind crises, to help individuals make developmental transitions, and to achieve permanency goals for children.

By our first review conference with Dorothy's family, Lisa had been moved into her aunt's home. Billy, separated from his sister and mother, looked more and more depressed. He continued to cling to his mother in sessions and said little. After family sessions, he would yell, scream, and occasionally break things in his foster family's home.

Billy had spent much less time with his aunt than Lisa had, and had no viable substitute for his mother. While Dorothy continued to earn positive reports in her alcohol program, Billy, as a 4-year-old, was losing faith. I pointed out his growing detachment and used this to keep everyone's focus on moving ahead with longer visits and the 1-year time frame for reuniting. My colleagues and I also began exploring whether Billy could join his sister in their aunt's home.

Each of the children were seeing one of my agency's therapists as well as participating in weekly family sessions with their mother. With Dorothy's approval, we worked out a plan for them to begin combined visits with their aunt for increasing amounts of time. Lisa still felt torn and angry, and I wanted to see if Lisa would be able to direct her anger toward her mother rather than against her brother, Billy. Dorothy recognized how Lisa felt left out following Billy's birth and how she had frequently taken Billy with her while sending Lisa to stay with their aunt. I asked for Dorothy's help in showing the children that she could hear how they felt during her visits and phone calls.

Each review conference provides the network with the opportunity to pull together and address family goals, signs of progress, and challenges in permanency work. Successful sessions require planning and preparation.* Before each session, we set priorities for the session, clarify the agenda, consider who needs to be included, and plan how to engage key network members. Invitations are coordinated with parents and referral sources and best made by phone with letters as reminders (see chapter 4). Sessions begin with engaging and safety messages about individuals not having to talk about anything and the time frame for the session. Introductions of new members and their relationships with family members are important. We thank everyone for coming and reinforce our need for their help and role as facilitators of the permanency work.

We share the agenda, which includes what has to be addressed for court, funding, and accrediting bodies, and invite network members to bring up issues they would like to address. We invite foster parents or child care workers to describe the child's behavior over the last few weeks, improvements, and how the child behaved before and after visits. This should not be a formal analysis covering a series of scripted questions but rather an expression by someone who cares about the child of what he or she sees working and not working. I avoid bad/good labels about anyone. "We are here to see how things are working, not to blame anybody."

If diagnostic labels are brought up by family members or practitioners, I carefully explore what clusters of behaviors mean, each individual's potential for change, and how family members can help. For instance, if a traumatized child dissociates and shows psychotic behaviors, it's important to stress how hallucinations and irrational thinking reflect the child's reaction to stress and that all of us will act in psychotic ways if the stress in our lives is high enough. We can then focus our work on reducing stress with the help of the network and increasing skills for managing stress.

To help us understand what the child is showing us, we need to hear the details of what has happened and how that fits with family members' goals. The actions of children and parents reflect the reality of the work being done. Problems indicate the beginning of another

---

*Please see Schlosberg's outline for permanency meetings for a step-by-step guide (Kagan & Schlosberg, 1989, pp. 190–192).

crisis cycle. A child may confide in a child care worker that she does not feel safe at home. A foster parent may experience a well-behaved child become a terror after a visit to his mother's home. If these issues are not addressed, someone in the system will eventually act out what has not been said and disrupt efforts toward reunification with much more dangerous behaviors. A child may steal again or get kicked out of her foster home for having sex with another foster child. A parent who had been presumed to be sober may violate his probation and end up incarcerated for driving while intoxicated.

Frequent conferences help to prevent collusions and secret under-standings between individuals. Parents and children are invited to review what they have seen happen, what they thought was helpful and not helpful, differences of opinion about what has been shared, and what they see needing to happen. Service providers are asked to share perspectives on progress and concerns. I am curious about who has been able to talk to whom about these changes, how family mem-bers understand what led up to any progress, and what network members believe needs to happen in the future to maintain improve-ments. Complaints or concerns can be used to generate goals for the future.

To avoid confusion and misunderstandings, I have found it helpful to end sessions by double checking and reaffirming my understand-ing of messages by family and network members. Who will do what and by when? I try to end sessions with a sense of hope based on real signs of progress. This may be limited to family members showing up for a session, allowing us in their door, or expressing their willingness to work over the course of a year to decide whether a child can come home or needs to grow up somewhere else. We validate the hopes, needs, and efforts of family members and outline a plan for work in the next four to six weeks.

Review conferences provide a forum for dealing with predictable roadblocks to change. Parents and children will likely test whether they really need to work on the goals and plans agreed upon. For example, parents will cancel visits complaining of work overload or car problems. This is to be expected and the importance of family visits and sessions should be emphasized when visitation plans are developed. Messages that "we need your help" reinforce the contract begun in initial sessions. I stress that parents are sending their kids a message about whether they are really willing and able to do what is necessary to take them home.

Cars, of course, do break down, employers may not let a parent take time off, and people get laid off. We work with real people and real situations. Visitation schedules have to be realistic for the distances involved and job demands of clients. Funding is often needed to help poor families with transportation and sometimes lodging expenses.

When real crises happen, we work with parents and children to manage problems without falling back on old patterns of running away, getting drunk, getting into fights, and giving up. Parents need to help their children share frustrations and fears that once again Mom or Dad is not going to come through. Mom or Dad can then work on ways to show that things are different. Missed visits can be made up. Daily letters and phone calls can be maintained with parents demonstrating what they have done to get visits back on track.

Work with the Messages to the Children

After six months of work with Dorothy's family, she had moved into the final phase of her alcohol treatment program and we had arranged for steadily increasing unsupervised visits. Billy had been moved into his aunt's home which was a relief to Dorothy and allowed for more frequent visits. Dorothy saw each child individually as well as together, and in counseling sessions she told her children that she wanted to hear what they felt, even their anger, fears, and pain. The children and Dorothy were able to talk briefly about about some of Lisa's memories of their mom getting hit by boyfriends when both were drunk. Billy and Lisa looked forward to visits, became more tolerant of each other, and began spending two-day weekends with Dorothy.

By the eighth month, however, during weekend visits with her mother, Lisa returned to her old behaviors of staying away from her mother's home without permission and getting into fights with peers in her mother's neighborhood. After weekend visits, both children bickered, occasionally fought, and screamed when asked to do things by their aunt. Billy began wetting his bed again. At our review conference, we learned that Dorothy's lease was being terminated in her current apartment for reasons Dorothy would not share. Dorothy told her county worker to relax and stop pestering her about obtaining a new apartment.

I asked what message Dorothy wanted to send to her children. In the past, evictions had been an early sign of renewed drinking. Was she giving up? Dorothy's eyes flared. "I will get a new apartment when I need to!" she insisted. Everyone should stop pressuring her; she was working one day at a time. I asked if it was still okay for the children to share their worries and anger. Dorothy's face softened and she shared that Billy had hung up the phone on her a few days earlier. I asked Dorothy if she could help Billy share more of his feelings with her and Dorothy said she wanted this.

Dorothy was offered help in locating a new home and we ended the conference on a positive note. Visits would be increased again as soon as Dorothy had arranged for a new home and Dorothy agreed to work in family sessions to show the children that she could manage hearing their feelings. Dorothy had always had to "stuff her feelings" as a child and drown them with alcohol as a teenager and an adult; she wanted Lisa and Billy to feel safe and strong enough to find another way.

GOING THE DISTANCE: BE REALISTIC

Reality-based work means giving up magical thinking about miraculous cures. Life means facing real crises, which don't stop after a few sessions. The wounds of the past will likely flare up again as family members face losses with deaths, illnesses, children growing up, and job or community changes. At the same time, I look for the courage, desire, and strengths in each family member that will enable them to move out of crisis cycles.

Every child has her own way of testing whether a parent has truly changed (C. Celmer, personal communication, 1994). This usually involves repeating behaviors that provoked desperate acts by parents and mandates for counseling, probation, and placement by authorities. We can utilize this natural tendency to predict what a child is likely to do and help parents show that things have changed by managing their children without being accused of abuse, neglect, or ending up hospitalized or incarcerated themselves.

Art, sand play, role plays, drama, and other creative approaches can be used to prepare for problem points in the future. Having family members create drawings, sculptures, or collages of their worst fears (see Linesch, 1993) can help to keep concerns from being submerged. Similarly, family members can talk about concrete ways they will deal with these fears or picture themselves coping in the future.

We expect that families will want to retrench and pull back after limited changes. This is normal behavior. No one wants to deal with pain; most of us simply want relief from stress (Pittman, 1984). Family members and supportive people in their communities make the difference in maintaining change with plans for continued sessions, work with service providers after a child goes home, and an understanding of how family members can call for help in the future before crises get out of control. Opportunities for going back to therapists at later times of stress are very important and provide a sense of continuity. Funding is needed for agencies to provide outpatient services that will continue the work begun with families of children in placement.

Discharge is a difficult time as issues of abandonment naturally recur. This is one of the primary reasons why a network approach is essential for crisis-addicted families. Permanency work means addressing each family member's need for attachment, support, and a home. Building up supportive ties among family and community members replaces the cut-offs and toxic relationships leading up to placement. Progress is shown by family members using their network to deal with problems. From this perspective, calling up and asking for help from a supportive relative, a minister, or a former agency represents change (Kagan & Schlosberg, 1989); family members are reaching out for support before someone in the family has to act out the pain once again.

Passages

At our next review conference, I learned that Lisa and Billy were fighting more than ever. Dorothy angrily denied reports that she had taken the children to various friends' homes for their overnight visits. The county worker believed some of these homes were unsafe.

I shared concerns about the visits and the childrens' behaviors but emphasized that this wasn't a question of finding someone to blame or who was being bad or good. The children loved their mother and wanted her to succeed. Dorothy had shown that she wanted her son and daughter to be free of the drinking, spousal abuse, fighting, and "stuffing" of anger with which she had grown up. I asked Dorothy what message she wanted to send to her children. Each week without a safe apartment told the children that she could not give them a lasting home and was probably on her way back to drinking.

Unsupervised visits had to be cut back. A month later, Dorothy lost her apartment and began moving from friend to friend. But, no one wanted to give up on Dorothy. Family and individual sessions continued focusing on Dorothy's message to her children. Would she find and maintain a home? Would she maintain sobriety now that she had completed her mandated alcohol program? In each of the next review conferences, we talked about the difficult task for Billy and Lisa of waiting to see if their mother could raise them. Could Dorothy provide a home for herself and her children?

Sadly, Dorothy did not find a home for herself. She did come to family sessions, continued to visit with the children, and attended review conferences. Billy screamed at her over the phone and cursed her one day; Lisa missed several visits so that she could go to birthday parties and soccer games. Dorothy accepted their anger and continued to call and visit, showing Lisa and Billy that they could be honest with her.

The family was drifting apart. My colleagues and I felt the loss of hope and more than a little anger at Dorothy's broken promises. Dorothy was not building a safe home for herself or her children. We heard a report that she was seen with a black eye. Dorothy denied this but agreed that her children were moving away from her and settling in with their aunt. She saw the sadness and the anger in their looks. I felt Dorothy had let us all down; but, at the same time, I knew that she had helped the children to be able to feel again and begin to grieve.

After 12 months of work, Dorothy tearfully decided to surrender her children. She had moved in with a friend and refused to take part in any urine checks for alcohol. Becky remained committed to caring for the children if Dorothy could not do it. Dorothy told Lisa and Billy that she wanted them to grow up with their aunt and she would take care of herself. She saw that they were making it in their aunt's family, doing well at school, and getting what she never had and felt she couldn't provide—a stable, caring family.

Billy and Lisa's aunt respected their need to care for their mother. She offered them a second home and validated their wish for their mother to change. They were never forced to choose one family over another and were able to use the months in their aunt's home to slowly strengthen their bond to their aunt, even while they held on to their hopes for their mother to provide them with a home. As time went by, Billy and Lisa faced the reality of their mother's failure to provide a home. With the support of both Dorothy and their aunt, the children were able to make their aunt's home their own, without having to be disloyal to their mother.

When a parent cannot raise his or her child, I have sometimes found it helpful to talk about the child finding a "second family." This is not a question of eradicating the child's "first family," but rather the necessity of facing what has happened and finding a home where a child can feel wanted and at the same time remember her past. Working with the "first family" helps everyone involved to understand what happened in previous relationships so that triggers for a child's fears and anger can be predicted. Just as in biological families working to reunite, children who have experienced abuse, neglect, or abandonment need to test and see that their new homes can implement safety plans which work.

SUMMARY

Permanency work begins with respect for a family's strengths and struggles to survive. I want to stress our need for parents, siblings, extended family members, community leaders, and other service providers to help a child and map out a plan showing who will do what to strengthen (or build) the attachment a child needs. Children do not have the capacity to wait long for a safe nurturing home and families need to understand how laws and funding contracts limit the time everyone has to work together on change.

Placement represents a child and other family members at great risk, typically with unresolved traumas threatening everyone in the family. Parents and children often feel torn apart and that their core sense of self and family has been wounded. Stressing these messages creates the urgency needed to make placement a crisis in itself, to keep time moving, and to engage families by showing that we can talk about what's painful.

When a child is placed, a family and service provider meeting should be held within the first two days to enlist the help of family members and service providers, to assess who is committed to parenting the child, to learn from a child's behavior and development, and to hear perspectives on what led up to the current crisis. If this is not the first placement, factors leading to the child's first move away from home may reveal much more about core conflicts than current behaviors.

A psychological assessment of the child can be very helpful to show parents that we recognize the risks shown by a child's behavior and to allow a child to share in his own way about primary conflicts, what can't be said out loud, who he looks to for support and comfort, who could be his protector in the future, the level of risk, and the forces and experiences which drive dangerous behaviors. This assessment helps map out who the child sees as his psychological family and who to invite into subsequent sessions.

By the end of the second family session, I show family members that I am sensitive to the split messages that lead to dangerous behaviors and that I respect the family's fears and loyalty. I frame the crisis of the child's placement with a metaphor and a dual centering message that reflects the child's struggle within his family. I invite family members to help the child resolve this struggle and, by so doing, to strengthen everyone in the family against threats of abandonment, violence, or other problems. Discussion of how a child's behaviors reflect the wounds and struggles of his parents and siblings helps to validate everyone, to move away from feelings of shame, and to focus the family on what can be done.

Healing and resolution of the crisis begins with family members becoming safe enough to share their experiences. This almost always requires bringing in extended family members, service providers, and community leaders who will commit themselves to helping a child and her parents avoid future problems. Involvement of supportive grandparents, aunts, uncles, and other extended family members and community resources begins within the first three sessions and is a primary factor in the success of permanency work.

Safety plans can then be developed to deal with the problems and patterns of behavior which have typically led to crises and traumatic events. Each member of the family's network needs to know and practice the safety plan, including who to go to for help if they fear that someone is once again in danger and who will be responsible for checking on the safety of children and helping parents to cope with the stresses of day-to-day life.

Metaphors and dual centering messages lead directly into concrete steps that parents and children can take to achieve goals of reuniting and resolving crises. Buying a bed and fixing up a room for a child, attending parenting classes, coming to every family session and visit, calling a child at regular times, validating a child's fears, and helping a child to tell what happened demonstrate a parent's committment to a child. Children and adolescents can be expected to test whether things really have changed and can be challenged to earn the privileges they desire by succeeding in school, sports, afterschool activities, and other areas in which they are interested.

Every child in placement needs a back-up plan for where they can grow up if their first family is unable or unwilling to do what is necessary to raise them. Who can they turn to if they are sick and with whom can they share important events and holidays? A child or adolescent without positive, ongoing connections is a child at risk, and in turn presents a risk for her community. Communities can provide links to religous organizations, mentors, foster families, and programs that will offer services to a youth past age 21.

By maintaining a perspective about what children need over time and working to help families help themselves and their children, we can make a significant difference and offer hope to children, parents, and communities in crisis. These are not "happily ever after" stories, but family members, like Dorothy, her sister, and her children, can make choices, slow down crises, and provide children at risk with a stronger, more secure attachment.

part three

turning points

chapter 7

People with broken hearts should break things.
Hitting something or somebody gives me relief.

*Fourteen-and-a-half-year-old girl in a long-
term substance abuse facility who disclosed
sexual abuse by her father and was
castigated by her parents and grandmother*

speaking up

TOMMY BURST THROUGH THE DOOR WITH A DETERMINED LOOK. "MY
dad's doing sex. You've got to stop him." To Tommy, I was an unknown man in a sport coat and tie talking with the supervisor of the
agency's crisis residence. My colleague introduced me and Tommy's
voice got louder. "Got to stop him . . . doing sex . . . up and down . . .
with Ronnie, now!" Tommy moved towards me with his eyes darting
back and forth between my colleague and myself. "Why don't you
stop him?"

Tommy was 12 years old but acted, spoke, and thought more like a
6-year-old. "Mild mental retardation" was reported for Tommy, his
twin brother, Ted, and his younger brother, Ronnie. Tommy and Ted
had first started talking about sex abuse five years before, but child
protective services determined that none of the reports had sufficient
validity to warrant placement, monitoring, or even listing in the
state's child abuse register.

Reading the scant information we had on the family, I was struck
by the ages of the boys' parents. Their mother was just 13 when she
became pregnant with Tommy and Ted. Ted Sr. was 28 at the time, a

case of statutory rape that had never been prosecuted. Instead, the couple married and lived together until Ronnie was born five years later. The boys' mother was diagnosed as schizophrenic at age 18, entered a psychiatric hospital, and gave Ted Sr. custody at his request. She started a new life with a new boyfriend and took the boys for visits a couple times a year. The boys' disclosures about sex abuse often followed these visits.

Ted Sr. claimed his sons made up stories about him in order to go and live with their mother. "She abandoned me," he complained. Ted Sr. had taken the boys to a mental health counselor for the last five years because of Tommy's and Ted's tantrums and fighting. The boys' therapist worried about Ted Sr. following through on his periodic threats to kill himself if he ever lost his sons. "What more can I do?" the boys' father insisted. "These boys are too much for me . . . but they're all I have." Each time the boys disclosed sex abuse, they recanted after interviews the therapist held with them and their father at the mental health clinic. Child protective staff would then drop their investigations.

Eight months before I met the family, Ted had set a fire near his father's shed and repeatedly ran away from home. Ted Sr. filed a PINS (person in need of supervision) petition and Ted was placed at a residential treatment center for a 30-day diagnostic assessment. In this group care placement, Ted urinated on himself, exposed his backside, wet his bed, and tantrumed. The diagnostic team recommended extended residential treatment for Ted.

Ted, however, returned home and outpatient counseling continued. Six months later, Ted Sr. placed all three boys at his sister's house after Ronnie (age 8) began talking vaguely to his teacher about "bad touching" in his home. Six weeks later, Tommy and Ted were placed in the crisis residence when their aunt said she could no longer safely care for them. She complained that they masturbated all the time and had threatened to rape her children and kill her when she tried to stop them from having oral sex with each other. Ted had also darted several times into the street and threatened to kill himself by running into a truck.

Now, in the crisis residence, Tommy was again disclosing sex abuse and asking if he could stay in the shelter "10 years." He told staff that his Dad was still seeing Ronnie alone at their aunt's house, "doing sex." Tommy claimed his father's former girlfriend also "did sex" with the boys, making them put their penises in her mouth.

Child protective services staff agreed to start another investigation into sex abuse but said they saw little chance of "indicating" this latest report. "Just more of the same." The boys had recanted each time before and were expected to do so again. County social services staff were relieved just to have the two boys temporarily in a safe residence.

Ted Sr. filed a second petition in family court complaining about Ted's running away and tantrums. He agreed to the county's plan to place Ted in a residential treatment center 80 miles from the family's home as a PINS. Ted Sr. wanted Ted to learn to control himself and thought that he could control Tommy and Ronnie without Ted at home.

"I did it before," Ted mumbled and nodded his head when he heard about his father's and the county's plan to send him to a residential treatment center for at least a year. Ted kept himself aloof from the other kids, said little to staff, and looked very much like his father, a bitter old man in a pudgy 12-year-old's body.

While Ted appeared resigned to live away from the family, Tommy became even more frantic. Tommy was shorter and thinner than his brother and made up for his smaller size with a shrill voice and a high level of energy that kept staff members chasing after him. He began going up to everyone he met including myself, searching for someone to "stop" their father.

Ted threw his brother against a wall one day when he heard Tommy talking about the sex. When their Dad came to visit, Ted hung back, compliant but removed. Tommy ran to his father and hugged him. "Take us home," he begged his father. "Just stop the sex."

I knew what Tommy wanted as he stared into my eyes. Somebody to do something. Somebody to act. Take the pain away. Make everything better. A man in a sport coat should be a hero who would save his family—Bruce Willis in tweed.

Not that he wanted to lose his father. Tommy had kept alive a fantasy of going to live with his mother over the last nine years but she had never taken care of him for more than a week at a time and had never petitioned for custody. His father and his brothers were all he had. He certainly didn't want his father behind bars.

I knew I wasn't a police detective but felt a pull to become this boy's hero. "That's a warning signal," I told myself, "First the hero. Then the bad guy. Soon the victim."*

---

*Based on Karpman (1968).

Still, it was hard to try to explain to Tommy, a 12-year-old thinking like a 6-year-old, what I could do for him and his brother. I said I'd like to talk to him, his brother, and his father about making things better but "I'm not a policeman." Tommy turned toward the crisis residence supervisor. "Just stop him," he implored. Then he darted out of the office as fast as he had come in.

Neither of us had given Tommy what he wanted to hear. I wished I could have promised him that there would be no more sex abuse in his family, that we had the power or tools to make it all better. But I knew we didn't. He ran out of the office leaving me feeling like I had failed once again.

In the space of five minutes, I had moved in Tommy's eyes from a would-be hero to another powerless mental health, social service, or education professional. Tommy and Ted's story seemed like one more tragic example of children growing up without the safety most of us take for granted. Ted was already giving up any hope of change and Tommy's desperate pleas would soon die down. The mental health, criminal justice, and social services systems were failing.

On the surface, Tommy and Ted's behaviors reflected a typical pattern of ongoing sex abuse. Excessive masturbation, oral sex, running away, setting a fire near their Dad's shed, threats to rape their aunt's children, and Ted's behavior at the previous diagnostic treatment center (showing his backside and urinating on himself) all fit with Tommy's current allegations and the allegations brought up by Tommy and Ted over the last five years.

These five years also corresponded to the age difference between the twins and their younger brother, Ronnie. I have often seen older children become suddenly much more provocative and dangerous to themselves and others when they see a younger sibling begin to experience the same stages of sexual abuse that had happened to them. What they as older siblings had become resigned to accept as an inevitable and unchangeable part of life becomes intolerable when their younger brother or sister starts to be hurt. While the older children learned to block out the pain, they cannot tolerate seeing it again in the looks and cries of younger siblings. Ronnie was now 8-years-old, the age when Tommy and Ted first began disclosing.

This was also the age at which Ted Sr. began bringing the boys to a mental health center for counseling to control their tantrums and defiant behavior. Despite the boys' aggressive behavior, they each showed fondness for their father. Their therapist had struggled to help the family stay together and to maintain the therapy sessions with the goal of nurturing the caring she saw between father and sons.

Ted Sr. presented himself as beaten down, physically disabled with a back injury from years before, and easily enraged. Even mild confrontations led to canceled appointments and no-shows with the therapist. The boys' periodic allegations of sex abuse to their teachers led to Ted Sr. questioning once again whether or not he'd be alive for the next session. This was a threat his sons could not tolerate.

OVERCOMING THE MONSTERS OF THE NIGHT

"Say the words," my colleague Shirley Schlosberg insisted when I felt stuck with a family. "What holds you back?"

All the monsters of my childhood, of course, fears of failure, humiliation, and self-blame if things went terribly wrong. Not to mention, a good dose of disaster fear, years of instruction to "go slow" with severe trauma cases, and administrative mandates to "keep your client engaged" and avoid precipitous discharges.

Ted really could run into a truck. He was certainly an impulsive boy, quite fast on his feet, almost totally closed off, and churning inside, ready to explode. Our facility was not locked and we didn't have the staffing to guarantee that he wouldn't run into the road again. Of more concern, I assumed that Ted's suicidal gestures were really a metaphor for his father, who I had not yet met. The family's therapist considered Ted Sr. a real risk.

We quickly pick up on the fragility and threats of a family in crisis. Crises and risk are a given in this work. When children are acting in ways that are dangerous to themselves or others, this usually means that the family secrets are seen as so dangerous that voicing them could be life-threatening. A mother may be threatening to kill herself. A 14-year-old boy is talking about killing himself with a gun he stole and hid in his house. A father stressed to his family that if he was disturbed too much, he would drive his city bus into a catastrophic accident. It would be their fault for pushing him over the edge with any talk of what was going on.

We can't help but feel these threats. We hear about cases where children, adolescents, and parents in treatment have killed themselves or others. "There but for the grace of God," one of my colleagues whispered after an 8-year-old drank a bottle of gasoline antifreeze and died. The child could easily have been in our program.

Many of us were taught the old adage, "If you don't have anything good to say, don't say it." Or, perhaps more to the point, "Let sleeping dogs lie." No one wants to get bit. In the families we work with, the lesson is often driven in much harder. A 16-year-old girl recalled her father stuffing a bloody sanitary pad in her mouth and being told, "Don't look or I'll kill you and your sister." She was 12 at the time and had learned to keep her mouth shut and to try to forget what her father and his friends did to her mother, her sister, and herself.

SLOWING DOWN

To help me regroup, I remind myself to slow down. Working with crisis-addicted families means helping families to slow down the pace of events. We can be quickly sucked up into the swirl of mayhem. Our clients are veterans of multiple therapies and have learned to be experts at evoking a therapist's own issues and blind spots (Masterson, 1989) in a game of high risk. I will quickly become stressed out if I throw myself into a battle as some kind of magician or Wild West hero.

I know I need to look at what's missing. It helps to remind myself of the basic tenets and steps outlined in table 4.1. I need a map to stay on course. What steps have I missed? What needs to be done? I knew only a fragment of what Tommy and Ted had experienced growing up. Yet, both boys had been involved with mental health and social services systems for a long time, with multiple assessments.

In the long run, Dad, the three boys, their aunt, the boys' mother, the family's therapist, and child protective services needed to work together. Child protective staff had been investigating Tommy's latest allegations but doubted that the boys would remain consistent in their allegations or provide the details needed to win in court. Each allegation had become another frustrating and seemingly pointless exercise. County social services staff continued to pursue an 18-month residential treatment program for Ted as a PINS. This, at least, would keep him out of trouble at home and possibly give him another chance.

At this point, we needed to show the boys that we were working to engage their father, to validate their love for him, and, at the same time, to voice their need for the sex abuse to end. Tommy and Ted needed to hear that people with some power (child protective workers, judges, police) believed what they had been trying to say for years about the sex abuse and would protect Ronnie. They also needed to see that their father would be okay, that people would be helping him to get help for himself, so that he would stop the sex abuse and overcome the shame that drove his suicide threats.

SAYING THE WORDS

We invited Ted Sr. to join us for an initial family session with Tommy and Ted. Tommy's level of agitation accelerated as the time of his father's arrival drew near. Ted appeared to grow even more sullen and tense, like a wound-up spring. The other children in the unit gave him a lot of space.

Ted Sr. arrived 10 minutes late, issuing a gruff "Let's get started" to the center's social worker. Deep lines furrowed his forehead. His gray hair and thin, gaunt appearance made him look more like 60 than 40. He barely looked at me as I introduced myself and shook his hand.

Tommy bolted from the meeting room before we could even say "Hello." I thanked Ted Sr. for coming to our session, recognizing that this was a very hard time for everyone. I shared that I knew about the sex abuse investigation and stressed that I wanted him to stop me if I asked about anything too upsetting. "I'm going to count on you to tell me when to stop."

Tommy ventured back into the room, leaving the door open. "Stop lying!" Ted Sr. ordered his sons. He glared at Ted and Tommy then turned to me and the center's social worker. "I just want them to stop lying. I'm not going to jail."

"Nothing happened," yelled Tommy as he darted out of the room again.

"Dad didn't do nothing," echoed Ted looking at the floor. "I want to go home."

"And I want you to stop setting fires. Stop this trouble," Ted Sr. ordered, glaring at Ted. "You're going to have to live away from home for a while. Mrs. Murdock (the county social services worker) and I are making the plans."

At this point in the session, I felt powerless and a bit threatened. Ted Sr. had five years of experience blocking child protective services. He knew his sons. He wielded the power to send them away and castigate any of them who defied him or, like Ted, caused too much trouble. The placements of his sons at our crisis residence were on a voluntary basis; he could end them at any moment, just like the counseling he had undertaken over the last five years.

REMAINING CENTERED IN THE STORM

When I'm feeling stressed and strained, I know I need to center my-self. What's most important? The most striking thing for me was the boys' loyalty and love for their father. Tommy had begged him to take them home, and implored Dad and everyone else to "just stop the sex."

"I like to be very straightforward," I told Ted Sr. He glowered and Ted Jr.'s head jerked upright, just about lifting his body out of his chair. Although one boy was already out of the room, I plunged ahead anyway. "When I hear boys of this age consistently talking about sex abuse, I believe them." Ted Jr. quickly looked at his father whose frown had turned back into a glare. "What really strikes me about your sons is how much they love you. They look to you. They keep saying they want to go home. And, they want the sex to end. I'd like to hear what you see happening and especially more on the good things going on in the family. About what keeps Tommy and Ted saying they want to go home."

At this point, Tommy stuck his head back in the door and caught the anger in his father's glare. "I'd like you to hear what I just told your Dad," I said to Tommy. "It's hard to say and I appreciate your Dad staying and talking with us about the hard stuff."

Tommy looked at Ted Jr. and held onto the door. "Get in here!" his father ordered. Tommy moved inside the room and sat on a desk by the door.

"I just told your Dad and Ted that I know you guys want to go home. He's your Dad. I can see you love him by the way you hug him and jump on him. I also told him that I believe what you have said about the sex abuse."

At the word "sex," Tommy was out of the room. He had heard enough. Yet I was pleased that he had stayed long enough to hear. Ted Sr. had not threatened suicide. And a few minutes later, Tommy was back in the room sitting near his father.

"This all started when they went to see their Mama. Last May," Ted Sr. complained. "That led to them going to live with their aunt. Their Mama put this stuff in their heads. She's been doing this for years and I'm sick of it. . . . Why doesn't someone take a look at *her.* . . . She's out of her mind and her boyfriend's a real loser! You know, she *left* me and the boys after Ronnie was born.

"I was in the hospital, hurt my back at work. Three weeks and she never even called. When I got home, I found she was seeing another guy, smoking weed. Who knows what else? I couldn't stand it!

"But the judge saw what she was doing. The kids are mine now. I don't know what she keeps putting in their heads, but she's never tried to get custody. She doesn't give them anything. She really doesn't give a damn!"

"Tell me about the good times you've had with the boys. What do you like to do with them?" I asked.

"He takes us fishing . . . got me a bike . . . everything!" yelled Tommy standing up again.

"Then why do you keep saying this stuff about me?" barked Ted Sr.

"They lied," Tommy mumbled.

"Who lied?" his father demanded, the glare returning.

"These guys," Tommy responded, pointing to the center's social worker and me. "Nobodies!"

"Did I ever sexually abuse you? Did I?" Ted Sr. demanded glaring at each boy. Tommy again bolted from the room while Ted Jr. mumbled a fast "No." His head was pulled down again. He reminded me of a turtle trying to pull into a shell which never quite covered his whole body.

I felt once again that any sense of safety was lost. Everyone was threatened and Ted Sr. was acting like his back was to the wall, fighting for his freedom. "We're not here to do an investigation. I'm not a child protective worker," I said.

Ted Sr. kept glaring alternately at Ted Jr. and the door. Clearly, my colleague and I had become "nobodies" by saying the evil words.

"I do believe what the boys have said. I also see how much they care about you. How much they worry about you. How much they want to go home. They need to see that the 'bad touching,' the sex stuff they talk about, is over."

"I've taught them all about 'bad touch,'" Ted Sr. countered. "I want them to tell me if anyone ever touches them down there. My damn fuckin' brother did that to my nieces. I'll kill him! Swear to God. Soon as he gets out of prison."

"Then the boys would lose you. I think that's what they're afraid of—losing you one way or another. Tommy's so scared he won't even stay in the room."

"Am not!" blustered Tommy who had returned to the room standing now near his brother.

"Are you going to be okay with us talking about these things today?" I asked his father. "These boys don't want to lose you. I hear what you've been saying about who raised them."

Tommy looked down. "He's really worried about you," I added, nodding toward Tommy.

"Nothing's going to happen to me," Ted Sr. replied. "Is that all? I'm just sick and tired of these meetings."

"I think the boys are too," I added. "I'm glad to see, though, that you keep coming in and your sons keep trying to get home and make things better at home."

Tommy was the first one out the door. Ted Sr. gave them each a quick hug and nodded curtly when asked to come back for another meeting with the county workers, the boys' therapist, and hopefully Ronnie and his aunt. The boys' mother had been refusing to come in, although she phoned the boys regularly. No miracle cure had taken place in our session, just a step toward validation of the split messages going to and from the boys.

STAYING THE COURSE

Crisis residence staff and I met with the child protective workers investigating the sex abuse allegations. "These boys always change their stories," we were told. "They don't give us anything to work with in court."

I stressed how the boys' behaviors and statements over the last five years fit a pattern of sex abuse, and how everyone involved was afraid of Ted Sr. hurting himself or someone else. The boys had already been interviewed by child protective staff; Tommy had mumbled vague references to sex acts by his father with Ted, Ronnie, and himself. Tommy was not going to give a judge the details of time, place, what happened before, and what happened after that were needed for a criminal court proceeding; his mind didn't think in that way. However, I felt that Tommy's statements and their consistency with the boys' behaviors was certainly enough for child protective to "indicate" the report and pursue a neglect petition if Ted Sr. failed to cooperate in a sex abuse treatment program. In the interim, we recommended only supervised visits and that the boys not go home.

Ted Sr. was scheduled to go for a psychological evaluation at the county's mental health clinic and child protective staff said they would await this report before doing anything more. That would take a couple weeks. In the meantime, the county social services department insisted that Ted Jr. go for an interview at a residential treatment center 80 miles away from the family's home despite our recommendations that the boys be placed together in a therapeutic foster home program designed for disturbed youths. Securing a safe bed was the county's first priority and the waiting list was too long for the few foster care programs capable of providing the close supervision, limited number of children, child care back-up, respite families, and therapists needed for boys like Tommy and Ted.

I was also distressed to hear that the family's mental health therapist had complained to the crisis residence coordinator about our discussing what the boys had said about sex abuse in front of their Dad. She feared that this would lead Ted Sr. to drop out of all counseling and quite possibly hurt himself or cut off contact with the boys. The therapist said she could not possibly join us for a permanency conference, cautioned against any further confrontations, and warned that these things were too delicate to discuss openly.

Ted Jr. was taken by county staff for his interview at the residential treatment center and Tommy became even more agitated and wild. In a phone call with their Dad, Tommy surprisingly blurted out that he did not want to go home. Ted Jr., was overheard in the crisis residence telling other children, "I'm really bad."

In phone calls to Ted Sr. before the permanency conference, I encouraged staff to repeat the message given at the family assessment about how much the boys were showing they loved their father and wanted him to change things at home so they could feel safe.

I was relieved when Ted Sr. showed up for our session and thanked him for coming in. "I was worried that Tommy thought you were mad at him and wouldn't come anymore because I had talked about the sex."

"I'm not mad at you," Ted Sr. said to Tommy. "I'm just tired of this stuff!"

"I ain't saying nothing," Tommy stammered.

I asked the child protective staff members who were present to review what was going on. Three staff members had come—the worker assigned to the case, her supervisor, and the county's child protective services coordinator. Clearly, anxiety was high. I worried that crisis residence staff and I would be left standing alone as the only ones who validated the sex abuse.

"We believe what Tommy and Ronnie have been saying," The supervisor stated in a soft but clear voice looking at Tommy and Ted. "And the boys are not going to be going home right away."

I breathed a sigh of relief, but the most difficult work lay ahead. The fear of Ted Sr. blaming and abandoning the boys or killing himself remained.

Ted Sr. was silent and I asked the group what could be done to help the family get back together. I explained, "These boys care about their father. Tommy is always trying to give his father a hug and climb in his lap. Ted Jr. tries real hard to please his Dad."

Tommy was looking up at his Dad like a mournful lost dog. "I think Tommy is looking for a hug now," I added.

"Come over here," his father mumbled and let Tommy sit on his lap. "I ain't mad at you."

Tommy sat quietly for a minute and then abruptly got up. Tommy had not sat in one place for more than a few minutes in the last two weeks. I was very glad to see him sit down by himself and listen quietly as we continued the meeting.

"The boys need to be able to see their Dad," I continued. "And to see Ronnie." Child protective staff agreed with this. "Who can their Dad work with if he wants to work on stopping the sex and getting the kids back again?"

"This we have to work out," the child protective supervisor replied, "but we will provide a place for everyone to get help, including Dad, if he wants. And Mom, if she wants." The boys' mother had again refused to come in for today's meeting. "We're looking at an agency closer to the family's home for the boys to go to."

We ended the meeting with dates set for the boys' next visits with their father and brother. These would be written on the boys' calendars to help them keep track of the time.

MOVING AHEAD

Tommy and Ted moved out of the crisis residence to a group home that was fortunately only a half-hour drive from the family's home. After the permanency conference, Tommy settled down and both boys did well in group care. The crisis center's director spoke to the mental health therapist by phone and I was pleased to hear that she later referred another child to the crisis residence.

Ted Sr. was formally indicated by child protective services for sex abuse. He refused to work in treatment programs and after a year of his sons' group care decided to surrender custody of the boys rather than continue fighting the case in family court.

For Tommy, Ted, Ronnie, and Ted Sr., this was not a fairy tale ending. But the boys were validated about the sex abuse. They heard repeatedly that practitioners saw how much they cared for their father *and* their need for him to "stop the sex." Ted Sr. did not commit suicide. He was able to give the boys a chance to become part of another family and to tell them that he was not mad at them. They didn't have to grow up as "nobodies."

MUSTERING COURAGE

If "no pain, no gain" is a maxim of therapy, it's also true that too much pain leads us all to freeze and for family members to frequently reenact the crises of the past. As I feel myself beginning to freeze, I know I need to back off, get some space, get in touch with what I am feeling, map out where I'm going, and get some feedback from colleagues who can be more objective.

I struggle to avoid some of my own triggers and myths, telling myself that I'm neither Solomon nor Sherlock Holmes. I don't expect to find the magic cure. Rather, I want to use the turmoil and tension I feel to help create a network that can work toward small changes. No heroes, martyrs, or villains. Just real people: parents, children, grandparents, friends of the family, other service providers, and very fallible psychologists like myself.

When children carry secrets about sex abuse and threats of beatings, abandonment, murder, or suicide, my impulse is to move slowly, "walk on eggshells," and get away. Yet, I know that my challenge is to gain the courage to go past obstacles and help family members make a change. It helps me to move ahead by remembering axioms of my training: the need to keep everyone from feeling trapped up against a wall, the need to validate everyone (victims and perpetrators), and the need to show respect *and* earn it by dealing with the messy stuff.

If we can't speak up, who will?

chapter 8

We make our Mom.

*Pregnant 17-year-old describing how she and
her two brothers are responsible for keeping
their crack-addicted mother out of trouble*

saying "no"

"I WANT TO SEE MY SON. . . . IT'S BEEN FIVE YEARS AND I'M DOING better." Phyllis came to the assessment with her halfway house worker. She had petitioned for weekly visits with her son, James, who was now 7 years old and living with his paternal grandparents. "I just want to see my son," Phyllis said in a monotone. "I take my pills."

Over the course of our session, I asked Phyllis what else had changed, how she understood what had happened five years earlier, and what she could say or do to show James he now had nothing to fear. "I don't want to talk about it," Phyllis insisted.

"Is there someone with whom you have been able to talk about it?"

"It's not anybody's business. I go to my counseling. I do what I'm told."

Phyllis was seeing a counselor weekly, had daily supervision from her halfway house worker, and saw a psychiatrist who monitored her medications every other month. "Phyllis is doing okay. She's working part time and takes care of her responsibilities," reported her halfway house worker. "In fact, she's petitioning the court to get out of our program, and it will probably happen."

When James was 2 years old, Phyllis stabbed him twice in the chest. By some miracle, he survived. At the time of the attack, Phyllis had been separated from her husband for a year and had wanted her husband back.

In police reports, Phyllis talked about voices ordering her to kill James. I asked her about the voices, "They're still there, but they don't bother me anymore," she replied as if I had asked her about the weather. "It's just not an issue."

I had been asked to do an assessment of Phyllis and her son James for family court. Phyllis had already had an individual evaluation at another center. James had also been evaluated. The clinician at that center had recommended that visits commence so that James could get to know his mother. The judge obviously had second thoughts and asked for a second opinion.

James's father had asked his mother and father to raise James and all three of them adamantly opposed any contact with Phyllis. James didn't know his mother at all. No one in the family talked about Phyllis or the scars on James's chest. This concerned me. James needed to know what had happened, how he got the scars, what had happened with his mother, and what would keep him safe. In many ways, James's father and grandparents were in as much denial as Phyllis.

THE BEST INTERESTS OF A CHILD

I was faced with Phyllis's wish to have a relationship with her child and the dilemma of whether or not that would be in James's best interest. In child and family services, such dilemmas often become a search for the least detrimental alternative (Steinhauer, 1991). Phyllis was doing what she had to do in her halfway house, but she had not faced the pain in her own life or what led to the voices ordering her to kill her son. The medications helped Phyllis to manage, but the voices remained, subdued but not vanquished.

Phyllis certainly did not appear dangerous. Yet, from her first messages to me I felt a strong warning: "Don't push me!" She spoke about the stabbing and her voices with an eerie coolness. I felt a need to keep an eye on her; I sensed that she could erupt again.

Nothing was really that different from the time she stabbed her son, except that now she was being supervised by the halfway house, and this supervision would almost certainly end in the near future.

No one could predict how long she would continue to take her medications.

I invited Phyllis back for a second session after reviewing the results of her previous assessment and consulting with colleagues. As she walked in the door, I felt my heart beating faster. I told Phyllis that I did not think ongoing visits would be in James's best interests at this time and that I would recommend a reevaluation in a year. I thought that she needed to do much more work in her counseling on dealing with her own past and the voices she continued to hear. She needed to demonstrate that she could deal with the pressures that had prompted her to stab her son—that would mean being able to talk about what led up to the stabbing and being able to show James and his father how things were different so that James could feel safe in her presence.

Phyllis pursed her lips, listened carefully, then stood up abruptly and left the room. I felt a momentary shiver as she passed by.

Did I say the right thing? Doesn't a child need to see his mother in person? Could Phyllis really be asked to face what she had done? Would family counseling have given her the help she needed to deal with her own issues and help her son? Wasn't she safe now that she was taking the medications?

That night, as I left my agency's outpatient clinic, I couldn't help but look back over my shoulder with a brief shudder. I realized that even supervised visits would put James into the same position that I felt that moment as I walked out to my car in the dark.

I urged James's father and grandparents to get into counseling and work on ways to deal with their ongoing terror that Phyllis would return. James would need to know where his scars came from and how his father and grandparents were keeping him safe. Someday, he would want to learn about Phyllis and meet her. Hopefully, by that time, she would have made progress in putting the pieces of her own life together and could show James that she could face the voices and that he had nothing to fear.

WINNING AND LOSING

"I want family counseling to tell me why he does these things," Patti demanded. Her soft voice sounded gentle but tasted like an overdose of saccharine. Andy shot a fierce look at his mother from across the room. He was a chubby 11-year-old with bright red hair and dark freckles. Patti had filed a PINS petition citing Andy's incorrigible behavior, including threats to kill her, grabbing her by the throat, breaking dishes in her kitchen, running away from school, and taunting her with a bat. Andy was placed by family court in a temporary shelter for boys and I was asked to assess him and his mother and to make recommendations to the court.

"I think he's got attention deficit," Patti said with a fixed smile. She, like her son, was overweight. Several weeks before, Patti had dyed her dark red hair a light blonde color. Now, she had a two-tone appearance—dark red eyebrows and artificial light blonde hair. "He should be put back on the Ritalin!" she insisted.

"I hate that stuff," Andy fired back. After three weeks in the shelter, Andy had calmed down considerably and was taken off the Ritalin.

"I think our visits have gone pretty good," Patti went on, ignoring her son. She fixed her eyes on mine, causing a momentary flutter in my stomach. "He's my only son and I want him to live with me. But until he stops being violent, he'll have to stay in a boys' home."

"Good Trouble"

I remembered meeting Andy and Patti two years earlier, when Andy was 9. Patti had petitioned family court to get Andy out of the foster home where he had lived for most of the previous four years. She had placed him voluntarily at age 5, saying that she had no place for him to stay. Andy's father had died when he was 2 and Patti spent the next three years moving Andy from friend to friend.

At age 7, Patti brought him back briefly to her home, but he was placed again after only a few months when Andy told a teacher that his mother drank, kicked him, and let him go without food. Patti denied this and no bruises were found. Andy was remanded to his foster home on the basis of his mother's PINS petition for ungovernable behavior.

Andy did well with his foster parents, Cindy and Kevin Karner, and earned good grades at school. However, if Cindy or Kevin made any loud noises or shouted, Andy would run into his room, slam the door, and return a few minutes later in tears. He would only go to sleep at night with Cindy lying down next to him. Before each visit with his mother he begged his foster parents to let him stay in their home. "I don't want to go."

Patti had smiled through every family counseling session and complied with court orders that she secure a source of income and an apartment for Andy and herself. She consistently denied hitting or kicking Andy and an alcohol assessment was inconclusive.

After Andy's visits with his mother were increased, his behavior abruptly changed. In the days before and after visits with his mother, he provoked fights with peers at school, was unable to focus on schoolwork, had tantrums in his foster home, complained of aches and pains before going to bed, and began getting up in the middle of every night and climbing into his foster parents' bed. After visits with his mother, he would climb onto Cindy's lap and refuse to let her get up.

Visits were steadily increased at Patti's insistence, leading to overnight stays at Patti's apartment. Andy returned in a rage, hitting, kicking, and attempting to bite his foster mother. Andy would only calm down after Cindy held him in her lap. He raged and eventually sobbed, "You can't make me go."

When Andy was 9, I had been asked to assess Patti and Andy at the request of the home-based counseling program that was working to help Patti reunite with her son. The program's social worker saw no progress by Patti and felt horrible taking Andy to weekly visits. Andy was growing increasingly defiant to the Karners as visits went on and return to his mother became more imminent.

During that assessment, I asked Andy to draw a picture of his family. He drew himself with the Karners. When I asked him to draw his biological mother and himself, he drew his mother pregnant with him. When I asked Andy what he would say if his mother, foster parents, or teacher called him, he said that he would "just hang up." If any of them came to the door, he said he would "shut the door and lock it."

My stomach tightened and I worried about where this would lead. When a child does not feel safe with anyone, he is likely to act dangerously. Andy knew that if he asked to live with the Karners, his mother would get angry at him. He was pulling away from everyone around him and becoming convinced that not even the Karners could help him. Like many children in foster homes, he blamed his foster parents for making him go on visits and felt they were sending him away instead of protecting him. The Karners took the brunt of his rage against a world that was steadily pushing him back into his mother's home.

I asked Andy where he'd tell his county social worker that he wanted to live. "I'll live here," Andy said referring to our clinic offices. I felt his eyes challenging mine for a brief instant in a look that said, "Why don't you do something?"

I asked Andy what he'd tell his mother. "No, I don't want to live with you! I don't want to see you!" Andy yelled and his whole body began to shudder. His voice dropped, "My mom's gonna get mad if she hears this."

Patti joined our session and sat next to her son, leaning toward him with her head almost resting on his shoulder. She gazed at her son with her unwavering smile. "You want to come home with me, don't you?" she cooed.

"Yeah," mumbled Andy, looking away.

Patti said that her visits with Andy went "pretty good." "I think what he's doing at Cindy's and at school just shows that he wants to see me more. He doesn't understand why he can't."

Andy shook his head. "It's the system," Patti complained.

I asked Andy and Patti to draw pictures and make puppet stories together. Andy took the paper and drew a line down the middle of the page. "That's your side," he told his mother. On his side of the paper, he wrote "KARNER." "That's my name!" he whispered. In puppet shows, Patti used her puppets to repeatedly court Andy. "You're making me sad," she had her puppets say while she maintained the same sugary smile and voice. "Don't you want to talk to me now? When are you going to say you love me?"

Andy built a house for the puppets and indicated that his mother should live there. Patti retorted that Andy should live there too. She leaned toward Andy, "Please kiss me Andy. Give your mom a big, big kiss." Andy spun in his chair, round and round until he nearly toppled over.

I had seen Patti alone as part of this assessment and asked her to draw a person. Patti, instead, sketched a stuffed doll she remembered from when she was a young child. Patti told me that she could not talk to her parents and wished that they would help her take care of Andy. Most of all, she wished that she could get her current boyfriend back. Patti denied Andy's claim that her boyfriend was abusive. "He's wonderful," she maintained.

Patti impressed employers with her ability to remember details, perform simple arithmetic, and work as a clerk. Nevertheless, she had great difficulty when asked to reason out problems, demonstrate practical judgment, see relationships between words and ideas, place events in a logical sequence, or denote the meaning of words beyond a sixth-grade level. Patti showed little understanding of what a 9-year-old boy would need, but emphasized repeatedly that she wanted Andy back.

After four years of foster care and two years of counseling, Patti remained a scary image that Andy resisted. "I get into trouble," he confided to me. "It's good trouble. It keeps me away."

My colleagues and I recommended to the judge that visits and continued efforts to help Patti reunite with Andy be terminated. Andy had consistently showed no attachment to his mother. She showed little or no sensitivity to his needs. Andy had continued to complain about his mother hitting him. His behavior, before and after visits, in individual counseling, and in my assessments, demonstrated his fear of being placed back in his mother's custody, even for a short visit.

Patti, at the time, had been considering surrendering Andy, and I had hoped that their relationship could improve once he did not have to fight off her efforts to bring him into her home. Periodic contacts could be maintained as part of an open adoption. Andy simply had no trust in his mother and was threatened whenever she tried to get him home. She had never given him a safe, loving home. While his mother and I were talking at the end of our session, Andy wrote in large letters on a piece of paper "KARNER."

Patti had six children before Andy and had given up each one. She could have no more children, had lost her most recent boyfriend, and was determined to get Andy back. Despite making no progress in gaining Andy's trust or establishing a stable home, Patti convinced the family court judge that she deserved another chance. After several more months of visits, Andy, at age 10, was once again returned to his mother's custody.

Split Messages

Now, two years after my first assessments, Andy had gained weight and grown taller. His face was tense and the little boy's charm was gone. He glared openly at his mother. "You hit me on the chest. You fight with your boyfriends. You lied about the bruises on your face."

Cindy Karner remembered Andy crying when he heard that he must return to live with his mother two years ago. The Karners had petitioned for custody but had lost in court. After Andy returned to live with Patti, they took care of him whenever Patti went away and for several days each week when Patti worked late-night shifts at a donut shop.

After Andy was placed in a shelter, the Karners were again granted temporary custody. Andy told the staff at the shelter that he wanted to go back and live with the Karners. He also repeated complaints that his mother hit him and drank beer.

Together, Andy and Patti looked like combative siblings with Patti trying to make Andy take on a spouse-like role. "Kiss me," she demanded and later added, "Do you want me to end up on the streets?" Andy's legs began to vibrate like a compressed spring and he jumped up several times, running to the door. I asked him to stay.

Later, I asked him if he could remember good times with his mother. "I get out of the house . . . I go to friends," he countered. When I asked about Patti's desire for him to live with her again, Andy roared, "Not in this lifetime!" and darted out of the room.

"She drinks, you know," Andy said when I saw him alone. "She calls me 'the animal.'" "Why can't I stay where I am?" Andy asked, referring to the Karners. They were the only family he had felt safe with.

Patti gave her son a double message, "Kiss me" and "You'll have to stay in placement until you are not violent any more." Calling Andy an "animal" was nothing short of emotional abuse. This had gone on for most of Andy's life. Whatever she did when they were alone, Andy felt like killing her. Nights meant particular stress and I visualized Patti demanding that Andy hold and comfort her in and out of bed.

I felt repelled by Patti. Just talking with her for an hour made me want to get away and I could understand why Andy kept running away from her. At the same time, I knew I should have more empathy. Patti was in many ways like a 4- or 5-year-old herself, unable to move on in her own development, lacking in reasoning skills, and desperate for someone to hold and kiss her. All she had ever had was her dolls and a series of boyfriends who she tried to cling to and with whom she eventually fought. Patti repeatedly ended up alone, empty, with no place to go. Andy looked like her last hope for a companion.

Under our legal system, biological parents have rights to their children unless significant abuse, neglect, or abandonment can be proven. Patti always showed up for visits and counseling sessions and reiterated her position, "He's got to stop getting into trouble . . . I want him back." Now she was asking for another year of counseling to change his behavior and another series of increasing home visits leading to his return.

Sometimes we simply have to say "No." The torture has to stop. Patti had not been able to build the trust and provide the caring that her son needed despite years of services. I wrote to the judge saying that further work on reuniting Andy with his mother would be damaging to Andy and would very likely push Andy to get into more trouble in order to avoid returning to his mother's home.

Andy wanted to grow up with the Karners and showed little or no attachment to his mother. I recommended that permanent legal custody be transferred to the Karners and that individual counseling be offered to Andy to help him understand and deal with his mother without getting into trouble. Any visits with his mother needed to be supervised and only provided as part of limited family counseling. In counseling, Patti could work on expressing the caring she said she felt for Andy and could take on a role more like a visiting aunt. Patti could be offered individual counseling to help her work on her depression and build a more positive life for herself.

"I get in trouble to stay away from my mom," Andy told me. When this didn't work, he raised the stakes.

Andy did well again back in the Karner's home. Despite my recommendations, the judge granted only temporary custody with an order for another agency to provide another year of counseling to help Patti work on reuniting. A year and a half later, Patti petitioned for custody again and was granted four-hour, unsupervised visits which were to be lengthened to day-long and weekend visits. Andy again fought with youths at school, was suspended twice, and threatened to jump off of a bridge. He was failing all of his subjects in school and spent most of his time brooding with his legs swinging from side to side. Andy was now 13, sneaking cigarettes, and rebelling more and more against the Karners' family rules.

Andy was fortunate to have the Karners stick with him. They endured Andy's agitation and defiance following each visit. They lived with Andy's outbursts and panic, fearing that with each court hearing they would lose Andy.

One day, Andy ran away from the Karners and headed toward the bridge. He was picked up before he got there and placed in a crisis residence. Another series of assessments reinforced what I and the home-based prevention staff had argued for several years. The judge ordered that permanent legal custody be granted to the Karners. However, he also ordered supervised visits and joint counseling for Patti and James at a separate agency selected by Patti.

In the first visit, Patti told Andy that these counseling sessions were being held to help her get him back. "You don't want me to end up on the street, do you?" Patti stroked Andy's hair as she complained to her new counselor about Andy's verbal abuse.

Patti appealed the judge's permanent neglect ruling, claiming she was a victim of "the system." A year later, an appeal's court judge ordered that custody be immediately transferred to Patti. Andy ran away from his school to the crisis residence and cried to staff, "My mom won." Patti took him from the Karners the next day.

Four weeks later, Andy was arrested for vandalizing a restaurant. He was 14 years old.

FINDING HOPE

Thinking of Andy, I feel frustrated and saddened. The appeals court destroyed Andy's hope that his needs would finally take precedence over his mother's wish for him to be her companion. Andy gave up on family court, foster parents, and therapists. He was headed toward the criminal justice system as his only way out.

It didn't have to be this way. I remind myself that the family court judge eventually listened to my and my colleagues' recommendations that permanent custody be given to the Karners. This kept Andy's hope alive for a few years.

Neglect of Andy began in his preschool years. Patti would certainly have been identified by a screening program for high risk parents from the time of his birth. If supportive services had been offered from his infancy and especially after the death of his father, Patti might have developed more empathy for Andy. With more feeling for him, she would have been more likely to give him what he needed or at least to have listened to his need to live away from her.

Patti's friends tried to help Andy and Patti by caring for Andy until they all became fed up with Patti's narcissism. This, unfortunately, cost Andy critical years when he needed to develop a secure bond. If a preventive program had been in place, Andy could have entered the county's foster care system at age 2 when she began leaving him with her friends. New York's Child Welfare Reform Act mandates diligent efforts to help a parent reunite. County departments of social services are also mandated to file petitions to terminate rights when parents like Patti fail to plan for their children's care despite a year of services and assistance.*

The lack of attachment between Patti and Andy marked her failure as a parent. Calling him names such as "animal" in fits of rage was just as destructive as hitting. While no bruises were found, Andy appeared to have been treated more like a pet animal than a son. Patti

---

*Note: not all states require diligent efforts to help parents reunite or use a one-year time frame for assessing permanent neglect. Federal law requires that parents make a decision about reunification within 18 months of placement.

gave him two choices: "Kiss me" and love me without question or "go to a boys' home." Getting into trouble was his only way out.

When I think about cases like Andy and Patti, I have an impulse to get away, just as Andy ran from his mother. But Andy showed me something else, which keeps me going. Year after year in his childhood, through assessments, family counseling, visits, and court hearings, he showed us all that he wanted the love and security he found at the Karners. I have to believe that as a young man he will retain that hope and give his children a better chance for a family.

The effort to help parents like Patti usually pays off for parents, children, and communities. But efforts to reunite cannot go on forever. The damage is too great and the cost too high. Sometimes we have to say "No."

the quest

chapter 9

It is the theory that determines what we may observe.

Albert Einstein

from practice to policy

JEN CAME TO SEE ME CLUTCHING HER STUFFED LION TIGHTLY AGAINST her chest. Her head hung down. Bright red hair partly covered puffy eyes. She looked like she might burst into tears at any moment.

"How are things going?" I asked speaking softly. Jen was the kind of girl who tugged at your heart. She was always in trouble, but she appealed to the rescuer in all of us. "Peggy took away my earrings. She said I wasn't taking care of my ears." Jen frowned. "It's not my fault."

Jen was 10 years old but two years delayed in school. Her mother had died when Jen was 5 years old and her father lost custody of his children several months later after leaving them unsupervised and returning home intoxicated. His mother took Jen, her younger sister, and two older brothers into her home, but after a year she asked the social services department to take Jen. Jen's grandmother complained that Jen wet herself day in and day out, ate too much, made a mess when she ate, and would not mind. Jen's grandmother was afraid she'd hurt Jen. Scratches on Jen's arms and old bruises on her back convinced social services workers that Jen was at risk if she remained in her grandmother's home.

Jen had been living with one of our foster families for six months but could only expect to leave in the near future—that was what happened at her grandmother's house and with the three foster families she'd lived with after leaving her grandmother. Jen's loss of her first pair of earrings came after Peggy, her foster mother, took a weekend vacation by herself—her first vacation since Jen had arrived. After Peggy returned, Jen failed more and more to follow directions, family rules, and to clean up after herself. Peggy, Jen's teachers, and other adults around her became exasperated.

Jen didn't talk back; in fact, she said very little. She just didn't do what she was supposed to do, leaving a mess for someone else. Now, the messes, along with the aggravation of her teachers and foster parents, were getting bigger.

Jen was especially irritable on the nights when her father was supposed to call. Jen had asked for a visit with him but he repeatedly missed appointments and usually forgot to call her. Jen's father refused to go for a substance abuse evaluation and said he could not work in family counseling. Yet he continued to tell county social services staff that he wanted Jen back and would not consider a surrender. Five years after her mother died, Jen remained adrift with no family she could count on.

I asked Jen how she got her lion. This was some time after the release of Disney's *The Lion King* and I wanted to see if her stuffed animal was something special or just part of *The Lion King*'s popularity. "From Peggy," Jen replied. Jen took the lion with her everywhere. I asked Jen what her lion could do. "It roars," Jen whispered.

I invited Jen to make up a story involving the little lion in her lap. "What happens when the little lion roars?" I inquired.

"He doesn't really," said Jen lowering her head.

"What would happen if he did?"

Jen looked down, clutching her little lion tighter. "If the little lion roared, the father lion would roar back."

"What would make the little lion want to roar?" I asked.

"First the father lion roars and then the little lion roars," Jen replied.

"Then what happens?"

"If the little lion roars, the father lion will roar back."

"Can the little lion ever really roar?" Jen shook her head and looked down at the floor.

"What would happen if one day he did roar back?"

"The father lion will bite off the mother lion's leg and maybe,

maybe knock her off a cliff," Jen's voice trailed off into a whisper. "She'll die."

"That's terrible!" I grimaced, caught up in the story and what Jen was probably feeling about her own mother's death. "What would happen then with the little lion?" I asked.

"He'd run away."

"Where would he go?" I added.

"To the monkeys," Jen replied. "They would help him."

"How would they help?" I asked. Jen shrugged her shoulders and clutched her lion.

"Let's think about that for a minute. What do monkeys do?" Jen shrugged again but looked up, lifting her lion slightly. "Monkeys are a lot like people," I continued. "They stay together. They help each other. They guard. If one of the monkeys sees something that's dangerous, that monkey warns everyone else. They protect each other. It's like a family should be."

Jen nodded her head.

"Do you think the monkeys could help the little lion like that?"

Jen nodded again.

We talked about the lion living with the monkeys and I asked, "What if the little lion wants to go visit his father? Sometimes he might feel like he ought to go back, just to check on what's happened."

"He could sneak back," Jen replied.

"But what if the father lion saw him?" Jen's mouth tightened and her eyes looked scared. She quickly dropped her head. "Is there anything he could do?"

"He'd have to run away again."

"Is there a way that the monkeys could help the little lion so that he could check on the father lion without getting hurt? Could they figure out a way to sneak back and take a peek without the father lion knowing? Monkeys can be pretty smart and the little lion could help them figure out a way."

Jen nodded.

"Could they make up a plan for how they could check on the father lion without the little lion being in danger? The monkeys could help her, don't you think?"

Jen clutched her lion tightly and nodded her head.

"Of course, the little lion is so much smaller than the big lion, right? The little lion is going to need a lot of help until he is big enough to roar safely at the big lion."

Jen nodded again.

"That's why he's with the monkeys," I continued. "But what if the little lion gets angry sometimes? You know, everyone gets angry sometimes. And this little lion saw his mother get her leg bitten off and knocked over the cliff by the father lion."

"He can't roar!" Jen replied sternly. "It would scare the monkeys."

"Is there anything that the monkeys could do to show the little lion that they wouldn't be scared away?" I asked.

Jen shrugged her shoulders.

"You know, monkeys can be very strong, but they would need to show the little lion that they could be strong enough to handle the little lion's roar. You know, monkeys can talk to each other. Maybe they could tell the little lion what they would do if the little lion roared. Maybe they could show the little lion that they wouldn't be scared away." Jen shrugged her shoulders but looked up with a half-smile.

"Of course, the little lion probably wouldn't believe them. He'd have to test them out. Do you think he could do that, find a way to test the monkeys?"

Jen nodded, more vigorously this time.

Jen and I talked about ways the little lion could test out the monkeys, beginning with little roars and maybe even a big roar with everyone forewarned. The little lion had lots to be angry about and he was a very nice lion.

Our time was up and we went off to join a review conference involving Jen's foster mother and social worker. Jen's father failed to come for this session, just as he had failed to attend previous conferences and family sessions. Peggy reported that each week a couple hours before he was expected to call, Jen became restless, couldn't sit for more than a few minutes and moped around with her head hanging low, leaving a trail behind her of half-finished art projects, opened magazines, and assorted papers. She bumped into furniture, accidentally knocked over a lamp, and occasionally wet her pants. Jen wouldn't talk about her father except to say she was mad that he didn't call. This had gone on until Jen's social worker terminated the calls and told Jen's father that he must attend a family session before calls and plans for visits would begin again.

Jen's aunt and her county social services worker had called to say they could not come in for this review conference. Given the three years of placements with no progress made by Jen's father, we had been urging Jen's county worker to file a petition to terminate rights.

She sent a message supporting the termination of phone calls and reported that a petition citing permanent neglect by Jen's father was being filed by the county's lawyers.

A few days after our session, Jen told her foster mother how she remembered her father having intercourse with her and seeing him sexually touch her younger sister. In counseling sessions with her social worker, Jen shared memories of her parents fighting, both parents leaving the children, and what happened when her father came in her and her sister's room late at night. Jen stopped wetting her bed each night, completed more of her assignments in school, remembered to do her chores in her foster family, and began to yell back at another foster child who teased her. Overall, she spoke up more and messed up less.

Jen had let out a little roar reflecting some of the hurt, the anger, and the courage she kept hidden inside. She had begun to feel safe enough to expose a little more of herself and to believe Peggy's commitment to continue caring for Jen, even if she shared some of her anger.

Jen began to trust that she could have a new home and a new life free from the abuse and secrets of the past. Storytelling and metaphor helped, but the courage and commitment came from Jen and Peggy.*

I have seen what abuse and neglect can do, from the photographs of murdered children to the rage and despair of survivors. I have shared parents' grief as they gave up the struggle to end their addiction and confirmed their children's greatest fear: Mom and Dad couldn't give up drugs or give them a home.

I have also seen depressed parents mobilize their courage and rebuild a family. I have seen parents who have hurt their children own what they did and show their children that they will not have to live in fear. I find that my faith in the ability of the human spirit to heal is renewed each time I see a child or parent move beyond the boundaries of silence, fear, and fury.

---

*Several months later I saw Jen beaming in the hall of our building. She looked two inches taller and spoke with a strong and clear voice. "Do you know what happened?" she asked. I had heard that her father had continued to refuse to work in any counseling program and then cut off all contact after the sex abuse investigation. The county filed a petition to terminate the rights of Jen's father and a court hearing was held. Jen's law guardian asked Jen if she *still* didn't want to go back to her father, a painful and disturbing question given the years of placement, sex abuse, and failure to work to help Jen. "My dad can't take care of me . . . I'm afraid he'd hurt me but I still love him," Jen replied. Jen's father surrendered her, giving Jen a chance to grow up in an adoptive family.

As I was writing this book, the New York Legislature and the United States House of Representatives, under the banner of cutting taxes, passed bills that slashed child and family services.* Block grants with massive cutbacks in funding felt like a slap of rejection from government leaders and represented a very real threat to the efforts of my colleagues and myself to help children and families.

Meanwhile, we worked day by day with children and families in crises that remained hidden from most Americans. The news shows the ugly aftermath of years of neglect with each report of gang violence, battered wives, or serial killers. Few, however, see the pain behind the violence. Fewer still see a way out of the morass.

The monkeys in Jen's story about the little lion provided the "safety net" a child needs to move past traumas and develop her talents and strengths. Jen's story reminds me of how foster parents, social workers, psychologists, and other practitioners can provide a healing community for children who are too frightened to roar.

But what happens to homeless cubs if there is no one to help or provide a substitute family? What if the monkeys don't work together or tell the little lion that he can only stay for a short time and then must go back to her father because that's all the food or time they can afford? "Thirty days, kid, and you're out! That's all your insurance covers."

The monkeys could argue about who should take responsibility and move the little lion from family to family every few months, saying in effect, "Sorry, but you're just too hard (or bad) for us to handle." The monkeys could even file a petition in court citing the little lion's running away as a violation of the law. The little lion could be taken in front of a judge, adjudicated to be in need of supervision, and sent hundreds of miles away to be reformed and disciplined.

The monkeys could also disparage the little lion's wish to see his family again and tell the little lion that he should simply accept them as his new family and forget his mother and father. If he started to

---

*New York state cut expenditures for foster care, child protective services, and prevention of placement services by 25% in 1995. Several months later, following the highly publicized abuse and murder of a 6-year-old child in New York City, New York's governor proposed increasing these funds by 18% over the 1995 reduced levels for the 1996 fiscal budget. Nationally, the Child Protection Block Grant approved by the House of Representatives on 3/24/95 would have repealed federal foster care and adoption regulations and reduced expenditures for abused and neglected children by $3.5 billion over five years including a 14% cutback in the year 2000 (Children's Defense Fund, 1995).

roar or misbehave, he could be sent away as ungrateful or sent for medical treatments for his genetic defects and impulse to roar.

I have seen children who have experienced each of these possibilities. I have also seen how the system can work.

THE CRISIS OF ATTACHMENT

America has become "the first society in history in which the poorest group . . . is children" (Phillips, 1990, p. 483). We are facing a growing number of children living with the greatest poverty of all: the lack of a bond to someone they can count on.

A family's referral to a child and family services, mental health, or criminal justice program represents an opportunity to stop the evolution of homelessness and violence. This opportunity only lasts a moment. Children like Jen simply can't wait. Development (social, emotional, moral, educational) stops when children lose faith that they will have someone to be there for them through maturity. Research has demonstrated the need of all human beings and especially children to have lasting emotional connections (Ainsworth, 1969; Bowlby, 1977; Brazelton & Cramer, 1990; Kaplan, 1988; Mahler, 1972). Studies of resilience have affirmed the importance of a caring, nurturing adult who children know will advocate for them and believe in them—an adult to whom they can turn and with whom they can identify (Brooks, 1994; Farber & Egeland, 1987; Segal, 1988; Weiss & Hechtman, 1993).

Practitioners working in child and family services have seen what leads children to give up hope and stop caring for themselves and for others. We have seen firsthand how violence, deprivation, abandonment, and abuse become ingrained into the very being of children. Studies have shown that physical and sexual abuse leads to biological changes (De Bellis, Chrousos, Dorn, et al., 1994a; De Bellis, Lefter, Trickett, & Putnam, 1994b; van der Kolk, 1984, 1988).* Suicidal ideation, suicide attempts, major depression, and dysthymia have frequently been found in adults who experienced sexual abuse as children (Briere & Runtz, 1986; Burgess, Hartman, & McCormack, 1987; Cahill, Llewelyn, & Pearson, 1991; Herman, Russell, & Trocki, 1986). Laboratory studies have also demonstrated how traumatic separation

---

*While trauma has been found to lead to biological changes, the genetic predispositions of individuals also play a major role in the vulnerability of individuals to develop depressive and stress disorders (De Bellis et al., 1994b).

of infant rhesus monkeys and rats from their mothers leads to biolog-ical changes, agitated behavior, and hyperactivity that continues into the animal's life (Suomi, 1991; Thomas, Levine & Arnold, 1968).*

Children become hypervigilant as victims who learn to always be on guard, ready to run or fight, and later often become aggressors themselves, like Kristin in chapter 3 and James in chapter 8. "When you got nothing, you got nothing to lose" (Bob Dylan).

The attachment of a parent to a child incorporates ongoing rein-forcement, respect, nurture, and security—the key ingredients to so-cialized and successful behavior. Parents who are able to provide this bond typically have strong ties and supportive relationships with ex-tended family, friends, and their community. Parents who abuse their children are more likely to be socially isolated (Strauss & Kantor, 1987).

The placement of a child represents a crisis of attachment. We must face the question of who will be there for the child and what will that person need in order to raise the child to maturity. Just like the little lion in Jen's story, children in crisis test whether those who care for them (parents, foster parents, teachers, and group care staff) can maintain their commitment when children let out the pain and rage locked inside. Will they be tossed out once again when their care-takers hear them begin to roar? Can they find a way to master the traumas of the past?

We can learn from what helped Jen and other children to heal from violence and use this understanding to develop effective legislation, funding priorities, regulations, and service management. In short, we have an approach to offer communities strained and frightened by the violent acts of children growing up with abuse and neglect. This is *not* a magical solution with happily-ever-after endings but, rather, an answer to critical questions that keeps the focus of policies and interventions on each child's need for attachment to a parent who can provide a safe and lasting home.

WHY BOTHER?

Practitioners in child and family services have witnessed how abused and neglected children who are repeatedly moved from one home to

---

*These studies are particularly poignant given the separation of Black children from their parents during slavery and the abuse and neglect inflicted by slavemasters. In later years, Native American children were separated from their parents and commu-nities and sent off to boarding schools.

another eventually lose hope, stop caring about others, and become violent themselves (Steinhauer, 1974). An old Navaho saying admonishes, "A child who is careless, wild, is a child without a family."

The community takes on the responsibility of protecting children in danger through provision of well-staffed child protective, family counseling, and emergency placement services. This is more than a moral challenge. All too often, today's severely abused and neglected children become tomorrow's violent adults. In one study, 74% of crimes committed by juveniles were found to have been committed by children who grew up in violent homes (Trieschman Center, 1994). A community's neglect of its children's safety will come back to haunt them in a few short years.

Research has shown how violence is largely learned and tied to experiences of child abuse, witnessing battering of parents, alcohol and drug abuse by parents, and criminal activity (O'Connor, 1993). Parents who were abused by their fathers or witnessed their fathers abuse their mothers were found to be much more likely to abuse their own children than parents experiencing the same level of stress who did not experience such abuse as children (Strauss & Kantor, 1987).

Children and adolescents growing up in violent or neglectful families often turn to youths in similar situations, developing their own family networks outside of the family. Groups of youths who have given up on getting nurture at home and who see little hope of succeeding in school or legitimate work find other ways to gain the respect that all humans need. This often involves demonstrating their mastery of the violence with which they lived. Anger and rage are directed outside the family. Control of a street, a neighborhood, or a community's drug trade can earn respect and a sense of control for a young person who grew up feeling shamed and rejected in what appears to a young child to be a hostile and out-of-control world.

Neglect, abuse, out-of-wedlock births, family violence, and community violence have been rising together in the last 10 years, along with an accelerating drug epidemic. The cocaine battlefield has created thousands of homeless children. In the United States, 40% of the nation's children were reported to be living in poverty, and child abuse and neglect reports increased 40% between 1985 and 1990 (American Orthopsychiatric Association, 1993). In 1993, nearly three million children were reported abused or neglected, 22,000 infants were abandoned in hospitals, and half a million young people were living without a place to call home (Liederman, 1994) At the same time, arrests of youths for violent crimes grew by 24% (American Orthopsychiatric Association, 1993).

Children in single parent homes are six times more likely to be poor, two to three times more likely to have emotional and behavioral problems, and more likely to drop out of school, get pregnant, abuse drugs and go to jail than children from two parent families (Whitehead, 1993). In 1994, 24% of children in the United States lived in mother-only families (Casey Foundation, 1995) and the number of unwed teenage mothers increased by 44% from 1985 to 1992 (Burrell, 1995).*

Everyone agrees that children are our future and critical to the health of a nation. Businesses need employees who are responsible, skilled, and function at a high level of social, moral, and educational development. To protect a child like Jen from abuse and neglect can save generations coming afterward. To let a child grow up without attachment will plague us all for generations to come.

WHAT ABOUT CHILDREN'S RIGHTS?

Jen should not have had to wait four years to find out if her father would stop his use of drugs, end the sex abuse, validate his children, and provide a safe home. She had little attachment to him. She lived for most of her life in terror.

The law, however, protects parents' rights. Children continue to be treated as property. In ancient times, a child's right to live depended upon acknowledgment by a father in some cultures and illegitimate children were especially likely to be abused or to simply disappear (Radbill, 1987).† Hitting adults leads to assault charges; hitting children by parents is permitted as long as it doesn't leave marks that can be verified by authorities.

In England the first laws for children's rights were not passed until the 1830s at which time the legal age for prostitution was raised from 9 to 13. In 1869 in America, about 30,000 children reportedly lived on the streets of New York City. In 1871, a battered girl, Mary Ellen,

---

*It is a myth that most welfare recipients are unmarried teenage mothers. In 1993, approximately 8% of the 3.8 million mothers who received welfare were unmarried and under age 18 (Del Valle & McNamee, 1995). Yet, advocates of teen pregnancy prevention programs have found that 60% of the women heading families receiving Aid to Families with Dependent Children had their first child as a teenager (Gottlieb, 1995). Moreover, children born to teen mothers have been twice as likely to become dependent on welfare than children born to older mothers.

†This was not true in all cultures. Illegitimacy, for instance, was an unknown concept in ancient African culture (Williams, 1976). In matriarchal Native American cultures, a child without a father was taken in by the mother's brother (Green, 1992).

sought protection from the Society for the Prevention of Cruelty to Animals; no such organization for children existed. Today, the United States has three times as many shelters for animals (3600) as for battered women and their children (Trieschman Center, 1994).

Child labor and child welfare laws were not passed until the 1920s and 30s. Historically, children were considered expendable—easy to replace. Children who have bonded to adoptive parents have been ordered to live with birth parents returning after years of abandonment. Focusing on the best interests of the child (Goldstein, Freud, & Solnit, 1973) remains secondary in many court decisions based upon legal precedent. Continuing this approach leaves everyone's future in jeopardy.

IS FAMILY REUNIFICATION ALWAYS BEST?

The needs of parents and children often conflict. Ann, a 20-year-old mother of three children, listed as her goals: a car, a better job, a new boyfriend. Ann's goals were very appropriate for her age but said nothing about meeting the needs of her children. They had already experienced periodic lack of food, abandonment by their father, fighting between their mother and her boyfriends, and prolonged absences by their mother.

Jen and other children who have grown up with violence and neglect need to learn that they can trust a parent to be there for them. Time and commitment from the child's primary parent are needed to build a secure attachment in the child's first years (see Bowlby, 1969, 1973, 1979; Gelles, 1993).

Children who have lacked safety in the past often need the level of attention and nurturing contact typical of the developmental age at which they lost their ability to trust their parents. Thus, an 8-year-old who experienced neglect from age 2 would emotionally need the level of support and emotional dependence typical of a 2-year-old. Caretakers would need the skills and commitment to manage whining and tantrums from a large child who is still struggling to master the challenges of "the terrible two's."

Most families with children in placement can be successfully reunited. For some families, however, making an adoption plan is the best outcome for both the parents and the child. The crucial question for Jen and all children in placement is whether the biological parents can develop a nurturing relationship with their child and establish a home free from abuse and neglect. Children's development is contingent upon the development of a secure, nurturing relationship with a caring adult who may or may not be a birth parent (Egeland & Erickson, 1991; Sroufe, 1983).

Family preservation and family reunification when a child has been placed into foster care has too often been touted as the ultimate goal and the primary outcome measure for evaluating the success of treatment programs. This, however, conflicts with the experience of practitioners that some parents cannot (or will not) do what is needed to parent their children. Small improvements in lifestyle over a 10-year period may be very real but not enough to save an 8-year-old who has never known a safe home or a secure relationship. A mother may learn to stand up to an abusive husband and stop drinking but continue to threaten her daughter with beatings or abandonment.

It is sobering to note that 30–50% percent of children murdered by parents or caretakers were killed after violence was identified by social services agencies when the children remained at home or were returned home after short-term placements (Anderson, Ambrosino, Valentine, & Lauderdale, 1983; Basharov, 1991; Daro, 1987; Mayor's Task Force, 1983; Mitchel, 1989; Texas Department of Human Resources, 1981). Gelles (1993) has argued that parents who severely hurt or kill their children are "categorically different" from parents who have neglected or maltreated their children *without* life-threatening harm; he estimated that family preservation may be most appropriate for 65–70% of abuse and neglect cases.

I don't believe that children can overcome the terror associated with a parent who has threatened to physically wound or kill the child, a spouse, or a sibling. All too often, I have heard stories from older adolescents and young parents of how they or a sibling had disclosed abuse as children. Their parent(s) held off abusing them during a 60- or 90–day child protective investigation and pretended to be decent and caring to their children. Beatings and threats resumed as soon as the investigation was closed, with parents telling their children that no one, including CPS, believed the children.

Threats of death and severe bodily harm invalidate a parent's potential to establish a secure, positive attachment. Children in such families need orders of protection, which block unsupervised contact with a threatening parent, and assurance that their primary caretaker affirms the risk experienced and demonstrates that he or she will work to protect the child from harm by the threatening parent. As a child gets older, she can be helped to understand what forces shaped the threatening parent and how the child can be different in her own life.

As practitioners, we see the conflict between our effort to empower families and children's need for safety and permanence. Remembering that Jen had very little time helped to keep us focused on putting her interests first while we worked to engage her father. Parents have the responsibility to make choices about caring for their children or giving up their role as the primary parent so that someone else can raise their child. These are difficult and painful questions but we cannot ignore them and risk another generation of children growing up without secure attachments.

PINS OR FINS OR PIN?

PINS (persons in need of supervision) petitions filed for truancy and other misbehavior focus on a youth's defiance without addressing what is going on in the family. In many if not most cases where PINS petitions have been filed, neglect is at the root of the problem (see Reid, Kagan, & Schlosberg, 1988).

Children like Jen display a range of behavior problems. A child who doesn't go to school is telling everyone that something is wrong. The child may be in a school program that is too frustrating, too boring, or simply inappropriate for her needs. For other children, skipping school is a way of telling their family and community that they just don't care or that they see no way to succeed. They may see school as a waste of time compared to other things going on in their lives. Skipping school can be a way of calling for help. I have frequently seen children in foster care fail to attend or work at school when their parents are failing to do what is needed so that their children can return home.

I always want to know where a child is spending her time when she is not at school. Some children feel a need to be at home watching over a depressed or suicidal parent, a parent who is medically ill and not caring for him- or herself, or a parent who has been threatened by a spouse or boyfriend. Often, siblings appear to take shifts over time with one sibling or another always ending up sick, expelled, or simply truant in order to keep an eye on a parent who remains at risk.

With the advent of family preservation programs and an emphasis in social services on avoiding placements of children, many parents have filed PINS petitions against their children as a way of arranging for long-term placements outside the home. Children barely into kin-dergarten are labeled as ungovernable and placed on probation with a message from the judge, "One more time and you're placed."

With this provocative challenge, children and adolescents are given control of whether they remain in their homes. In the eyes of the court, it's up to them. Youths who have heard this message are more likely than other children or adolescents involved in prevention of placement programs to end up placed away from home, often in a group care facility for twelve to eighteen months (Reid et al., 1988).

The child placed as a PINS or JD (juvenile delinquent) learns how to move "the system," may temporarily escape from family conflicts, and sees that the community has endorsed what her parents have said so many times, "You're bad and need to be punished." Many youths can do well in a new setting that offers an individually tai-lored educational program and skill-building activities. Many, how-ever, return to their previous behaviors as the time draws near for them to return home. Family problems can be put on hold for the term of the placement but, if nothing has changed in the family, these problems soon confront both parents and children, leading to re-newed conflicts and transgressions.

To look at the child's misbehavior and truancies outside of the con-text of her family misses the child's message. The child is taken before a judge and listed as the problem. The parent's role is ignored in the legal proceeding. This also means ignoring the key role parents can play as resources for change.

A child who is skipping school would be better served if court authorities would first mandate an evaluation of how parents have been carrying out their responsibilities to care for their child and get the child the help needed so that he or she can be successful in school. An evaluation of the appropriateness of the school program for a given child is also needed. Responsibility for change needs to be shared by the child, the parents, the school, and, optimally, extended family and community organizations.

Many PINS cases are more accurately defined as cases of educa-tional neglect by the family and/or the school. I have met many older adolescents placed for truancy who had to stay home from school to help take care of younger siblings. Families of PINS youths often need to be court-mandated to work to resolve conflicts and provide the parenting the children need in order to succeed at home, in school, and in the community. Educational studies and research have consistently shown that the single most important factor in a child's educational success is his or her parent (Klein, 1993).

In New York, a movement was launched to change the PINS statute to FINS (families in need of supervision). Another option would be to drop the "S" and simply designate these children and adolescents as PIN (persons in need). The question for the court could then more accurately be focused on how to mobilize the guidance, support, and opportunities the child needs to reach her potential. At the same time, the child can be challenged to succeed and to demonstrate the maturity expected of someone his or her age.

Discipline, after all, means learning a way to become a winner. It involves both a teacher (parent or educator) and a student. Running away, taking things that don't belong to you, throwing temper tantrums, etc., are typical behaviors of children at very young ages. Older children and adolescents who act in these ways are sending everyone a message that for some reason they have not been able to move past nursery school or even pre-nursery school behaviors. Both the youths and their parents need to set goals and make choices about what they are willing to do in order for the youth to grow up and succeed.

WHEN SHOULD A CHILD BE PLACED?

Parents need opportunities for respite and to say, "I need to place Johnny before I kill him. We're *both* getting out of control!" Crisis foster homes and group care facilities can provide a time out and a chance to assess what needs to happen for a family to safely reunite and prevent future violence or repeated placements.

Real crises (deaths, losses of jobs, neighborhood violence) do occur, just as Jen's family experienced the death of her mother. Families may need a time-out and a chance to regroup to prevent problems and violence from becoming a repeated pattern. Parents who can ask for such help and then work to make changes show their children that they can face real problems and do not need to live in cycles of crises.

When parents are not providing for a child's real needs, placement may be needed to provide an impetus for change. In many states, removal of children requires demonstration of "imminent risk" of severe harm. Meager care is tolerated. Lack of attachment is often ignored. Children are left living with chronic neglect and risks of harm that are very real to family members who have learned how dangerous an alcoholic or cocaine-addicted family member can become.

Overloaded child protective staff are prone to close cases where strong evidence of abuse is lacking and when county lawyers refuse to file petitions of neglect or abuse because they could be dismissed in family court or lead to time-consuming counter-suits by angry parents. Failing to "indicate" cases of neglect and go to court shows children that nothing will happen. Children who have disclosed abuse or neglect too often learn that no one will listen, that their parents' abuse will not be stopped, and that whatever caring they receive from their parents is all that they can expect.

WHEN SHOULD PERMANENCY WORK START?

Diligent efforts and permanency messages need to begin on the first day of placement. Otherwise, children and parents may wait months before adjudication of neglect or abuse petitions, months in which little happens. Children and parents need to hear what needs to happen for children to reunite and that placement in foster homes or group care is temporary.

Resolution of crises should take place within a few weeks for emergency placements. If longer placement is needed, everyone should hear that temporary foster care can last no longer than a year or eighteen months before a child is reunited with their family or a long-term plan is developed for the child to grow up with a relative or in an adoptive family.

Parents have the right to fight neglect petitions in court, but winning in court is not the same thing as showing commitment to one's child (S. Hunziker, personal communication, 1995). Parents who choose to fight in court can also start work from day one on what is needed to reunite. This shows children that reuniting and making things better are Mom and Dad's priorities and that Mom and Dad will care for them.

GROUP CARE, HOSPITALIZATION, OR FAMILY LIVING?

I have often been asked whether a child in an emergency placement needs a psychiatric hospital, a residential treatment program, a "therapeutic" foster home with child care, clinical, and other supports, or a less costly "specialized" foster home for children with mild behavior problems. This, I believe, depends to a large degree on what messages a child receives from the significant people in her life—parents, CPS workers, therapists, and extended family members.

The level of care needed typically increases with the child's perception of the risk of renewed trauma in her family and the lack of a family-community network that is able and willing to address this risk. Highly staffed group care and hospital settings can create the safety needed by a child and family to address painful issues. However, short-term hospitalization and placement has often been limited to reduction of acute and dangerous symptoms for one family member, leaving painful family issues to be addressed later in outpatient or community residences with far fewer resources. As most practitioners know, the effectiveness and intensity of therapy is tied more to the willingness of family members, family therapists, foster parents, child care workers, educators, and program managers to face difficult issues than to the restrictiveness of a program.

For most children placed in a crisis residence, the length of time needed in group care depends on how long it takes to mobilize a positive and supportive network of family members, service providers, and community resources. A child needs to see that the network is addressing critical issues, for example, Mom's suicide threat or Dad's cocaine use, and that people can talk about what led to placement. Jen, like many children in placement, felt that she must continue to hold in toxic secrets and doubted that her father had developed the strength, determination, and supports to make a safe home.

In brief, the network needs to demonstrate that (1) the child can regain or build a bonded relationship to someone she can trust; (2) the child's experience is validated by important people in the family; (3) a safety plan is implemented by family members, extended family, friends, and authorities, protecting family members from violence or dangerous behaviors; and (4) family members have succeeded in passing the child's test of whether neglect, abuse, or lack of discipline will repeat.

Some children have been so damaged in the first years of their lives that they appear unable to ever trust again. Any close relationship to a mother- or father-figure triggers memories of terrible abuse. Such children may need a more detached environment. This could be a professional foster home with child care support, clinical staff, and respite back-ups for foster parents who operate on a more structured and less intimate basis, essentially implementing a group care model within their home.

IS THE PERMANENCY PLAN WORKING?

Children and youths who have shown severe behavior problems have been able to do well in permanency-focused foster homes and small four- to six-bed group care units that involve child care workers, weekly respite for foster parents, social workers, psychological and psychiatric staff, supervision of foster parents, intensive training of foster parents, and respite. These services help keep youths and children in foster families and family-style group homes while focusing on what has to change for them to return to their biological families.

When children continue to act out and need longer residential treatment or psychiatric hospitals, they are telling us that they do not believe the critical dilemmas in their family have been (or will be) resolved. The child may oscillate from positive strides in self-development to repetition of past dangerous behaviors. In these cases we need to double-check the permanency plan. Are significant people missing in the network? What messages are being given to a child about the permanency work? Does the child understand what has to happen for her to return to her parents? Does the child feel that staff members respect her family? Do the parents and the child have the capacity to attach? Who is truly working to make positive changes? How can the child's family, social services, practitioners, and community meet the child's test of whether things have truly changed?

Adolescents often give staff only a short time to demonstrate that they truly respect their hopes, loyalty, and dilemmas. Messages of disrespect will not be tolerated for long. For example, Greg, a 15-year-old youth, became extremely agitated and ran away after a senior child care worker repeatedly criticized him for referring to a family friend as "Uncle John." This was not a biological uncle and the child care worker was trying to teach the youth reality. For the child, however, "Uncle John" was more of a parent than anyone in his biological family. Lack of recognition by the child care worker meant lack of understanding and lack of respect. It was time to leave.

Many children and adolescents in placement can benefit from medications for symptoms of attention-deficit/hyperactivity disorder, posttraumatic stress, depression, psychotic tendencies, and many neurological impairments. Psychotropic medications and physical restraints have also been used to reduce a child's behavioral outbursts and maintain sufficient safety for a child to remain in a foster home or group care program. Overreliance on restraints, however, can block healthy forces in a child's struggle to heal and give the child the message that dealing with her pain is not possible in this setting or that only chemicals can provide relief from her pain.

For many youths, placement in group care means learning to hold in their anger. In cases where the biological family has made no change or has given up custody, youths who have "stabilized" may be referred to a foster family. Such youths may quickly return to their original dangerous behaviors as soon as they feel themselves interacting with people who remind them of the fathers, mothers, brothers, and sisters who hurt them before.

Group care staff can use a child's behaviors to understand what she and her family cannot say and use this understanding to focus on what needs to change within the child's network so that she can be validated and have the lasting connections she needs. Nurses are in an excellent position to empathize with a child who comes to them with aches and pains. Youths are naturally interested in their bodies and can turn to a nurse or physician in a confidential and very productive relationship, which allows expression of intimate concerns about their sexual development, sexual experiences, or physical growth and which can lead to positive steps to help them feel better about themselves.

IS IT UNFAIR TO ASK PARENTS TO CHANGE?

I often feel compelled to "walk on eggshells" with parents or children who covertly threaten to hurt themselves or others. When I feel myself hesitating to say what's important and fearful of a child's or parent's reactions, I remind myself that treating families as fragile or incompetent is disrespectful to the family as well as to myself and other staff. Engaging family members and developing a context for change requires being genuine and saying what people are afraid to voice.

When I met Beverly, she was sitting under a large, draping plant that hung from the ceiling over her couch. The plant was dead. Beverly's three children had been placed in a foster home after she threatened to kill herself. In our review conferences, Beverly would tell everyone that she might not be there for the next meeting. Her children would stiffen and distance themselves from everyone. Their mother's suicide threats meant that they could say nothing.

It helped me to remember that Beverly had been able to raise that dead plant to an enormous size before her hospitalization. She had also survived years of abuse and neglect as a child. I needed to build on her wish that her children have a better life and asked Beverly to show her children that she would keep herself safe and not kill herself. At the same time, we continued to work with her on reuniting

with her children within a one-year time frame or making a decision
about placing them for adoption.

A permanency-based approach means truly believing that children
and communities cannot wait months and years for parents like Beverly or Jen's father to slowly change. It's the responsibility of parents
and extended family members to face the real challenges involved in
providing a safe, secure home and a bonded relationship for their
child. Family members have choices to make within the time frame of
a year or year and a half of permanency work. This is a model of
respect *and* responsibility.

DO CHILDREN HAVE RESPONSIBILITIES?

Children in placement have choices to make and jobs to do that fit
their age. Succeeding in school, developing skills in activities, learning how to manage in their communities, respecting the rights of
others, helping other people, and taking care of themselves are all
important. Children like Jen also need to find a way to discover
whether parents have changed and whether safety plans can work
without anyone getting hurt again.

THE CRISIS IN CHILD AND FAMILY SERVICES

Working with families when abuse and neglect is mild or moderate
offers the best chance for strengthening families and preventing extended placements. Yet these are the cases that often end up being
dismissed or put on waiting lists for preventive services that last
months or years.

Pressure toward mediocrity continues throughout children's services. While program funding on a state-wide or national basis increased overall in the 1980s, funding has not kept up with increased
caseloads or cost-of-living increases.

The gap between private, nonprofit agency salaries and state or
private for-profit salaries has grown increasingly over the past 15
years. Masters level social workers who deal with high-risk cases involving violent or self-abusive family members in agencies such as
my own began at $22,050 in 1993. In the same region, the *very lowest*
starting salary for beginning bachelor's level, public school teachers
working a 10-month year was $3,250 more with better benefits and

annual step and cost of living increases. Frequently, staff leave social work positions to become analysts for managed care companies or to work as a regulator in a state department with an immediate salary jump of $5000–$10,000, better benefits, and annual step increases.

Many states are now moving from capped rates to capitation plans in which nonprofit agencies are asked to absorb the risk of cost over-runs for foster care and family services. Cutbacks in funding are being passed on to direct service providers with a call for more efficient work. Yet, court system and child protective delays remain outside the control of service providers. Minor mandate relief coupled with demands for more accountability has often meant more paperwork.

"Do more with less" and "Do the paperwork first or no one gets paid" have been the dominant messages in social services over the last 20 years. Time for engaging youths and parents, providing consistency in therapeutic relationships, evaluating outcomes, training staff, and developing innovative programs has been steadily stripped away. This has resulted in bare bones services, which in turn lead to high staff turnover and mediocre outcomes. As state governments cut funding of family services and move toward managed care approaches, many child and family services agencies have found themselves poorly staffed and lacking the data on cost-effectiveness needed to garner managed care contracts.

Children's and society's need for safe, consistent, and nurturing families has been overlooked in many areas. Instead, short-term, home-based work has been pressed as a panacea for chronic, dangerous situations. Channeling Medicaid funding through managed care has restricted services to specific, time-limited problems when children referred for placement are usually demonstrating long-term attachment disorders and symptoms of multigenerational abuse and neglect. Children and families who fail to respond often end up in family court with PINS and JD petitions, leading to placement within the criminal justice system.

Practitioners have been feeling the burdens of increased demands and reduced resources. While funding to serve individual families has been reduced, the levels of child abuse and domestic violence in communities have increased. Agencies and individual practitioners remain liable for services limited by restricted funding.

Child and family services have been described as toxic environments marked by high risk, high responsibility, poor supportive services, and little or no control—a prescription for high stress and burn-out. This in turn means that children like Jen face a high risk of losing their workers before any real change occurs. As both demands and constraints have mounted, some agencies have taken on a war mentality with administrators taking a "need-to-know" orientation and feeling tremendous pressure to control what is increasingly becoming an out-of-control situation. The oft-cited three "Rs" of management—respect, recognition and remuneration—are too often lacking in child and family services.

THE ROLE OF THE PRACTITIONER

Practitioners in child and family services work at a critical juncture. The conflicting needs and demands of parents, siblings, children, schools, child protective units, probation departments, lawyers, judges, legislatures, accreditation bodies, and taxpayers are played out by real people in crises leading to a child's placement. This juncture is also the best place to learn what is essential for change and what practices and policies can help children and parents rebuild their lives, foster supportive networks, and promote safety and security within families and their communities.

Practitioners can work together with children, parents, administrators, and community leaders to voice what is essential for a child's development, what helps, what gets in the way, and how to build the most effective services. In the next chapter, I will outline several tenets for advocacy and change.

chapter 10

building a better future

WE CAN CREATE A BETTER FUTURE FOR FAMILIES AND COMMUNITIES BY focusing our efforts on what is most essential, developing a shared agenda, and streamlining our work. We can then strengthen coalitions and mobilize a strong lobbying effort. I suggest the following steps as a starting point.

MAKE ATTACHMENT THE FIRST PRIORITY

We know how to create psychopaths in the child welfare system (Steinhauer, 1974). We also know how to foster attachments. From parent support programs for high-risk pregnant mothers to foster care and adoption programs, child and family services need to focus on attachments that can last and provide secure homes for children and adolescents at risk.

In all phases of work, this means focusing on what clients need in order to build (or rebuild) positive attachments. Children entering placement programs should be encouraged to bring in special items from home, for example, pictures of people important to them. Phone contacts and visits with siblings and relatives should be encouraged, unless they are harmful to the child. Foster families who could become adoptive parents if necessary provide an opportunity for continuity and a reassurance to birth parents that their child will be safe if they cannot care for her.

Kinship foster or adoptive homes should be explored whenever possible; however, relatives should not automatically have preference. Custody determinations should be based on assessments of a child's attachment to potential guardians and the capacity of the adults petitioning for custody to provide the care and help a child needs to overcome experiences of abuse and neglect.

"Independent living" should never be a goal for a child. Each of us needs connections throughout our lives. Teaching youths day-to-day living skills and providing supervised apartments are valuable services for older adolescents who cannot live in a family, but our stress must remain on working to build or rebuild positive ties within an extended family and community. If a 17-year-old cannot live in her family, I want to know where she would like to spend holidays and birthdays. Youths with no one are very much at risk. Connections to teachers, foster families, and volunteers who are willing to serve as mentors; ongoing relationships with agencies as volunteers; and links to religious organizations provide some options.

Innovative programs that foster bonding and support networks in a child's first years have been found to be especially cost-effective in reducing the incidence of neglect and abuse. Hawaii's Healthy Families program (Breakey, Uohara-Pratt, Morrell-Samuels, & Kolb-Latu, 1991) has been implemented in several states. Families are screened at the time of a child's birth to identify risk factors for abuse and neglect. A home visiting program is then offered to high-risk families of children in their first five years, including medical services and parent training. These are true prevention programs focused on fostering attachment and preventing long-term neglect.

Family preservation programs are most effective when they include a comprehensive assessment of a family's needs and provide a range of services such as mentoring programs, parent-child activity groups, family therapy, parent training, direct assistance with housing, education, job-hunting, and integration of services into a community (Daro, Jones, & McCurdy, 1993). Recruitment of skilled staff who can engage parents and work in a nonjudgmental and supportive manner is essential. Services need to be offered before problems have multiplied,

family members have given up, and judges have warned juvenile offenders, "One more incident and you're placed."

DESIGN COMMUNITY-BASED SERVICES THAT FOLLOW
FAMILIES, NOT PROGRAMS

If child and family services were a game of basketball, most agencies
would be playing with a zone defense. Families needing placement of
their child tell their stories to an intake worker and then to various
staff from a placement program who may or may not admit their
child. Success and continuity of care has been visualized as well-or-
chestrated moves from one therapeutic team to another, leading eventually to a positive discharge from the agency. Each team is an expert
in its own zone. However, family members move from zone to
zone—for example, from a home-based counseling program to an
emergency foster home service to a day treatment program; and each
transfer means loss of relationships to staff. Parents and children are
obliged to tell their stories again to new workers from the next programs, with whom parents and children are supposed to develop
trusting relationships.

This process can disrupt the good intentions and efforts of staff and
family members struggling with crises. For instance, when Laurie's
four children were placed into foster homes by child protective services, the home-based counseling she had begun three weeks before
was terminated. She was asked to work with an emergency foster
care social worker on a temporary basis until it could be determined
whether her oldest daughter would need a group care program because of her disruptive behavior. A second social worker was assigned to begin working with her regarding her other three children.
In the course of three months, Laurie was asked to work with three
different family workers, none of whom assumed they would be able
to work with her for more than a few weeks. At the same time, the
county child protective worker who had arranged for placement of
the children transfered the case to a county foster care worker.

A family may have a social worker assigned for every program in
which one of their children or a parent attends even if siblings are in
different programs in the same agency. In foster home programs, it is
common for social workers to be assigned to foster families in order
to create a close and united therapeutic approach with foster parents.

If siblings are unable to get along together in the same foster family, this can mean different social workers and sometimes different supervisors, psychologists, or psychiatrists working with the same parents, attending the same meetings, or asking parents to meet with them in separate meetings—an unwieldy process. For example, Sandy said she wanted to bring her five children home from a myriad of placements. She had just completed a drug rehabilitation program and was asked to work with two social workers from foster homes in one agency, a social worker from a residential treatment agency, and staff from a psychiatric hospital. Sandy complained bitterly about all the appointments she had to keep and how this prevented her from getting a job to pay for a better apartment.

Such families typically have histories of rejection and abandonment. With high rates of staff turnover and the zone defense model of family service, it really isn't any wonder that families have little trust in any new worker. The zone defense model maximizes integration of services in each program but cannot provide continuity of service for families who need different services for several family members. The zone defense model fails to link families with service providers they can count on over time.*

Implement a Network Approach

Permanency-focused services can be provided by emphasizing a network approach that links agency staff to communities† and works with a family from admission to an emergency placement program to a child's return home and the provision of after-placement services. Figure 10.1 diagrams a possible service flowchart for a multiservice agency, offering teams that provide continuity and community-based services.

Each team would be responsible for building working relationships

---

*The zone defense model is also used in many social services departments to allow county workers to develop an expertise and connections in a given area, for example, adoption. For a child, however, this system typically means repeated transfers from one worker to another. For instance, a child initially placed because of abuse may very well experience transfers from an intake CPS worker to a long-term CPS worker to a foster care worker and finally, if necessary, to an adoption worker. Just as the child is beginning to trust in a worker and begins to make another transition, the child may learn that it is time to get a new worker.
†Parsons Prevention Program, Albany, NY, developed outreach family services based within or near local departments of social services. My thanks to Jenny Frank for emphasizing the value of staff assignment to communities during discusssions of our seminar.

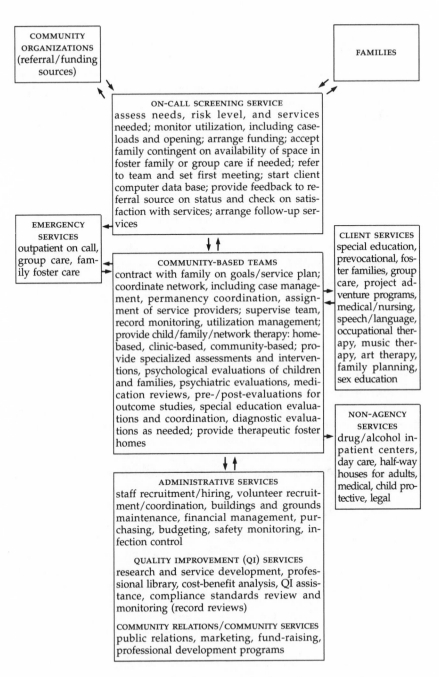

COMMUNITY ORGANIZATIONS (referral/funding sources)

FAMILIES

ON-CALL SCREENING SERVICE
assess needs, risk level, and services needed; monitor utilization, including caseloads and opening; arrange funding; accept family contingent on availability of space in foster family or group care if needed; refer to team and set first meeting; start client computer data base; provide feedback to referral source on status and check on satisfaction with services; arrange follow-up services

EMERGENCY SERVICES
outpatient on call, group care, family foster care

CLIENT SERVICES
special education, prevocational, foster families, group care, project adventure programs, medical/nursing, speech/language, occupational therapy, music therapy, art therapy, family planning, sex education

COMMUNITY-BASED TEAMS
contract with family on goals/service plan; coordinate network, including case management, permanency coordination, assignment of service providers; supervise team; record monitoring, utilization management; provide child/family/network therapy: home-based, clinic-based, community-based; provide specialized assessments and interventions, psychological evaluations of children and families, psychiatric evaluations, medication reviews, pre-/post-evaluations for outcome studies, special education evaluations and coordination, diagnostic evaluations as needed; provide therapeutic foster homes

NON-AGENCY SERVICES
drug/alcohol inpatient centers, day care, half-way houses for adults, medical, child protective, legal

ADMINISTRATIVE SERVICES
staff recruitment/hiring, volunteer recruitment/coordination, buildings and grounds maintenance, financial management, purchasing, budgeting, safety monitoring, infection control

QUALITY IMPROVEMENT (QI) SERVICES
research and service development, professional library, cost-benefit analysis, QI assistance, compliance standards review and monitoring (record reviews)

COMMUNITY RELATIONS/COMMUNITY SERVICES
public relations, marketing, fund-raising, professional development programs

Figure 10.1. Family and community-based service plan

and liaisons between an agency and their community. Ideally, teams would be based within that community as part of a neighborhood resource center approach—settlement houses for the 1990s. A typical team would have one network/case manager, four child/family/network therapists, one or two family support workers, an assigned psychologist or psychiatrist, and a group of specially trained foster parents. When special education or group care is needed, special education staff or coordinators and child care workers would become part of the team.

Caseloads would be determined by the demands for service time for each child at risk, with consideration to pending litigation for custody or neglect, the need for networking with family members and other service providers, the level of violence, and required travel time to biological and/or foster families. If necessary, family work could be reassigned from one practitioner to another, while retaining other team members working with a family. Network/case managers would be responsible for permanency coordination, team supervision, and keeping the work moving with each family.

Establish a One-call Intake Service

A "one-call" intake service would suffice for acceptance into agency services and initiation of funding for services to a given family. A coalition of agencies could unite to provide complementary services for a region or to develop their own managed care service with an integrated intake department. Intake workers would conduct a brief assessment of family needs and level of risk to determine if a family should be referred to an emergency outpatient, group care, or foster home service or directly to a community-based team.

The intake service would determine how services can be funded, denote the length of stay or number of sessions initially authorized for funding, arrange for billing with funding sources, set up the initial computer database for each client, and arrange for the initial contracting session with service providers. An agency's intake service would also monitor the number of families served by teams and channel referrals to maintain targeted utilization levels. Ongoing evaluation would begin with assessment of timeliness in arranging for services and initial family and referral source satisfaction. The intake service would also arrange referrals to post-discharge programs when necessary.

Comprehensive assessments would be carried out by the community-based team rather than by specialized services, which only see an individual or family once. Pre- and post-outcome assessments would also be the responsibility of teams and used as part of ongoing efforts to improve services. This model would link assessment to services from intake to discharge and promote accessibility, networking, and ongoing relationships with practitioners. By reducing the number of practitioners involved with a given family, agencies can maximize funding for direct services, avoid redundant assessments, create incentives for efficient services, and reduce the gaps in service typically found when families move from program to program.

Include Foster Parents in Working Teams

Effective foster home programs require close ties, a common approach, and a relationship of trust developed over time between foster parents, social workers, child care workers, and consultants. Family workers often need to move children from one foster home to another over the course of placement. Trust is facilitated when foster parents are recognized as key players within an integrated service that includes respite, child care support, and clinical services. Therapeutic foster parents, like child care workers, need to be part of a working team addressing client issues, strategies of intervention, and development of innovative approaches.

Training sessions, team meetings, and ad hoc work groups should include foster parents and child care workers in order to promote shared values, understanding, and interventions. Family therapists can involve foster parents in therapy sessions, so that foster parents can continue interventions in their homes as cotherapists.* Similarly, child care workers play a critical role in maximizing the impact of any placement program. After therapy sessions, foster parents and child care workers need to be prepared for a child's reactions.

Close ties between family workers and foster parents can also be facilitated by placing siblings in the same foster family and assigning all children from a given family to the same family worker. Thus, a family therapist with a caseload of ten children in placement could be working with three biological families, two foster families, and a group home. A therapeutic-level foster parent with two to three foster children would work closely with one or two family workers at a

---

*Henderer, B. (1995, October 20). Personal communication.

time and optimally would always take in children from the same community-based team.

Initial contracting sessions and four- to six-week review conferences can be used by foster parents, child care workers, family workers, and other practitioners to plan services conjointly with family members. Foster parents and child care workers should read the files on the children and families they are serving. Foster care supervisors and team staff would also be assigned to help foster families manage children and develop practice skills on an ongoing basis following recruitment and orientation.

Invest in Permanency Specialists

Effective community-based programs must recruit and train skilled practitioners who understand permanency, can assess what drives a child's dangerous behaviors, and who can work directly with families and other service providers. This model would represent a shift from practitioners operating as specialists in circumscribed areas such as foster homes, group care, day treatment, or home-based work *to* practitioners as specialists in permanency work, coaching family members to build attachments, and promoting healing beyond the limitations of a specific program.

The impact and legitimacy of interventions depends on clients' perceptions that practitioners have recognized both the problems and the strengths in the family. Psychologists and psychiatrists can help engage clients, focus services, and substantially reduce lengths of stay by centering child and family assessments on permanency needs and working directly with families. Assessments need to explore attachments, capacity to parent, obstacles to permanency, cognitive and communication skills, attention and concentration abilities, legal and economic issues, biological problems, recurring traumas, and, most of all, what is working in a family.

Assessments should be conducted as soon after placement as possible, when a family is experiencing the crisis that led to placement and when family members and service providers are struggling to identify permanency goals and to agree on an initial contract, in other words, the service plan. It is very valuable to schedule an individual evaluation of a child within the first week of placement, followed very soon after by a family assessment (see chapters 4–6). The power of a psychological evaluation is greatly increased when the psychologist serves as an ongoing member of the treatment team and participates in review conferences to reinforce metaphors, healing from traumas, messages about time, and the choices family members are making.

SHOW COMMUNITIES THAT PERMANENCY WORK PAYS OFF

Recently, the mayor of New York City requested that the funding from the state government for social services be cut back further so that the city could avoid having to put up matching funds. The mayor was quoted as saying that he wanted to put more money into police forces. In contrast to social services workers, he knew what police did.

Child and family services cannot survive without telling the stories of children at risk to the public and showing "customers"—including mayors and governors—why the best interests of the child are also the best interests for each community's fiscal and social health, both now and into the future. Escalating costs for crime, prisons, special education, lost tax dollars from businesses leaving the city and tourists staying away, public health expenses, and increased drug usage are the symptoms of neglected children growing into alienated and violent or self-abusive adults. These are costs that the citizens of New York and all communities are paying today and will pay for decades to come.

It is our responsibility as practitioners to show what can save a child who has been growing up with addicted parents or moving from placement to placement. We must present an alternative to simply adding more police and building more jails. Advocacy for children means articles in newspapers and magazines, speaking to citizen organizations, working with politicians, and research (see below) to get the facts out and to demonstrate how permanency-based programs serve all of our customers, from mayors to businesses and taxpayers.

LISTEN TO PARENTS AND CHILDREN AND HELP THEM TO SPEAK OUT

Involving parents in task groups, parent councils, and development projects is part of an empowerment approach. The testimony of children and parents to funding bodies can refocus fiscal cost-cutting exercises into working sessions on how real needs can be met. It's much harder to slash a program when legislators and government managers see and hear children and parents,* especially if testimony and narrative accounts of children in crisis are coupled with statistical reports of how services help families at risk.

Parent groups have formed to advocate for families involved in mental health and social services programs, to provide badly needed support to parents, to guide parents on how to obtain needed services for their children, and to serve as an alternative to professional programs when parents feel poorly served or mistreated. These groups can play a valuable role in developing supportive networks for families in crisis. We need them to be our allies as members of service coalitions and programs.† Developing shared goals and service plans for communities can begin this process.

ADVOCATE FOR PERMANENCY-FOCUSED LEGISLATION

Legalization of open adoptions would make it easier for birth parents to make an adoption plan when they cannot do what is needed to raise their children. Open adoptions allow birth parents to make a reality-based plan without fearing that they will never be able to see their children again. Contact with children after adoption should be based on what is in the best interests of the children. This hopefully would include visits a few times a year, periodic letters and phone calls, and sessions with family therapists as needed. Adoption subsidies are needed to cover the costs of treatment for traumatized and handicapped children.

Provisions for permanent legal guardianship offer a viable option especially for older children and adolescents with conflictual attachments to dependent or mentally ill parents. This option is also very helpful when a child can be raised to maturity by an extended family member and when adoption would be seen as a transgression or inappropriate within the family.

At the macro level, funding for child and family services should be centered in one state agency rather than splintered into often conflicting and competing departments of mental health, social services, cor-

---

*Schimmer, R. (1995). Personal communication.
†At Parsons Child and Family Center, a leader of a parent advocacy organization was invited to work within the agency.

rections, probation, and education. Splintered systems mean splintered services.

ADVOCATE FOR WELFARE REFORM THAT FOSTERS ATTACHMENTS AND STRONG FAMILIES

Many current proposals advocate eliminating benefits for poor parents who appear to be living off the backs of taxpayers. Teenage pregnancies, in particular, have been seen as a way for teenage girls to get money and an apartment of their own. This perspective neglects the drive to create a new attachment. Simply changing fiscal contingencies ignores the social, cultural, and emotional issues involved in teenage pregnancies and the larger problem of poverty in the United States and other countries.

"These girls aren't dumb, it's just that they need somebody who really cares" (Hernandez, 1994, p. 9). Having a baby is a way to escape from the neglect and abuse of one's own parents and to start over again with a new life (see Louis & Louis, 1980; Schaffer & Pine, 1972). Young people need a way to succeed and someone who values their success and gives their achievements meaning.

Teen pregnancies are also a way to gain an identity and sense of respect. "A 14-year-old without a child is a 'teenager'; one with a child is a mother" (Waldman, Shackelford, Wingert, & Bogert, 1994, p. 34). These are often girls who have given up on rebuilding bonds with their parents, extended family, or foster families. They may search for idealized, romantic relationships to make up for the lack of nurture in their own lives (Pines, 1988).

In one study of pregnant teenage girls, 69% were found to have insecure attachments with their own parents (Ward & Carlson, 1995) In a study comparing pregnant and nonpregnant sexually active teenage girls, security of attachment was significantly correlated with desire to have a baby, use of birth control, and becoming pregnant (Fruchtman, 1995). Pregnant girls were also found to have had more traumatic experiences, including losses of significant people in their lives.

The near universal appeal of a cuddly, dependent baby can break down when toddlers start asserting their autonomy. As the burden of running after the increasingly mobile and challenging toddler increases so does the recognition by a young parent of all she has given up. The 2- or 3-year-old child may also begin to remind her mother of characteristics she cannot tolerate, for example, looks, gestures, and mannerisms of the child's father or the mother's own parents.

We cannot afford to continue the neglect of fathers. In the 1960s it was said "that a woman needs a man like a fish needs a bicycle." Children do best with love and care from two parents. Parents need a support system from extended family and community in order to be able to provide the attachment and security their children need.

Engagement of fathers in raising their children appears directly tied with legitimate opportunities for young men to succeed. Boys and young men growing up need to be able to succeed in school and to see models for success in their community, ethnic group, and, optimally, extended family. At the same time, men need to be held accountable through requirements that fathers be identified on birth certificates* and enforcement of "statutory rape" laws† and child support legislation (see Blankenhorn, 1995; De Angelis, 1995; Freeman, 1989; Meyer, 1991; Nichols-Casebolt & Garfinkel, 1991; Watson & Kelly, 1989).

Poor parents of all ages and society as a whole benefit when parents are successful in providing economic resources, nurture, and safety for their children. Mandates that parents are in school, a training program, or working are legitimate, but none of us can work and care for our children without adequate and safe child care. And vocational training programs have little value if they do not include work experience and job placement to develop realistic hopes for success in employment. Mandating that parents return to work when children reach a certain age, capping the number of years on welfare, cutting off aid for failing to keep children in school, and forcing teenage mothers to remain with their parents will fail without provisions for child care, job training, job placement, health insurance, and help to young people trying to escape from generations of abuse and neglect.

STRENGTHEN CHILD PROTECTIVE SERVICES

Protection of children and the provision of foster care are essential for the well-being of children and the future of our communities. Government must maintain the responsibility for providing child protec-

---

*An exception should be provided whenever a mother is at risk of being harmed if she identifies the father of her child.
†The Alan Guttmacher Institute recently reported that half of the fathers of babies born to teenage girls (ages 15–17) were 20 years old or older (Wycliff, 1995).

tive services (CPS), including investigations, assessments, court petitions, service referrals, and monitoring. Well-trained CPS staff are needed, along with realistic caseloads. Moreover, funding for child protective services, foster care, adoption assistance, and prevention of placement programs should be maintained by statute as separate from any block grants for welfare reform.

CPS also needs the authority to maintain records of suspected neglect and abuse. Current laws in some states require agencies to expunge any reference to abuse or neglect allegations which were not proven sufficiently to be indicated. This prevents CPS from being able to monitor patterns of abuse (for instance, a child who is treated repeatedly in emergency rooms for minor injuries) and leaves agencies without the information they need to deal with ongoing neglect. Such laws foster the secrecy under which tragedies occur.

MASTER THE LANGUAGE OF MANAGED CARE

The risks of managed care's increasing dominance are clear to most practitioners. For-profit health management organizations (HMOs) pay off investors and increase revenues from subscribers by reducing health care expenditures. This often means cutting reimbursements to service providers and limiting services to patients while increasing expenditures for advertising. After profits and management expenses are deducted, only 70% of a HMO's income may be left to cover patient care (Taylor, 1996). Chief executive officers of the seven largest for-profit HMOs earned an average of $7 million in 1994 (Denn, 1995). Meanwhile, practitioners face reduced fees, increased time requirements for paperwork, daily calls to managed care auditors for approval of services, prohibitions against talking to clients about problems in HMO services, and reduced ability to provide the services that clients expect and need for long-term change.

HMOs share the mission of child and family services to serve a community in a cost-effective manner, but services to children and parents with attachment disorders and other chronic and severe problems do not mesh well with most models of managed care. Moreover, even not-for-profit HMOs have a built-in press to use limited funds for their own administrative staff (the care managers) and to provide high salaries for executive officers.* When direct service staff leave

---

*Earnings in the Albany, NY, area during 1994 for chief executive officers of the three largest HMOs averaged $210,000 (Denn, 1995).

child and family services and mental health programs for much higher paying jobs as analysts with HMOs, it is hard for the remaining practitioners to envision how this process will not lead to further funding cutbacks for treatment programs. After all, every time $40,000+ is spent on hiring an HMO analyst, $40,000+ in waste must be discovered and eliminated *or* direct services to clients must be cut by the same amount.

Without neglecting the risks of managed care, we need to recognize the opportunities this model can provide for improving services to clients. Managed care organizations need to demonstrate quality services or subscribers (businesses and governments) will take their funds elsewhere. The focus of managed care on cost-effective services should be the focus of any program dedicated to serving children and families.

What most agencies and programs are lacking is the information needed (the vocabulary) to speak the language of managed care. And learning to speak this language is not an elective if agencies want to survive in the 1990s. Nor is this language requirement just the responsibility of executive directors. Speaking the language means collecting data on who we are serving (client characteristics), the costs of providing specific services by problem and community, the risks for taking responsibility for treating all clients needing services, and service outcomes (see below) in the short and long run.

Child and family agencies are in a good position to offer a package of high-impact, permanency-based services for children in turmoil, services that have been shown to effectively help children succeed in school, live in families, and avoid hospitalization. Staffing and management in most agencies is lean and staff members have learned how to handle the paperwork demands of regulatory bodies, from Medicaid to the Joint Commission. Lengths of stay in temporary foster homes and expensive hospital or group care placements can be shortened by utilizing the permanency and network interventions outlined in chapters 4–6.

Agencies can offer a full range of services, from preventive bonding and parent education programs to home-based family counseling, crisis residences, group care, and long-term foster care or adoption. The family and community-based service plan outlined above would work well within a capitated contract in which a multiservice agency provides ongoing services to clients and is allowed flexibility to provide families with a wide range of services based on actual client needs.

On the other hand, accepting capitated contracts without consideration of legal, court, and child protective delays presents an inordinate
risk. Similarly, contracts need to provide for services to match client
risk factors, including chemical abuse, neurological disorders, mental
retardation, and developmental disabilities. Capitated service plans
should allow practitioners to be creative and much more flexible in
helping families overcome crises.

Coalitions of agencies can negotiate with governmental funding
sources and HMOs from a stronger position, manage allocation of
resources, share some costs, and coordinate a network approach for
an identified population. In this way, child and family agencies could
become the contractors, rather than remaining dependent on whatever contracts HMO's are willing to offer.

Viable contracts need to ensure adequately staffed child protective
services and timely processing of court petitions for neglect, exten-
sions of placement, and termination of rights as well as funding for
supervised visitation, transportation for visits, parent training, day
care, family- focused substance abuse treatment, special education,
vocational training, and job placement for parents. For every family
with a child in placement, the service plan needs to identify who will
work with parents and children to reunite, who will provide any
needed substance abuse or parent training, who will provide transportation for visits, who will manage any needed court petitions, who
will provide medical care, and who will be in charge of coordinating
all services and keeping time moving. We cannot afford to forsake the
effectiveness of integrated approaches in a rush to obtain contracts for
specific services.

The Home Rebuilders program in New York (Kaladjian, Semidei, &
the Home Rebuilders Workgroup, 1992; Ryder, Courtney, & Ellis,
1994) demonstrated how a capitated rate system can increase the
number of children returned home from foster care. Nonprofit agencies were allowed to allocate funding based on specific client needs
for services. Funding incentives promoted use of assessments and intensive work soon after placement with provision of a wide range of
services for children and parents.

IF IT DOESN'T HELP CLIENTS, JUNK IT

Improving service delivery begins with eliminating requirements and
practices that contribute little to accomplishing goals and that waste

precious resources, especially staff time. For each activity, from administrative meetings to group therapy to mental status evaluations, I ask myself, "How does this accomplish the primary mission of the agency and the priorities of clients and customers? Is this service mandated by funding or accreditation bodies? Would I include this activity as part of a new program being developed today? Is this service redundant?"

Ongoing committees are a luxury in a fast-changing world. Time-limited task groups with a few clear objectives can address challenges to an agency, consider alternatives, and develop plans. Timely decisions involving staff at all levels of the agency can prevent an agency from becoming as crisis-driven as its clients. Input from parents and older adolescents who have been involved in programs, leaders of funding organizations, and representatives from referral sources ensures that an agency remains committed to service.

MAKE PAPERWORK PART OF THERAPY

Paperwork, the bane of most practitioners, is also terribly difficult to cut within an agency. The "useless" form or question for one clinician is highly valued by another. Most records represent compilations of everchanging record requirements from the multiple regulatory bodies that govern agencies and clinics. Even when the regulations change, forms can take on a life of their own. As paperwork mounts, the time needed for quality services declines.

What in the record actually helps to achieve permanency? What is still needed to meet today's requirements of funding and regulatory bodies? What do we need to demonstrate the effectiveness of services? The rest may be of interest, but is this a priority over other badly needed services?

Goal and objective setting can become an onerous task. I've seen records with 20 objectives. Human beings can keep at most six or seven items in short-term memory at a time. Having multiple specific objectives typically causes everyone to become problem-focused; headaches from the strain are also common. People lose sight of the critical factors that led to a child's placement.

I believe goals listed for a child and family should be limited to two or three key areas necessary for successful completion of work (criteria for discharge). In most cases, these need to focus on: (1) what parents and the network will do so that children can live in safe, nurturing homes; (2) development and maintenance of enduring bonds between children and birth parents or substitute parents; and (3) life skill development as shown through mastering developmental challenges appropriate for each family member.

For each goal, measurable behaviors that tie in directly with permanency work can be listed. For example, Dave's mother needed to complete a drug treatment program, show she could stay off drugs with weekly random drug testing, secure an apartment, show Dave and his siblings that she could acknowledge what had happened leading to placement, and put in place safety plans to protect against renewed drug use or violence in the home. Dave needed to show he was taking care of himself by completing schoolwork, passing his courses, making it to football practice, telling his mother what he saw happening in the past, and showing everyone how he was implementing his own safety plan when he began to get frustrated and angry. Accomplishment of objectives goes hand in hand with beginning unsupervised visits and expansion of visits leading to a return home.

Permanency-centered objectives focus progress reports on what's most important for discharge from placement. Lengthy narratives are helpful in supervision but no one is reimbursing staff for the time or secretarial help needed. I've always believed that record keeping would shrink dramatically if clients were given access to records on a regular basis.

The traditional process of the professional writing reports about a family reinforces family members' feeling disempowered (Imber-Black, 1988; Roberts, 1994). In contrast, we can actively involve clients in writing service plans, reading all assessments, and helping to write up final reports (see Imber-Black, 1988; Roberts, 1988; Roberts, 1994). Documentation of the facts required for court proceedings (e.g., participation in sessions, cancellations or no-shows for visits) should be shared directly with clients.

Required notes could be done conjointly with clients at the end of a session. Sharing "what struck me most" in a session (Anderson, 1991) could be done with the family worker's sharing what will be put in the session's progress note. Principles of narrative therapy (White & Epston, 1990) could also be tied into record keeping. Practitioners can use mandatory progress notes as an opportunity to develop a healing story with clients, including the split pressures encountered, what the client has been able to do or not do thus far to overcome dilemmas, the choices that a client is facing, and signs of hope.

I've been sharing psychological evaluations with clients for many years, usually at the request of clients who are angry, distrustful, or looking for ammunition in upcoming court hearings. Sometimes I've shared reports on my own initiative, for instance to ensure that clients are informed and truly giving permission to share personal information with a school. Whatever the reason, I've asked for clients to help me correct any inaccuracies in what I wrote and have usually ended up with a better report and a higher level of trust with the client. They might not like a report, but at least it's not some secret to be shared only between professionals.

Cowriting and editing reports empowers clients and makes the record part of the therapeutic process. On the other hand, an agency should never release information about children or parents that could lead to someone getting hurt. If parents are separated or divorced, each parent should only be allowed to see information about their child and him or herself.

Gina, for example, described her father as a monstor who harassed and threatened her mother and she repeatedly expressed fears that her father would kill her mother. With her father present, she kept her head down, looked away, and refused to talk. The girl's father demanded to see all reports about his daughter and about how his ex-wife and daughter got along. In view of the risk presented, we only shared with the father reports of sessions involving him and his daughter and urged him to work in family therapy to show his daughter that she could share her feelings with him and not have to worry about what he would do.

From a fiscal perspective, paperwork needs to be reimbursed and not just another unfunded mandate that takes priority in a worker's day. For practitioners, this also means completing paperwork within the allotted time for each client.

OUTCOME RESEARCH IS NOT A LUXURY

Most practitioners are used to entering pages of notes and completing multiple required forms. "Don't ask me to do anymore" is a typical response. Yet the viability of programs depends on being able to show HMOs and governmental bodies what works for whom. "I don't know" means little funding.

The choice for practitioners is to allow external funding directors to determine what data must be collected, or to design our own research that contributes to day-to-day work. We can keep outcome research focused on permanency objectives with measures of parental care and affection for children (see Magura & Silverman-Moses, 1986), children's adaptive behavior and general functioning (see Gresham & Elliott, 1990; Shaffer et al., 1983; Sparrow, Balla, & Cicchetti, 1984), variations on attachment interviews (see chapter 4; Fruchtman, 1995; Main & Goldwyn, 1989), and behavior problem checklists (Achenbach, 1991a, 1991b; Conners, 1989). Parent and child ratings of the value of services are very valuable. Perhaps the most objective measures are indicated reports of abuse and neglect, length of time in temporary placements, school attendance, and academic achievement test scores.

Completing a few minutes worth of research instruments at intake, three to six months, one year, and two years can provide a wealth of data. Linking outcomes with costs of services delivered allows agencies to negotiate contracts with the data needed by HMOs and government agencies.

Many programs evaluate the percentage of children reunited with biological families as their primary criteria for success. This is the ideal goal for children in emergency placements, but adoption or a plan to live with legal guardians through maturity may be the only realistic and best outcome for some children. Moreover, avoidance of placement or return of a child from placement may have as much to do with changes in the orientation of authorities making placements as with improvements in family functioning (Rossi, 1992).

Permanency work cannot be expected to cure behavioral problems based on serial traumas and organic damage. However, when permanency and network interventions are successful, most children can learn to function well enough to return to family living. I believe outcome measures should assess whether a child is living in a family (biological, kinship, permanent guardianship, or adoptive) with whom they can form an attachment and expect to grow to maturity.

COMBINE PRACTICE AND ADVOCACY

I ask family members who they can count on to listen to them, to support them, to be on their side. "Nobody," say a large number of children, adolescents, and parents. "Only my boyfriend," said a 14-year-old in a group care facility for substance abusers. "I met him a month ago."

With each break in ties and positive connections, the fragility of families grows. Single parents, relatives not talking to one another, and poverty lead to vulnerability and often trauma. Without the safety of a warm embrace and validation from someone who can be trusted, family members cannot face losses and traumas. It simply isn't safe enough. Conflicts and pain must be forced underground. Spiraling crises reflect what can't be talked about.

When a child is placed, she implicitly challenges practitioners to demonstrate how this placement can somehow help her and her family overcome fears of engulfment and abandonment and stop the repetition of destructive cycles of behavior. This is a challenge that cannot be ignored. The child and her family need to see that somehow this placement can be different and that the dilemmas generating crises can be addressed in a nonshameful and respectful manner. This does not mean searching for miracles but rather working with reality in a way that can revive hope.

Therapy serves as a bridge, a positive channel, that can be used to replace dangerous behaviors. Instead of acting out calls for help, secrets of family violence, demands for nurture, etc., a therapeutic alliance provides connections to say the unspeakable and to build upon hopes for change.

Working from the designated client outward to larger and larger groups, we help to create a network of positive connections to family, friends, and service providers. Within this context, a child and parent can begin to address the wounds that underlie dangerous behavior. The network serves like a protective shield under which new growth can occur.

But this network cannot function outside of the community. Without community understanding and support, no one will be there for children and families in crisis. Or, if some policymakers have their way, services will be limited to behavior modification approaches for specific symptoms.

This overemphasis on behavior change for specific problems was illustrated in a recent audit of a crisis residence. An 8-year-old boy began to trust staff members and after a few days disclosed sex abuse by his stepfather, beatings by his mother, memories of chairs, beds, and bones broken, and fears that everything would happen again. The boy also was a bedwetter. When the facility was reviewed that week for relicensure, the state auditor criticized the program for failing to implement a behavior management plan to stop the boy's bedwetting. Enuresis, after all, was a definable problem and the auditor ordered treatment to begin at once.

Children in placement don't fit the standard paradigms of managed care. We are dealing with attachment failures, serial traumas, chronic neglect, and homelessness. Quick fixes don't exist. Yet, children and parents in the most damaged families show a healthy drive to get what they are missing. We can join family members and bring in extended family and community resources, building upon everyone's need for safety, commitment, and family. This is the quest to help children get the bonded nurturing relationships and safe, consistent homes they need—homes in which they can grow up and develop competence to function as adults in our society and someday to provide the parenting their own children will need. To get there, we need practitioners who can be more than kind and caring. Like Jen in chapter 9, we need to roar from time to time.

chapter 11

It's not the critic who counts. Not the man who
points out where the strong man stumbled or
where the doer of great deeds could have done
them better. The credit belongs to the man who
is actually in the arena. Whose face is marred by
dust and sweat and blood. Who strives valiantly,
who errs and comes up short again and again.
And who, while daring greatly, spends himself in
a worthy cause so that his place may not be
among those cold and timid souls who know
neither victory nor defeat.

*Theodore Roosevelt**

breaking through the storm

"SOMETIMES I WAKE UP IN THE MIDDLE OF THE NIGHT AND WORRY . . .
did I do enough?" a colleague confided in me. The children we strive
to help have slashed at their parents with butcher knives and at-
tempted to kill themselves by tightening electrical cords around their
necks or hanging by their fingertips from third-floor balconies, threatening to jump. Parents may look hopelessly depressed or like the
vengeful stalker from the latest horror movie. Our job is to work with
them all.

Without practitioners† like my colleague, the boy found hanging by
his fingertips would have little hope for change. No amount of legislation, funding, theory, or policies can provide the human connection
this boy needs. Someone has to be willing to touch this kind of pain

---

*Cited by Edelman (1992, pp. 42–43).
†Throughout this book, I have referred to practitioners as including child care workers,
special education teachers, foster parents, nurses, social workers, psychologists, psychiatrists, and other trained professionals who have devoted their careers to helping children and families at risk.

and risk. However, worrying in the middle of the night is a sure sign of overload and impending exhaustion. Helping families in crisis means taking steps to protect oneself.

HIGH RISK AND LOW CONTROL

Beneath the often angry exterior of children in trouble, we see bodies tense or tremble at the mention of someone's name and the tracks of tears shed alone in the night. We hear the howl of abandonment from a 4-year-old in his fifth placement who has never known a secure home. To care for and work with children at risk means to feel their terror and rage, their desperate hopes and dark despair, their valiant struggles and pent-up rage.

We come in eager to help, feeling a rush of excitement as a new child is referred for an emergency placement. We know it's a seduction, but we're pulled in nevertheless to rescue, to be the hero. Family members and colleagues look to the latest practitioner to help a child and family at risk. What can you do? Will you make things better or just add to the shame?

The glory doesn't last long. Constrictive forces seem to come in from everywhere at once. There simply is no time. Decisions must be made without sufficient information. Most agencies lack funding for the assessments, network coordination, and time needed to transform a crisis situation into an opportunity for change. Contracts fund only limited services, a roof, beds, staff to maintain order. Too often, children and parents end up waiting for assessments, network meetings, and court hearings.

But children in placement cannot wait long and soon escalate crises. Threats to burn houses down, fights with peers, or running toward busy streets draw everyone's attention and defuse a child's fear of staff getting to know what is really happening at home.

Stressful situations are defined by high risk, low control, and feelings of responsibility. We deal with the traumas that most people never want to touch—the risk of people hurting themselves or others, of children's lives spiraling downhill toward the fate of their parents. We fear another generation of addicts, prostitutes, delinquents, battered spouses, and neglectful parents in the making—or worse, a runaway girl killed while prostituting for drugs or a child who slips on his chair with a rope around his neck.

I've struggled for years with my own tendency to dump on myself and worry in the night, to do everything that stress management experts tell us not to do, to accept unrealistic responsibilities, to expect miraculous changes from people afflicted for generations with severe problems, and to hold myself accountable for what is out of my control.

I've seen myself and my colleagues move in less than a day from being the hero to the new scapegoat, the target for blame. A typical situation begins with a late day or evening call from a distraught parent or anxious referral source. We hear a message of desperation, danger, and need. "I'm *really* going to do it this time," Mrs. Kinman told Toni, her prevention of placement therapist, late one night. "I'm sick of that kid. Why did I ever take him back home? He's going to get what he deserves . . . gonna break his neck."

Toni left her husband and 3-year-old to run out and calm Mrs. Kinman. She got back home at one in the morning still worried about whether she had done the right thing by helping the family stay together. No one could really predict what Mrs. Kinman would do. Would her son be safe?

A few restless hours later, Toni arrived at work and anxiously checked for messages from Mrs. Kinman or the police. With no messages, she continued to fret and started to make plans for her next visit to the Kinmans. Just then, her supervisor walked in and chided her for not getting her reports in on time. The county children's services department was being audited by the state social services department and any agencies with overdue reports would be sanctioned. This meant fines and cutbacks in services and staff.

Toni glared at her supervisor. "I can't do everything!"

"This is serious!" her supervisor retorted and marched off to her office. The day had barely begun and Toni felt exhausted.

PROGRESSIVE TRIANGLES

We're drawn in to save, to be the hero, only to quickly find ourselves scorned or hated. A needy child, birth parents, and a foster family (or group care workers) present a natural set-up for caring people to become victims, heroes, and persecutors. Karpman's triangle, the victim-rescuer-persecutor cycle (Karpman, 1968), is alive and well in child and family services.

Problems develop when we feel locked into one predominant role. Victims are often depressed, taking out their anger on themselves.

Rescuers may see themselves as driven to heal, to cure, to save at the expense of everything else. Persecutors may see their only way to survive as striking out first, taking aggressive steps at the first hint of threat.

For most of our clients, victimization, terrifying rage, hopelessness, and rejection/abandonment drive spirals of crises. This works like a progressive series of triangles,* which spread a family's conflicts outward incrementally to larger groups of people. The individuals at the hub of the triangles often feel less and less empowered and more and more constricted with each additional triangle. Moreover, the original conflicts continue unresolved and are often magnified with new players.

Abandonment, violence, and failures shape a narrow role for a child growing up with both economic and emotional poverty. For instance, a child scorned for looking like his abusive father may begin life as a victim, neglected by both parents. He learns that getting into trouble draws at least some recognition and leads to a fleeting sense of control. The boy becomes "a devil" in his mother's eyes with no protection or support from his father. Over time, he gives up on getting emotional support and acceptance from either parent. The boy changes from the victim of two parents' neglect into a perpetrator himself.

As a young victim, the boy draws in concerned adults to play out roles in the triangle. A concerned teacher's call leads a CPS worker to a hungry boy sleeping on a dirty mattress in a barren, unheated room. "Just punishment," the boy's parents assert, "He's a demon." "Neglect," retorts the CPS worker and petitions the judge to order the parents to attend parenting classes, work with a family counselor every week, and endure weekly monitoring visits with the threat of placing their child.

A family therapist comes in and sees a sullen, angry boy, a replica of the neglect that Mom and Dad experienced growing up. The therapist tries harder and harder to engage parents who feel driven to battle what they see as persecution by "the welfare." If crises escalate and risks increase, the CPS worker brings in new agencies or the youth's defiant behavior leads to PINS or JD petitions with additional court-ordered treatment programs. To the new agencies involved, the first family worker may appear hopelessly locked into an advocate

---

*I am using the term triangles in the sense of people becoming locked into constricted roles (see Bowen, 1978).

role with a family that is becoming more and more dangerous. Battles ensue between the agencies with practitioners repeating the original cycle from rescuer to victim and then needing to leave (the non-protecting parent-figure) or becoming what is seen as an unfeeling, uncaring persecutor themselves.

I know I'm feeling locked into such a progressive triangle when I feel tense and can see only very limited options with clients who seem to be in so much danger that someone has to move in and take over. The pull to rescue may be acute—a sure warning sign. The next step will almost certainly be a feeling of shame at what I did or failed to do. When I find myself anticipating criticism from another practitioner or, conversely, find myself becoming angry at the obvious incompetence of colleagues, I know I am slipping once again into the victim-rescuer-persecutor cycle and am on my way to becoming part of a family's crises.

PUTTING COUNTERTRANSFERENCE TO WORK

The first step in avoiding the role of rescuer, persecutor, or victim is to shed some of our myths and utilize the natural forces that we can't help but experience. Countertransference* is not a failing of practitioners. It is an essential tool. To the trained clinician, the feelings that swell up inside can be an "aha" moment of insight. I expect to feel the pain, rage, and fears of a family; I would be inhuman if I didn't. In fact, I want these feelings to come out. I want to welcome them as clues to the struggles that family members cannot voice.

"One can only face in others what one can face in oneself" (James Baldwin cited by Ventura, 1994). Countertransference marks the monsters and nightmares that the child in placement has experienced and is often dramatizing for everyone to see. I will know these monsters because, in truth, these are the same monsters and phantoms that I and everyone else has to deal with from birth to death. These are the monsters in life that connect all of us and help us as practitioners to avoid taking a one-up position with family members in crisis.

I want to show each child and parent that I won't crumble, run away, or demean family members. I have to protect myself. Yet at the same time, I know that it is my own vulnerability that allows me to

---

*I am using the term countertransference in a very broad sense to reflect a wide range of feelings and conflicts stirred up by work with clients. These feelings and conflicts can then interfere with our effectiveness as therapists.

engage sullen adolescents, depressed grandmothers, or shame-ridden parents.

Harnessing the Monsters Inside

Countertransference is my primary instrument. I need to pull it out, tune it, and make it work. My reactions can guide me to the conflicting forces which propel a family's struggle. Feelings, images, and associations help me tie a child's or parent's provocative stance with the tear in their lives, the place in time where a child's and often a parent's emotional development stopped.

To be a therapist means facing our own monsters. I don't mean eliminating them. I respect the forces in my own family's history that led to my beliefs about what I can and cannot do. I worked in a therapist's own family program (see Bowen, 1978; Titelman, 1987) and have utilized many other forms of therapy to help me understand what makes me freeze, run, or attack and to break out of my own narrow role in my family.

If I was going to ask families to look at their own fears and demons, I needed to first do this myself. Learning to speak out was hard for me. I needed to confront my own fears of being rejected or hurting those I loved and my tendency to detach, intellectualize, and avoid anything connected with the serial deaths I experienced early in my life.

The children and parents who come to us can tell who has the courage to face what troubles them. Their threats to run away, pitiful looks, failures to show up for sessions, and angry outbursts quickly test what we will do and whether we can be trusted enough to share their pain and rage (see chapter 4). Courage, of course, doesn't mean fearlessness, but rather the ability to confront what we dread without running away or becoming abusive ourselves.

Respect, from the Inside Out

Understanding that all of us share the same fears, impulses, and healthy drives helps me to perceive a parent or child's struggle to make things better. Respecting clients goes hand in hand with respecting myself. I never want to push someone up against a wall— that's when people explode like cornered animals. I always want to give them options, choices, and recognition for the good things they are doing and any signs of their effort to help others and to promote healing. At the same time, I want to keep myself out of constricted roles, narrow limits, and the feeling of being trapped in any way.

Fear of perpetrators is magnified when we are unable to voice our concerns, to talk directly to alleged abusers, to give both/and messages (see chapters 5 and 7), and to offer help to everyone on working to overcome a child's and other family members' fears. As a family therapist and member of a foster care, crisis residence, or psychiatric hospital staff, I want to avoid taking on the responsibilities of judges, CPS workers, county attorneys, or the police. I need support from colleagues and supervisors and a schedule that separates client time from time with my own family. This is not the kind of work anyone can do alone.

PULLING OUT THE MAP

Courage also means having a clear sense of direction and knowing the landmarks that will guide my work (see chapter 4). I am especially mindful of three principles that focus my work and help me find a sense of direction in stormy seas.

1. A child needs a primary parent (hopefully a mother *and* a father) who will care for him, protect and guide him now and into adulthood, and help him to own and share his life story, a life story that makes sense and includes what the child saw, felt, heard, thought, and did over time. This may or may not be a biological parent.
2. Most children in crisis placements have experienced neglect and emotional, physical, or sexual abuse. The length of time a child acts out in dangerous ways is directly related to the time it takes for a supportive network to come together and prove to the child that significant people in his life can talk about toxic secrets and put into effect realistic safety plans. The child needs to see that his experience is heard and believed by significant people (parents, guardians, relatives, foster parents, community leaders).
3. The child in placement needs to learn and practice what he can do in place of previous behaviors that got him into trouble and to find out who cares enough to believe in him, set limits, implement safety plans, and keep the monsters of the past away.

For a child in placement, therapy means finding powerful people in his life (parents, CPS workers, foster parents, group care workers, family therapists, psychologists, psychiatrists, law guardians, and judges) who can make it safe enough to tell his story and help him move beyond blaming and to find a way to trust again. New and more adaptive meanings are constructed with other people (Roth & Chasin, 1994). The child, in effect, needs to rework his life story and can only do this with the help of a supportive network.

Building a supportive network reduces the pressure on practitioners to take on parent-like roles with family members. Parents and children confront traumas and develop safety plans with the help of network members. This helps family therapists to avoid becoming the only bulwark against overwhelming feelings of abandonment. The family therapist's role and the frequency of sessions can gradually be reduced as the network becomes stronger.

With these principles in mind, I can center my work on building (or rebuilding) trust between a parent (or, if necessary, a substitute parent) and a child and fostering a supportive network that can sustain both of them. Interventions focused on these principles shorten a child's length of stay in temporary placements and focus scarce resources (staff time and funding) on what is most important for the child and family over time.

FINDING THE SPLIT

In every assessment, I look for the conflicting struggle shown by a child and his parents (see chapter 5). What can't be resolved? My own often irrational responses can guide me to the conflicting messages and underlying threats that drive dangerous behavior. My job, then, is to voice the struggles of both the child and parent(s) and help them search for a way to counter the forces ripping them apart. Framing a dual centering message in the first two family sessions validates family members and demonstrates that I am able to talk about both what family members fear and their struggle to make things better.

Often, split messages reflect a time in a parent and child's lives when they felt terrified and helpless. Current crises reflect a struggle to master what could not be managed in the past. I want to show parents and children that it is okay to pull out both the hurt child from the past and the struggling adolescent or adult of the present, to be both 5 and 45. Opening up new perspectives of time (past, present, and future) leads to new solutions.

I want to validate both sides of a conflict and help parents and children set their own goals, where they would like to be. Then, we can work on mobilizing the resources to help them overcome the tears in their lives.

Goals lead directly to concrete steps that family members take to rebuild a safe, loving home or make a decision that a child is best off growing up in another family. Actions become messages about who can and will parent a child.

Scary Voices

Eleven-year-old Alex was a strikingly handsome boy, a good student, and well-liked by teachers and friends. After running away to a friend's home and refusing to return home, he was placed into a foster home. Alex said that his mother had thrown him against a wall because he bought bread with money his mother gave him to buy her cigarettes. Several old scars on Alex's back appeared to be belt marks but when asked about them, Alex became silent. The family's apartment lacked food and adequate clothes for a child.

Placed in a foster home, Alex told his school counselor that he was going to hang himself because he got his Mom in trouble. "I'm going to hell for what I did." He wanted to go back to his mother but was afraid because his mother often acted like different people. When he would ask his mother to stop, she would yell in a deep male voice, "Shut up, you little slut! Do you hear me?"

Alex would run to his room and hear his mother respond to the deep voice with what sounded like a young woman's cry, "No, don't do it. Please don't do it." As Alex listened, his mother acted out a struggle in which she started to gag and sounded like she was choking. Then, an older woman's voice came in to say, "Don't touch my girl!" Later, he often heard what sounded like a little girl's voice giggling or crying.

Alex's father reportedly was never involved in his life. His mother, Sandra, a petite black woman, arrived for our family session at CPS wearing a tight-fitting mini-skirt. "I was just talking to myself, that's all," Sandra said with a fixed smile. "Alex has got to learn to mind me. I'm not going to have him run the streets with his friends." Regarding the male voice, Sandra added, "I think it's God." When asked about her son's fears of the voices, Sandra continued to smile and said, "I have to laugh it off."

A week later, when I saw Sandra alone for a psychological evaluation, the smile and mini-skirt were replaced by tight lips, a stern look, and a business suit. Sandra warned that if she did not get her son back soon, she would kidnap him. "I'm on my way out of this country anyway." Sandra said she would tell the judge to stop the "propaganda." She saw Alex in a "catch 22" and interjected later in our session that she just might join the Marines.

I saw Alex and his mother a few months later in a review conference to assess the progress Alex's mother was making toward reuniting with her son. Sandra had refused our requests that she see a psychiatrist, consider medications, and work in psychotherapy, but she did come to some of the supervised visits scheduled each week. Sandra arrived late for our conference and stood at the door glaring at each person in the room. Alex cringed in a corner, sitting close to his foster mother.

"I'm not going to take this any longer," Sandra declared. "You keep this up and I'm taking Alex out of this Goddamn country. . . . You don't know who you're dealing with." Looking straight at Alex, Sandra added, "And you, stop this nonsense! Or you'll never see me again!"

I felt Sandra's words hit me like a blow to the stomach and her threat to Alex sent a shiver up my spine. I asked Sandra for her help to get Alex out of the "catch 22" and that I knew from what she had shared before that she wanted her son to have a good life. I also knew that Alex loved his mother and always worried about her.

Sandra relaxed her glare a bit and stepped a few feet into the room. "You know Alex loves you," I ventured on, "he just needs to be able to share how scared he felt without having to worry about losing you." I reminded Sandra of her pledge to me that she would not want to endanger Alex. "We need your help," I added.

Alex looked up at his mother and I hoped for a brief moment that Sandra would come through. Instead, Sandra fired back, "You're all a bunch of racists." She again glared at me, her county worker, her family worker, Alex's foster mother, and Alex. "I work for military intelligence . . . I know what you're up to," Sandra jabbed a finger at me and headed toward the door.

I wanted to jump up and bring Sandra back, but I didn't dare face her hate. I had become just one more persecutor, a racist stealing her child. Our group was made up of black and white professionals and a black foster mother but, still, Sandra's words were like acid and the charges stung.

I felt rejected and despised, that I had failed to convey my belief that the voices must have made sense in Sandra's own life. I could imagine the abuse and helplessness she faced as a young child. Now, Sandra was abandoning her son and leaving him with a terrible choice, love his mother and accept her as she was or be condemned to lose her forever.

Sandra had shared enough with me in our individual session for me to know that the rejection I felt was nothing compared to her experience as a young child. Sandra's mother was a former alcoholic who was loved by Alex as someone who cared for him, but who was hated by Sandra for everything that had happened when Sandra was a child. As a young woman, Sandra had gone from one violent relationship to another, repeating, no doubt, the abuse she endured as a child. When Alex was born, Sandra was forcibly hospitalized in a large city psychiatric ward for several months, a terrible experience for her. Now, she felt we were trying to steal her baby and lock her up again.

I looked over at Alex and saw him being wrenched apart. Half of him was in the chair, half was out. He could chase after his mother, the loyal son searching for the love that he remembered from the past. He felt responsible for her pain and to blame for all of us pressuring her to go into treatment. At the same time, he had shared with me that he couldn't stand the beatings, the voices, or being locked up in their apartment. He wanted to get away.

Alex struggled with a real "catch 22." He had taken care of his mother until he could no longer stand his mother's rages and voices. As Alex tried to go out more with his friends, Sandra set stricter and stricter limits. When he was late or snuck out, she beat him. I had asked Sandra to work with us and a therapist of her own to deal with the voices and show Alex that it would be safe to talk about the good times, their caring, *and* their fears.

Sandra hesitated at the door. I wanted to bridge the gap between my urge to chase after her and my fear of her rage. Alex was being split in half and felt like he was going to hell. I wanted to change the impossible "either/or" message to a "both/and" statement that would show respect for both Sandra and Alex, validate their struggles, and offer a ray of hope that they could overcome the split.

"I know you raised your son all these years," I said, still seated but looking into Sandra's fiery eyes. "We need your help to make it safe for you and Alex."

Sandra fixed her eyes on me. "I don't have time for this," she mumbled and left the room.

Alex's eyes filled and he began to cry. I had failed to keep his mother in the room but I could still help Alex avoid being ripped apart. "I think your Mom knows you love her. You always did. You can still love her and not want to face the voices or her anger. She's the only one who can decide if she can make things better, if she can face the voices. . . . We'll keep offering her help . . . that's our job. . . . The hardest part is waiting to see what your Mom decides to do."

Sandra came to a few more family sessions and eventually left the area. After a year in foster care, I learned that Alex went to live with his grandmother. Alex had asked to go to his grandmother if his mother could not change and, under the law, she had priority in seeking custody. I worried that the split between Sandra, her mother, and her son remained.

Alex's first months in a foster home were terrible but he learned to accept that he could neither change nor save his mother. He began to understand his mother (and her mental condition) more and to blame himself less. Alex felt accepted for himself in both his foster family and his grandmother's home. He did well again in school and made no more threats to hang himself. While Sandra remained at risk, her son had a chance to live the life she had wanted for him, a chance to escape from the overwhelming terrors that broke her apart.

The Split Message Exercise

When I feel stuck, I expect that I am caught up in a split message and am feeling the bind that has driven parents and children into serial crises. To preserve my own sanity, I want to find the split and frame it in a way that pulls both sides together (see chapter 5).

Sharing difficult case sessions with colleagues helps me to understand where I get stuck. I need to separate my own issues. Is this my frustration with passive dependent mothers coming out again? Exercises by Sallyann Roth and Richard Chasin (1990; 1994) have been very helpful to me in utilizing how I feel stuck and my own family's experience to develop ways to help a family. With their outline as a model, I developed a split message exercise (see appendix) that helps me to identify conflicting messages which have led to an impasse and to use this understanding to construct centered "both/and" messages.

Staying Alive*

Getting stuck often means thinking in "either/or" terms. "If I don't do this, something terrible will happen." It means taking on responsibility for someone else—a parent, a judge, a CPS worker—and often trying to take on everyone's roles in a network of family and service providers. Getting stuck means setting unrealistic goals for parents and children who are not clients, who don't feel respected, and who don't respect practitioners. It means ignoring very real biological, legal, and economic factors and the tremendous impact of traumatic memories implanted into a child's neurons. We can easily feed into the invalidation that spurs a family's cycle of crises. We can also very naturally begin to manifest symptoms of traumatization ourselves, including narrowing our perspectives, invalidating ourselves, becoming brittle, and obsessing about case issues (after van der Kolk, 1984, 1987). Losing one's sense of humor and compassion for clients is another sign of becoming overwhelmed and losing the balance we need in our own lives to work effectively with high-risk clients.

The antidote for me is to stay real, to speak out, to define roles, to develop a workable contract with my colleagues and myself, and to coordinate an effective network for each family in crisis. I need to validate my own feelings in order to be real enough to show a parent or child that I can genuinely validate their own dilemmas. I also need to separate my personal life from my professional work. A few minutes of meditation in the middle of the day and consultation with colleagues helps me to keep my balance[†] but I often fail to allow myself time for phone calls and find myself rushing to my next session without time to complete required reports or progress notes from the session before. Cardiovascular exercise at the end of the day helps me to sweat out the emotional toxins and release soothing endorphins, followed by a cleansing and soothing shower.

If I wake up thinking about a case, I most likely didn't say what I felt or thought during a session. I know I can only handle a limited number of trauma cases each week. When I go beyond that number, I

---

*Shirley Schlosberg and I listed some of the most common hazards for practitioners working with crisis-oriented families along with steps practitioners can take to stay alive and effective. Please see chapter 11 of *Families in Perpetual Crisis* (Kagan & Schlosberg, 1989).
†Please see Yvonne Dolan (1991), Beverly James (1989), and Pearlman & Saakvitne (1995) for other techniques to avoid secondary traumatization.

begin punishing myself. I need to respect my own needs for time and support if I am going to work effectively with crisis-oriented families.

Sharing my many mistakes, staying honest about my feelings, and setting limits about what I can and cannot do helps me keep my focus on the needs of family members to develop a supportive network and a sense of permanency for a child and a parent. I can then use my own reactions to understand the conflict splitting a family apart and how a child in placement needs to learn if his parent will make it safe enough so he can face what happened, share his feelings, and look to his parent to raise him to maturity.

FRAMING CHOICES

Assessment is just one part of my work. I go to my agency each day to help families make a difference in their lives, to work together with colleagues to make things a little bit better. This means engaging children and parents in the struggle for change, something most of us work very hard to avoid.

Crises serve as a powerful form of avoidance (Kagan & Schlosberg, 1989), but crises also reflect energy and a struggle, however fruitless, to make things better. We can use the risks acted out by children and parents to stress the need for family members to slowly and carefully begin making changes before it is too late for another generation.

By framing choices for family members, we raise the ante and offer hope. This shows both respect for family members' capacity for change and the courage on our part to talk about real choices and real consequences.

Therapy means helping each person reconnect with his or her feelings, memories, beliefs, and hopes that have been split apart. We can help a child to say aloud, show through drawings, or share in stories his struggle to bring his parents back and his fears that the horrors of the past will recur. With validation from his parents, a child can begin to let go of his self-blame, shame, and anger at his parents and the world.

If Mom or Dad can't make their home safe from the traumas of the past, we need to look for a substitute parent who can do this. Ideally, parents who can't raise a child will still be able to validate their child's experience and need for a safe, nurturing home with new parents. When this is not possible and parents abandon their children or when parents' rights are terminated by a court, the child needs to see that everyone has struggled to help his parents. The "diligent efforts" required in permanency work allow a child like Alex to learn that it is okay to move on with his own development, to learn how to succeed in a new home and school, to risk caring for new parents, and to show affection to an adult in a safe way.

MOVING BEYOND "I CAN'T . . ."

"I can't hear any more, not now," Susan sighed. "I want them to tell me what happened . . . but if they do, I'll leave the room." Susan's eyes watered and her head hung low. She thought her two daughters had been abused by their father during visits; but neither daughter would answer her directly. Her oldest daughter, Tonya, came into placement at age 12 after asking Susan to hold a knife while she ran into it. Tonya had also attemted to suffocate herself by putting a plastic bag over her head, and had told a teacher that she kept thinking of jumping out of a window. Both girls said they wanted to see their father but came home after visits looking terrified. Tonya began refusing to go on visits and frequently got into fights with her mother or threatened to kill herself on weekends when her younger sister went on visits alone.

"I'm afraid I'll end up in a hospital and then my husband will get the kids," Susan added trembling as she spoke. I sensed both her fragility and the warning she was giving me. "Don't push me or you'll lose me." I felt I would lose her. Given Tonya's suicide gestures, I believed the girls sensed a real threat that Susan would kill herself in addition to very real dangers posed by the girls' father. A series of therapists had tried to work with the family and each reported their own sense of fear when Tonya's father tried to intimidate them with threats of lawsuits and demands to see all reports about his wife and children.

"I just had a panic attack two days ago," Susan continued, her body continuing to shake. Susan wrung her hands in and out. "I just can't take any more."

"You need to listen to your body," I said watching Susan wring her hands in a clenching motion. "We can only go so far. . . . I know from what Tonya has said and did that she is terrified of losing you, that her father would kill you or you'd kill yourself." Susan nodded; she recognized how scared Tonya was as well as how scary she could become. This was not our first meeting and Susan had shared with my colleague in the crisis residence about her own history of sexual abuse.

I emphasized my belief that each of us has a limit to what we can take. "You look like the kind of person who takes in and takes in."

Susan nodded. "I've been stuffing it since I was a child," she answered.

I told Susan that our job, as therapists in a crisis residence, was to help her and not to push her into anything she was not ready to do. I tried to speak slowly and softly, matching Susan's body posture and pace. No one was going to rush her.

Susan's trembling slowed and her hands seemed to relax. I wondered aloud how she used her hands when she was nervous and Susan shared how she would knit sweaters for hours at a time. I shared my admiration of anyone who could do that and how her knitting gifts for her children was a good way to show how much she cared.

Watching Susan knit with her hands gave me a sense of hope. I often think of our work in therapy as helping people to knit together parts of themselves that have been torn apart. Here was a woman who needed to knit the pieces of herself and her children back together. To do this, Susan needed to master the trauma that had split her apart and left her unable to protect her children. As with so many other victims of childhood physical and sexual abuse, abandonment or threats of abandonment were tied in with trauma and had stunted Susan's development of herself and her ability to show her children that she could remain with them. I hoped that we could use the crisis of Tonya's placement to help Susan and her children begin reworking these traumas and end the threats of suicide or abandonment Tonya showed in her behavior. I knew that I was feeling the same threat of Susan's leaving me that had led to Tonya's desperation.

I asked Susan what kept her going. "My girls," she replied with more energy than I had heard the whole session. "I know I have to be there for them."

Susan's childhood terrors were rekindled by the intimidation and harassment she reported from her husband. She was too frightened of him becoming violent to even meet with him in the same room and we had to arrange for separate sessions with each parent.

Susan wanted to raise her daughters but at the same time resorted to messages of abandonment in order to protect herself. These, most likely, were the same messages that kept her so fragile as a young girl that she was only now beginning to deal with her own experiences of abuse as a child. I wanted to help Susan begin knitting together the two sides of this split; this meant helping Susan and her daughters counter the abandonment threat.

"Tonya keeps asking to see you, but at the same time she doesn't want to go home yet. She's still not feeling safe at home. She sees that you want her. But, you can't be there for them if you're filled up, if you can't hear what they have to say."

I knew I had to be honest with Susan. Tonya needed to know if her mother could deal with the fears in their lives and whether Susan was going to kill herself. At the same time, I did not want to push Susan into a corner or demand that she do certain things. It was her choice. I wanted to foster Susan's strengths and desire to care for her children and then challenge her to decide whether or not she would slowly and carefully work to make their lives safer from the threats they *could* control.

"Tonya's afraid of losing you," I continued. "And I hear you saying that you can't take any more, so I start worrying about you killing yourself. And I think Tonya worries about that too, plus her fear that her father might hurt you. No one can live like that. From the way you describe your husband, we can only expect that he will continue to do what he's done before. The girls keep looking to you to see if you are going to run away or hurt yourself. The stronger the girls see you, the more they will be able to deal with whatever is scaring them. We can work with you on getting some of the pain out. Or, you can leave it like it is. If you do want to show your daughters that you can be the one to parent them, we and the other counselors working with you and your children would work very slowly, a very little at a time."

Susan and I met later with other service providers and worked out plans for ongoing family and individual therapy for Susan and her daughters that would begin while Tonya was in placement. Each of the service providers supported a court petition requiring visits with Tonya's father to be supervised until he worked in counseling and showed his children they no longer needed to be afraid of him.

As with most of our work, nothing magical happened. Yet my colleagues and I voiced Tonya's fears of her mother running away or killing herself as well as her fears of her father hurting her mother. We respected Susan's fear of collapsing and offered her a way to work with a network of service providers to slowly release some of the anger and fear she "stuffed" inside.

Susan obtained an order of protection against her ex-husband and filed petitions in court, again seeking supervision of his visits with the children. She began working with an outpatient counselor on what she had started in her sessions with my colleagues and me in the crisis residence. Tonya asked to go home and no longer felt compelled to kill herself. She had heard the side of her mother that wanted to find a safe way to deal with their terrors and to end the threat of someone running away or killing herself.

TURNING POINTS

The Chinese symbol for crisis stands for opportunity as well as risk. My goal is to discover and unlock hidden opportunities for change that can help the next generation avoid the traumas experienced by their parents and grandparents. My colleagues and I strive to help parents who typically grew up with no one they could rely on for ongoing nurture, safety, and caring. This means working with their goals and, at the same time, their children's need for safety and attachment to parents they can count on to nurture, protect, and care for them now and into adulthood.

I want to work within the shortest possible time to empower parents to do what is necessary to raise their children. If this is not possible, we need to address the need for children to be freed—emotionally and legally—to grow up in another family. Children cannot afford to wait without sacrificing their development and potential, and communities cannot afford the costs of children growing up more damaged than their parents.

Therapy typically means painful and difficult work to break cycles of abandonment, abuse, and depression and to search with family members for the best solutions to chronic dilemmas. This means touching a family's pain without becoming overwhelmed, frozen with fear, or traumatized ourselves. Therapists have to be strong. If I can't talk about the risks and distress that family members have experienced, I can't be of much help. Our effectiveness comes from our ability to know and use ourselves, to be at once removed and in touch with the pain in a family.

Therapy for these parents and children means finding strengths and rekindling hope that traumas can be faced, that attachments can be strengthened or developed anew, and that children like Alex and Tonya will be heard and protected. Our challenge in evaluations and therapy is to put together a network including family members, friends, child protective workers, therapists, foster parents, child care workers, teachers, physicians, nurses, lawyers, and judges to work together to counter threats of abandonment, to overcome constraints, to mobilize resources, and to support and maintain change. The network provides an umbrella under which parents, children, and practitioners can work to regain trust and to reknit torn parts of their experience.

We need to validate that we have heard family members' and service providers' hopes, frustrations, anger, needs, and fears. At the same time, we must respect our own reactions as invaluable clues to what must be addressed. We need to develop contracts which provide for a team approach and the resources needed to work with traumatized and traumatizing families.

Every session centers on the search for attachment, to rebuild, strengthen, and create bonds between parents or parent-substitutes and children. I wanted Alex and Tonya to know what their parents were going to do to get them back, what they needed to do while in placement, and who was going to be there to help each of them. As Solomon understood in the story of the two women fighting over a baby, every child needs to know who will protect him from being split apart.

By finding the hope lingering in the most crisis-addicted families, we can engage children and parents to face the challenge of building secure attachments and to break out of the cycles of crises and emptiness that have put themselves and their communities at risk. Placements can be used to mobilize family members and create turning points in the lives of children and parents.

I haven't seen miraculous recoveries in this work. The rewards come in small but real changes in a child's trust and a parent's commitment, a child who entered a crisis placement at great risk of hurting himself or someone else who now feels believed and can learn and develop age-appropriate skills within a family he can call his own. Over time, these changes make the difference between perpetuating histories of trauma and giving the next generation a better life.

appendix

split message exercise

IN THIS EXERCISE, TWO PRACTITIONERS CAN HELP EACH OTHER IDENTIFY CON-
flicting messages. One practitioner takes on the role of facilitator and the
other becomes the presenter. The client giving the conflicting messages to the
presenter is called the "message-giver." The facilitator helps the presenter
move through a series of questions and helps the presenter focus on conflicting messages and traumatic dilemmas which lead to impasse.

This exercise is based on the understanding that a presenter can and will
stop at any time that he or she feels going ahead would be in any way harmful (after James Sacks cited by Lee, 1981). Suggestions are given for how the
facilitator can help the presenter with each step, and these are followed by an
example of a presenter's response to illustrate how this can work.

1. Describe a situation with a family in which you felt stuck.

Facilitator: "Who was there? What were the most powerful messages that you
gave and received? Often these were nonverbal. What was your greatest
fear?" Focus on how the presenter feels stuck rather than on the details of the
case.

Presenter: "I have frequently felt manipulated and hopeless when working
with a mother of a 5-year-old who had spent two years in placement. I've
been asked by the county and family court to provide diligent efforts to reunite for another six months. She recently terminated a visit with her son
early, complaining that I had reserved the wrong playroom. She yelled at me,
told me she never wanted to see me again, and told the receptionist that I
should go to 'fucking hell!'"

2. How did you experience messages given to you?

Facilitator: "Who gave the message? [Note: This will be the person referred to
below as the message-giver.] How did it conflict with your own message and
other messages you heard? See if you can condense your experience into a
conflict between two or more messages."

Presenter: "What disturbed me the most was this mother telling me: 'I'm doing everything' and 'I'm leaving; it's all your fault!'"

3. Imagine yourself as the message-giver.

Facilitator: "How do you look? How do you act? How do you feel in this situation? What are you most afraid will happen? What is most important for you?"

Presenter: "My face is drawn, head down, arms swinging up and down, I'm yelling. I'm afraid I'll be blamed again. I need to get away. I want to say: 'What about me?' 'You [referring to the presenter] are attacking me!'"

4. What messages did the message-giver experience in his or her life?

Facilitator: "Think of the message-giver feeling and sensing messages similar to how you felt as a therapist in the impasse situation. Imagine yourself as the message-giver. How did you learn this was the only way? Who might have given you these messages? What was the conflict for you? Try to picture a critical time or event in the message-giver's life that corresponds to the developmental level shown by his or her behavior."

Presenter: "I was placed as a young child, moved from foster home to foster home, got into trouble, sent to DFY, stole cars. I kept hearing from my parents and later institutions: You're too bad. Get out!"

5. What would the message-giver need to have experienced in his or her life in order to give a more useful message?

Facilitator: "Continue to imagine yourself as the message-giver. What would you have wanted to hear? Who needed to give this message? Give this person a name, for example, the message-giver's mother. In what dilemma or traumatic situation would you as the message-giver have needed this message?"

Presenter: "As a 10-year-old girl sent into placement, she needed to hear from her mother or father or someone who could give her a family: 'You're not to blame for your parents' sending you away. Somebody will take care of you now and for as long as needed.'"

6. With the facilitator taking on the role of the message-giver, have the presenter give more positive messages to the message-giver.

The presenter takes on the role of the person named above in step 5, for example, the message-giver's mother. Then, acting as this person, the presenter gives more positive messages about a traumatic situation to the message-giver. In this enactment, the facilitator takes on the role of the message-giver at the age when the dilemma or traumatic situation occurred. The presenter should consider what in this person's (e.g., the message-giver's mother) life could have led to better messages and actions. What messages would have helped the message-giver grow up with more security and trust? Healing messages would include, for example, an apology for previous hurtful messages, a way of understanding what happened, and how the message-giver would see over time that things would be different.

Presenter: "The grandmother's (message-giver's mother) saying, 'I'll get you home. It's not your fault. It's my job to protect you from the drinking and fights. I'm not going to let anyone hurt you or me anymore.'"

7. Return to the impasse situation first described by the presenter.

a. How does the impasse look to the presenter now?

Facilitator: "What ideas do you have now about what you could say to the message-giver?"

b. How did the messages received by the message-giver match the messages received by the presenter in the impasse situation?

c. What does the message-giver need now? Consider messages the presenter could give that would match split messages received.

d. If you wish, try these messages out in a role play in which the presenter acts as him- or herself and the facilitator acts as the message-giver.

Presenter: "I felt like I had done everything I could and ended up being yelled at and told I was bad. I felt hopeless and I wondered if that was how you felt every time you came to my agency for a visit. . . . I was also struck by how this seemed just like what you told me you experienced when you were 10. . . . And, now it seems like your son is hearing the same messages."

e. Tie healing messages into what the message-giver and the children need to hear to break this cycle.

Presenter: "What do you as a mother need to hear when you come for a visit with your son? Will you tell me if I start sounding like I'm blaming? How can you find out if your son is feeling blamed and hopeless? What does your son need to hear so he doesn't feel hopeless and blamed?"

references

Achenbach, T. M. (1991a). *Manual for the child behavior checklist/[ages] 4–18 and 1991 profile.* Burlington, VT: University of Vermont, Department of Psychiatry.

Achenbach, T. M. (1991b). *Manual for the youth self-report and 1991 profile.* Burlington, VT: University of Vermont, Department of Psychiatry.

Ainsworth, M. D. (1969). Object relations, dependency and attachment: A theoretical review of the infant-mother relationship. *Child Development, 40,* 969–1025.

American Orthopsychiatric Association (1993). Call for Proposals for 71st Annual Meeting, Silver Spring, MD.

American Psychiatric Association (1994). *Diagnostic and statistical manual of mental disorders (4th ed.).* Washington, DC: Author.

American Public Welfare Association (1989). *W-Memo, 10*(1).

American Public Welfare Association (1994). *Child substitute care flow data for FY '93.* Washington, DC: Voluntary Cooperative Information System.

Andersen, T. (Ed.). (1991). *The reflecting team: Dialogues and dialogues about the dialogues.* New York: Norton.

Anderson, R., Ambrosino, R., Valentine, D., & Lauderdale, M. (1983). Child deaths attributable to abuse and neglect: An empirical study. *Children and Youth Service Review, 5,* 75–89.

Auerswald, E. H. (1983). The Gouverneur Health Services Program: An experiment in ecosystemic community health care delivery. *Family Systems Medicine, 1*(3), 5–24.

Ausloos, G. (1978, October). *Delinquency and family dynamics.* Paper presented at the International Psycho-education Seminar, Paris.

Ausloos, G. (1981a, October) *Acting out adolescents: Systems in conflict.* Keynote address presented at the Second Annual Parsons/Sage Fall Institute, Albany, NY.

Ausloos, G. (1981b). Systemes, homeostase, equilibration. *Therapie Familiale, 2,* 187–203.

Ausloos, G. (1985, April). *Systemic approach to acting-out youth in and out of placement.* Symposium conducted at Parsons Child and Family Center, Albany, NY.

Ausloos, G. (1986). The march of time: Rigid or chaotic transactions, two different ways of living time. *Family Process, 25,* 549–557.

Bandler, R., & Grinder, J. (1976). *The Structure of Magic II.* Palo Alto, CA: Science and Behavior.

Basharov, D. J. (1991). Reducing unfounded reports. *Journal of Interpersonal Violence, 6,* 112–115.

Bateson, G., Jackson, D., Haley, J., & Weakland, J. (1956). Toward a theory of schizophrenia. *Behavioral Science, 1,* 251–264.

Beck, A. T. (1978). *Depression inventory.* Philadelphia: Center for Cognitive Therapy.

Beck, S. J., Beck, A. G., Levitt, E. E., & Molish, H. B. (1961). *Rorschach's test I: Basic processes.* New York: Grune & Stratton.

Berenson, D. (1976). *Family therapy theory and practice.* New York: Gardner.

Bergman, J. S. (1985). *Fishing for barracuda: Pragmatics of brief systemic therapy.* New York: Norton.

Bettelheim, B. (1960). *Surviving and other essays.* New York: Vintage.

Blankenhorn, D. (1995). *Fatherless America.* New York: Basic.

Boszormenyi-Nagy, I. (1972). *Invisible loyalties.* New York: Harper & Row.

Bowen, M. (1978). *Family therapy and clinical practice.* New York: Jason Aronson.

Bowlby, J. (1969). *Attachment and loss: Vol. 1. Attachment.* New York: Basic.

Bowlby, J. (1973). *Attachment and loss: Vol. 2. Separation anxiety and anger.* New York: Basic.

Bowlby, J. (1977). The making and breaking of affectional bonds. *British Journal of Psychiatry, 130*(1), 201–210 [Part I]; *130*(2), 421–431 [Part II].

Bowlby, J. (1979). *The Making and breaking of affectional bonds.* New York: Tavistock.

Brazelton, T. B., & Cramer, B. G. (1990). *The earliest relationship.* New York: Addison Wesley.

Breakey, G. F., Uohara-Pratt, B., Morrell-Samuels, S., & Kolb-Latu, D. (1991). *Healthy start training manual.* Honolulu: The Hawaii Family Stress Center.

Briere, J., & Runtz, M (1986). Suicidal thoughts and behaviors in former sexual abuse victims. *Canadian Journal of Behavioral Science, 18,* 413–423.

Brooks, R. B. (1994). Children at risk: Fostering resilience and hope. *American Journal of Orthopsychiatry, 64*(4), 545–553.

Bronfenbrenner, U. (1979). *The ecology of human development.* Cambridge, MA: Harvard University Press.

Buck, J. N. (1948). The H-T-P Test. *Journal of Clinical Psychology, 4,* 151–159.

Burgess, A. W., Hartman, C. R., & McCormack, A. (1987). Abused to abuser: Antecedents of socially deviant behavirs. *American Journal of Psychiatry, 144,* 1431–1436.

Burns, R. C., & Kaufman, S. H. (1970). *Kinetic family drawings (K-F-D): An introduction to understanding children through kinetic drawings.* New York: Brunner/Mazel.

Burrell, C. (1995, April 24). Number of fatherless children in U. S. quadruples in 45 years. *Times Union,* Albany, NY, p. A8.

Cahill, C., Llewelyn, S. P., & Pearson, C. (1991). Long-term effects of sexual abuse which occurred in childhood: a review. *British Journal of Clinical Psychology, 30,* 117–130.

Carson, M., & Goodfield, R. (1988). The Children's garden attachment model. In R. Small and F. Alwon (Eds.), *Challenging the limits of care.* Needham, MA: Trieschman Center.

Casebeer Art Productions (1988). *Projective storytelling cards.* Reading, CA: Northwest Psychological Publishers.

Casey Foundation (1995). *Kids count data book.* Spokane, WA: Annie E. Casey Foundation.

Children's Defense Fund (1995, September 29). *Reject the child protection block grant.* [Newsletter]. Washington, DC: Author.

Combs, G., & Freedman, J. (1990). *Symbol, story and ceremony: Using metaphor in individual and family therapy.* New York: Norton.

Conners, C. K. (1989). *Manual for Connors' rating scales.* North Tonawanda, NY: Multihealth Systems.

Daro, D. (1987). *Deaths due to maltreatment soar: Results of the Eighth Semiannual Fifty-State Survey.* Chicago: National Committee for Prevention of Child Abuse.

Daro, D., Jones, E., & McCurdy, K. (1993). *Preventing child abuse: An evaluation of services to high-risk families.* Chicago: National Committee for the Prevention of Child Abuse.

De Angelis, T. (1995, February). Calling all data to inform welfare-reform debate. *APA Monitor,* 38.

De Bellis, M. D., Chrousos, G. P., Dorn, L. D., et al. (1994a). Hypothalamic-pituitary-adrenal axis dysregulation in sexually abused girls. *Journal of Clinical Endocrinology and Metabolism, 78*(2), 249–255.

De Bellis, M. D., Lefter, L., Trickett, P. K., & Putnam, F. W. (1994b, March/April). Urinary catecholamine excretion in sexually abused girls. *Journal of the American Academy of Child and Adolescent Psychiatry, 33*(3), 320–327.

Denn, J. (1995, May 7). HMO bosses own up to big pay hikes. *Times Union,* Albany, NY, p. B2.

Del Valle, C., & McNamee, M. (1995, March 13). Welfare surprises. *Business Week,* 44.

Di Leo, J. H. (1983). *Interpreting children's drawings.* New York: Brunner-Mazel.

Dolan, Y. (1991). *Resolving sexual abuse.* New York: Norton.

Duhl, B. (1993). Metaphor in action. *Family Therapy Networker, 17,* 49–52.

Edelman, M. W. (1992). *The measure of our success: A letter to my children and yours* (pp. 42–43). Boston: Beacon.

Egeland, B., & Erickson, M. F. (1991). Rising above the past: Strategies for helping new mothers break the cycle of abuse and neglect. *Zero to Three, 11*(2), 29–35.

Erikson, E. H. (1986). *Childhood and society. 35th anniversary edition.* New York: Norton.

Farber, E. A., & Egeland, B. (1987). Invulnerability among abused and neglected children. In E. J. Anthony & B. J. Cohler (Eds.), *The invulnerable child* (pp. 253–288). New York: Guilford.

Ferreira, A. (1960, October). The double bind and delinquency. *Archives of General Psychiatry, 3,* 359–367.

Figley, C. R. (1989). *Helping traumatized families.* San Francisco: Jossey-Bass.

Finkelstein, N. (1980). Children in limbo. *Social Work, 25*(2), 100–105.

Finkelstein, N. (1991). *Children and youth in limbo: A search for connections.* New York: Praeger.

Fong, R. (1994). Family preservation: Making it work for Asians. *Child Welfare, 73*(4), 331–341.

Fossum, M. A., & Mason, M. J. (1986). *Facing shame: Families in recovery.* New York: Norton.

Freeman, E. M. (1989). Adolescent fathers in urban communities: Exploring their needs and role in pregnancy. *Journal of Social Work and Human Sexuality, 8,* 113–131.

Fruchtman, D. (1995). *Attachment relationships of childbearing adolescents.* Unpublished doctoral dissertation, California School of Professional Psychology at Alameda. (See Adolescent Attachment Interview.)

Galanter, M. (1993). *Network therapy for alcohol and drug abuse: A new approach in practice.* New York: Basic.

Gardner, R. A. (1975). *Psychotherapeutic approaches to the resistent child.* New York: Jason Aronson.

Garrison, J. (1974). Network techniques: Case studies in the screening-linking-planning conference method. *Family Process, 13,* 337–353.

Gelles, R. (1993). Family reunification—family preservation: Are children really being protected? *Journal of Interpersonal Violence, 8*(4), 556–562.

Gil, E. (1991, October 25). *Post-traumatic play in children: Facilitating and Intervening.* Workshop presented at the Parsons/Sage Fall Institute, Albany, NY.

Giordano, J. (1994). Mental health and the melting pot: An introduction. *American Journal of Orthopsychiatry, 64*(3), 342–345.

Goldstein, J., Freud, A., & Solnit, A. J. (1973). *Beyond the best interests of the child.* New York: Free Press.

Gottlieb, J. (1995, October 26). Groups seeking more funds to prevent teen pregnancy. *Times Union,* Albany, NY, p. B2.

Green, R. (1992). *Women in American Indian society.* New York: Chelsea.

Gresham, F. M., & Elliott, S. N. (1990). *Social skills rating system manual.* Circle Pines, MN: American Guidance Service.

Haley, J. (1976). *Problem-solving therapy.* San Francisco: Jossey-Bass.

Haley, J. (1977). Toward a theory of pathological systems. In P. Watzlawick & J. Weakland (Eds.), *The interactional view* (pp. 31–49). New York: Norton.

Harlow, H. F., Harlow, M. K., Dodsworth, R. O., & Arling, G. L. (1966). Maternal behavior in rhesus monkeys deprived of mothering and peer association in infancy. *Proceedings of the American Philosophical Society, 110*(1), 58–66.

Hartman, A. (1978). Diagrammatic assessment of family relationships, *Social Casework, 59*(8), 465–476.

Herman, J., Russell, D., & Trocki, K. (1986). Long-term effects of incestuous abuse in childhood. *American Journal of Psychiatry, 143,* 1293–1296.

Hernandez, M. (1994, August 22). Cited by K. Brandon, Home visiting: An avenue to stability. *Chicago Tribune,* Section 1, p. 9.

Imber-Black, E. (1988). *Families and larger systems: A family therapist's guide through the labyrinth.* New York: Guilford.

Imber-Black, E., Roberts, J., & Whiting, R. (Eds.) (1992). *Rituals in families and family therapy.* New York: Norton.

James, B. (1989). *Treating traumatized children; New insights and creative interventions.* Lexington, MA: Lexington.

Kagan, R. M. (1986). Game therapy for children in placement. In C. E. Schaefer & S. E. Reid (Eds.), *Game play: Therapeutic uses of childhood games.* New York: Wiley.

Kagan, R., & Schlosberg, S. (1989). *Families in perpetual crisis.* New York: Norton.

Kaladjian, G. M., Semidei, J., & the HomeRebuilders Workgroup (1992, March 10) *HomeRebuilders: A family reunificaton demonstration proposal.* Presented at the Family Preservation Conference, Washington, DC.

Kaplan, P. S. (1988). *The human odyssey: Life-span development.* New York: West.

Kaplan, L., & Girard, J. L. (1994). *Strengthening high-risk families.* New York: Lexington.

Karpman, S. (1968). Script drama analysis. *Transactional Analysis Bulletin, 26,* 39–43.

Klein, A. F. (1975). *The professional child care worker: A guide to skills, knowledge, techniques and attitudes.* New York: Association Press.

Klein, J. (1993, September 6). Michigan's tuna surprise. *Newsweek,* p. 21.

Klein, R. (1989). The art of confrontation. In J. F. Masterson & R. Klein (Eds.), *Psychotherapy of the disorders of the self* (pp. 215–230). New York: Brunner/Mazel.

Kliman, J., & Trimble, D. (1983). Network therapy. In B. Wolman & G. Stricker (Eds.), *Handbook of family and marital therapy* (pp. 277–314). New York: Plenum.

Kotulak, R. (1993, December 28). In search of the roots of violence. Part 3. *Times Union,* pp. A1, A8.

Landau-Stanton, J. (1990). Issues and methods of treatment for families in cultural transition. In M. P. Mirkin (Ed.), *The social and political contexts of family therapy* (pp. 251–275). Needham Heights, MA: Allyn & Bacon.

Landau-Stanton, J. (1994, March 3). *A family systems-network approach to preventing the next generation of MICA clients.* Workshop presented for the Sidney Albert Institute, Albany, NY.

Landau-Stanton, J. et al. (1993). *AIDS, health and mental health: A primary source book.* New York: Brunner/Mazel.

Lankton, C., & Lankton, S. (1989). *Tales of enchantment: Goal-oriented metaphors for adults and children.* New York: Brunner/Mazel.

Lauri (1984). *Familiar people.* Phillips-Avon, ME: Author.

Lazarus, A. A. (1971). *Behavior therapy and beyond.* New York: McGraw-Hill.

Lee, R. (1981). Video as adjunct to psychodrama and roleplaying. In J. L. Fryrear & R. Fleshman (Eds.), *Videotherapy and mental health* (pp. 121–145). Springfield, IL: C. C. Thomas.

Liederman, D. S. (1994, December). Letter. Washington, D C: Child Welfare League of America.

Lindemann, E. (1944). Symptomatology and management of acute grief. *American Journal of Psychiatry, 101,* 141–148.

Linesch, D. (1993). *Art therapy with families in crisis: Overcoming resistance through non-verbal expression.* New York: Brunner/Mazel.

Louis, R., & Louis, M. E. (1980). *The parents' guide to teenage sex and pregnancy.* New York: Berkeley.

Madanes, C. (1990a). *Metaphors and paradoxes.* New York: Jossey-Bass.

Madanes, C. (1990b). *Sex, love and violence: Strategies for transformation.* New York: Norton.

Madanes, C. (1995a, September 28). *Sexual abuse and sex offenders.* Workshop presented at Parsons Child and Family Center, Albany, New York.

Madanes, C. (1995b). *The violence of men.* San Francisco: Jossey Bass.

Magura, S., & Silverman-Moses, B. (1986). *The child well-being scales.* Washington, DC: Child Welfare League of America.

Mahler, M. S. (1972). On the first three sub-phases of the separation-individuation process. *International Journal of Psycho-Analysis, 53,* 333–338.

Main, M., & Goldwyn (1989). *An attachment classification system.* Berkeley, CA: University of California, Department of Psychology.

Mason, M. (1993). Shame: Reservoir for family secrets. In E. Imber-Black (Ed.), *Secrets in families and family therapy* (pp. 29–43). New York: Norton.

Masterson, J. F. (1976). *Psychotherapy of the borderline adult: A developmental approach.* New York: Brunner/Mazel.

Masterson, J. F. (1989). In J. F. Masterson & R. Klein (Eds.), *Psychotherapy of the disorders of the self* (p. 275). New York: Brunner/Mazel.

Mayor's Task Force on Child Abuse and Neglect. (1983). *Report on the preliminary study of child fatalities in New York City.* New York: Author.

McGoldrick, M., & Gerson, R. (1985). *Genograms in family assessment.* New York: Norton.

McGoldrick, M., Pearce, J. K., & Giordano, J. (Eds.). (1982). *Ethnicity and family therapy.* New York: Guilford.

McMillen, J. C., & Groze, V. (1994). Using placement genograms in child welfare practice. *Child Welfare, 73*(4), 307–318.

Meyer, V. F. (1991). A critique of adolescent pregnancy prevention research: The invisible white male. *Adolescence, 26,* 217–222.

Mills, J. C., & Crowley, R. J. (1986). *Therapeutic metaphors for children and the child within.* New York: Brunner/Mazel.

Minuchin, S. (1974). *Families and family therapy.* Cambridge, MA: Harvard University Press.

Mitchel, L. (1989). Report on fatalities from NCPCA. *Protecting children, 6,* 3–5.

Murray, H. A. (1971). *Thematic apperception test.* Cambridge, MA: Harvard University Press.

Nace, E. (1987). *The treatment of alcoholism.* New York: Brunner/Mazel.

Nichols-Casebolt, A., & Garfinkel, I. (1991). Transient paternity adjudication and child support awards. *Social Science Quarterly, 72,* 83–97.

Nichols, M. (1984). *Family therapy concepts and methods.* New York: Gardner.

O'Connor, W. (1993, September 14). Cited by Alan Bavley. Research: Violence learned. *Times Union,* Section C, p. 5,

Papp, P. (1983). *The process of change.* New York: Guilford.

Pearlman, L. A., & Saakvitne, K. W. (1995). *Trauma and the therapist: Countertransference and vicarious traumatization in psychotherapy with incest survivors.* New York: Norton.

Phillips, K. (1990). *The politics of rich and poor: Wealth and the American electorate in the Reagan aftermath.* New York: Random House, as cited in A. Hartman (1990, November). Children in a careless society. *Social Work, 35*(6), 483–484.

Pinderhughes, E. (1989). *Understanding race, ethnicity and power: The key to efficacy in cliniical practiace.* New York: Free.

Pines, D. (1988). Adolescent pregnancy and motherhood: A psychoanalytical perspective. *Psychoanalytic Inquiry, 8,* 234–251.

Pittman, F. S. (1987). *Turning points: Treating families in transition and crisis.* New York: Norton.

Pittman, F. S. (1984). Wet cocker spaniel therapy: An essay on technique in family therapy, *Family Process, 23,* 1–9.

Radbill, F. X. (1987). Children in a world of violence: A history of child abuse. In R. E. Helfer & R. S. Kempe (Eds.), *The battered child (4th ed.)* (pp. 3–22). Chicago: University of Chicago Press.

Rattray, R. S. (1956). *Ashanti laws and constitution*. London: Oxford University Press.

Reid, W. J., Kagan, R. M., & Schlosberg, S. B. (1988). Prevention of placement: Critical factors in program success. *Child Welfare, 67*(1), 25–36.

Reynolds, W. M. (1986). *About myself*. Odessa, FL: Psychological Assessment Resources.

Roberts, G. E. (1982). *Roberts' apperception test for children*. Los Angeles: Western Psychological Services.

Roberts, J. (1988). Use of ritual in "redocumenting" psychiatric history. In E. Imber-Black, J. Roberts., & R. Whiting (Eds.), *Rituals in families and family therapy* (pp. 307–330). New York: Norton.

Roberts, J. (1994). *Tales and transformations; Stories in families and family therapy*. New York: Norton.

Rossi, P. H. (1992). Assessing family preservation programs. *Children and Youth Services Review, 14*, 77–97.

Roth, S., & Chasin, R. (1990, March 10). *An exercise to stimulate variety and versatility when the therapist feels stuck*. Presented at the Family Therapy Networker Conference, Washington, DC.

Roth, S., & Chasin, R. (1994). Entering one another's worlds of meaning and imagination: Dramatic enactment and narrative couple therapy. In M. F. Hoyt (Ed.), *Constructive therapies*. New York: Guilford.

Rowland, C., Taplin, J., & Holt, A. (1983, August). *Home-based crisis therapy: A comparative outcome study*. Paper presented at the 91st Annual Convention of the American Psychological Association, Anaheim, CA.

Ryder, M., Courtney, J., & Ellis, B. (1994). *Home rebuilders: The first year's experience at Little Flower Children's Services*. New York: Little Flower Children's Services.

Schaffer, C., & Pine, F. (1972). Pregnancy, abortion and the developmental tasks of adolescence. *Journal of the American Academy of Child Psychiatry, 11*, 511–536.

Schlosberg, S. (1990, June 1). *Working with families in perpetual crisis*. Workshop presented for the Parsons/Sage Workshop Series, Albany, NY.

Segal, J. (1988). Teachers have enormous power in affecting a child's self-esteem. *Brown University Child Behavior and Development Newsletter, 4*, 1–3.

Shaffer, D., Gould, M. S., Brasie, J., Ambrosini, P., Fisher, P., Bird, H., & Aluwahilia, S. (1983). A children's global assessment scale (CJIS). *Archives of General Psychiatry, 40*, 1228–1231.

Sparrow, S. S., Balla, T. A., & Cicchetti, D. V. (1984). *Vineland adaptive behavior scale*. Circle Pines, MN: American Guidance Service.

Speck, R., & Attneave, C. (1973). *Family networks: Rehabilitation and healing*. New York: Pantheon.

Speck, R. (1967). Psychotherapy of the social network of a schizophrenic patient. *Family Process, 6*, 208–214.

Spitz, R. A. (1945). Hospitalism: An inquiry into the genesis of psychiatric conditions in early childhood. *Psychoanalytic Study of the Child, 1*, 53–74.

Sroufe, L. A. (1983). Infant-caregiver attachment and adaptation in the preschool: The roots of competence and maladaptation. In M. Perlmutter (Ed.), *Development of cogniton, affect, and social relations* (pp. 41–81). Hillsdale, NJ: Erlbaum.

Steinhauer, P. (1974, April). How to succeed in the business of creating psychopaths without even trying. Unpublished manuscript.

Steinhauer, P. (1991). *The least detrimental alternative: A systematic guide to case planning and decision making for children in care.* Toronto: University of Toronto Press.

Strauss, M. A., & Kantor, G. K. (1987). Stress and child abuse. In R. E. Helfer & R. S. Kempe, (Eds.), *The battered child (4th ed.).* Chicago: University of Chicago Press.

Suomi, S. J. (1991). Adolescent depression and depressive symptoms: Insights from longitudinal studies with rhesus monkeys. *Journal of Youth and Adolescence, 20,* 273–287.

Taylor, H. (1996, January 7). A mixed diagnosis for HMO's courtship. *Times Union,* Albany, NY, p. A9.

Texas Department of Human Resources (1981). *A study of child deaths attributed to abuse and neglect.* Austin, TX: Child Abuse and Neglect Resource Center.

Thomas, E. B., Levine, E. S., & Arnold, W. J. (1968). Effects of maternal deprivation and incubation rearing on adrenocortical activity in the adult rat. *Developmental Psychobiology, 1,* 21–23.

Titelman, P. (1987). *The therapist's own family: Toward the differentiation of self.* New York: Jason Aronson.

Trieschman, A. E., Whittaker, J. K., & Brendtro, L. K. (1969). *The other 23 hours.* Chicago: Aldine.

Trieschman Center. (1994). *Shattered vows: The impact of domestic violence on children, youth, and their families in group care* [Brochure]. Needham, MA: Author.

Trimble, D. (1980). A guide to the network therapies. *Connections, 3*(2), 9–22.

Trimble, D. (1981). Social network intervention with anti-social adolescents. *International Journal of Family Therapy, 3,* 268–274.

Trimble, D., & Kliman, J. (1981). Community network therapy: Strengthening the networks of chronic patients. *International Journal of Family Psychiatry, 2,* 269–289.

van der Kolk, B. A. (Ed.). (1984). *Post-traumatic stress disorder: Psychological and biological sequelae.* Washington, DC: American Psychiatric Press.

van der Kolk, B. A. (Ed.). (1987). *Psychological trauma.* Washington, DC: American Psychiatric Press.

Ventura, M. (1994, May/June). Solutions to everything. *Family Therapy Networker, 16.*

Waldman, S., Shackelford, L., Wingert, P., & Bogert, C. (1994, December 12). Welfare booby traps. *Newsweek,* pp. 34–35.

Walk, R. D. (1956). Self-ratings of fear in a fear-involving situation. *Journal of Abnormal and Social Psychology, 52,* 171–178.

Ward, M. J., & Carlson, E. A. (1995). Associations among adult attachment representations, maternal sensitivity, and infant-mother attachment in a sample of adolescent mothers. *Child Development, 66*(1), 69–79.

Waters, D. B., & Lawrence, E. C. (1993). *Competence, courage, & change: An approach to family therapy.* New York: Norton.

Watson, F. I., & Kelly, M. J. (1989). Targeting the at-risk male: A strategy for adolescent pregnancy prevention. *Journal of the National Medical Association, 81,* 453–456.

Watzlawick, P., Bavelas, J. B., & Jackson, D. D. (1967). *Pragmatics of human communication: A study of interactional patterns, pathologies, and paradoxes.* New York: Norton.

Wegscheider, S. (1981). *Another chance: Hope and health for the alcoholic family.* Palo Alto, CA: Science and Behavior.

Weiss, G, & Hechtman, L. T. (1993). *Hyperactive children grown up: ADHD in children, adolescents, and adults.* New York: Guilford.

White, M., & Epston, D. (1990). *Narrative means to therapeutic ends.* New York: Norton

Whitehead, B. D. (1993, April). Dan Quayle was right. *The Atlantic Monthly,* 47–84.

Williams, C. (1976). *The destruction of black civilization.* Chicago: Third World.

Wycliff, N. D. (Ed.). (1995, August 13). Enforce the law to make a point. *Chicago Tribune,* Section 4, p. 2.

Wylie, M. S. (1990, November-December). Are we neglecting the children? *Family Therapy Networker, 14*(6), p. 12.

index

abandonment, 51–52, 116, 119, 124, 126,
  130, 154, 197, 233
Achenbach, T. M., 227
acting out, 48, 107, 113, 116, 125, 145
  duration of, 236
  permanency work and, 204
adolescents, 53, 96, 97, 107, 142, 198
  assessing attachments of, 94–95
  group care programs and, 146–47
  independent living by, 210
  medication and, 204
  in parenting roles, 98
  "perverse triangle" and, 112
  pregnancies of, 111–12, 196, 219
  respecting of, 204
  in split double bind, 112
  violence of, 51, 195
adoption, 227
advocacy
  combining practice with, 227–29
  in communities, 217, 219–20
  for families, 217–18, 219–20
Aid to Families with Dependent Children, 196n
Ainsworth, M. D., 193
Alan Guttmacher Institute, 220n
Aluwahilia, S., 227
Ambrosini, P., 227
Ambrosino, R., 198
American Orthopsychiatric Association,
  195
American Psychiatric Association, 50, 137
American Public Welfare Association,
  xiii, 49, 143
Andersen, T., 100, 225
Anderson, R., 198
Angelou, Maya, 134n
Arling, G. L., 56, 89

Arnold, W. J., 194
art, 93–94, 103–4
attachment, 35, 87–89, 121, 180, 218
  crisis of, 193–94
  as first priority, 209–11
  in group care, 145–47
  psychological evaluations of, 91–95
  rebuilding, 127–29
  reunification and, 197–99
  support network and, 210–11
  teen pregnancy and, 219–20
  visits and, 148–49
Attneave, C., 134
Auerswald, E. H., 120
Ausloos, G., 53, 74, 79, 82, 112, 116, 117,
  118, 141

Balla, T. A., 227
Bandler, R., 127
Basharov, D. J., 198
Bateson, G., 109
Bavelas, J. B., 112
Beck, A. G., 60
Beck, A. T., 94
Beck, S. J., 60
behavior
  control of, 107–9
  delinquent, 112
  double bind and, 109–10
  psychotic, 109–10
  split messages and, 109–10
  teen pregnancy and, 111–12
  of 2-year-olds, 107–9
  violence as learned, 195
Berenson, D., 106, 116
Bergman, J. S., 100
Bettelheim, B., 121
Bird, H., 227

Blankenhorn, D., 220
block grants, in funding of child and
        family services, 192
Bogert, C., 219
Boszormenyi-Nagy, I., 126
"both/and" dilemma, 119, 120, 121, 240, 241
Bowen, M., 233n, 235
Bowlby, J., 35, 48, 121, 193, 197
Brasie, J., 227
Brazelton, T. B., 193
Breakey, G. F., 210
Brendtro, L. K., 54
Briere, J., 193
Bronfenbrenner, U., 134
Brooks, R. B., 193
Buck, J. N., 93
Burgess, A. W., 193
burnout, 14
Burns, R. C., 93
Burrell, C., 196

Cahill, C., 193
capitated rate system, 223
Carlson, E. A., 219
Carson, M., 88n
Casebeer Art Productions, 92
case examples
    Alex, 238–41, 247, 248
    Alice, 114–16
    Amy, 138–39
    Andy, 176–84
    Beverly, 205, 206
    Billy, 131–33, 134, 140–41, 143, 149,
        152–53
    Celene, 89
    Cheryl, 99–100
    Cindy Karner, 177–81, 182, 183, 184
    Dorothy, 131–32, 134, 140–41, 149–50,
        152–53
    Ed, 114–16
    Ellen, 138
    Gina, 138–39, 226
    Greg, 204
    Jackie, 102–3
    James, 174–76, 194
    Janet, 62–67
    Jen, 187–92, 193, 194, 196, 197, 199,
        203, 206
    Joan, 121
    Karen, 30–43, 45
    Kelly, 138–39
    Kevin Karner, 177–81, 182, 183, 184
    Kristen, 46–48, 49, 52, 53, 54, 57–67,
        71, 84, 96, 100, 120, 122, 123, 194

    Laurie, 211
    Lisa, 132–33, 134, 140–41, 145, 146,
        149, 152–55
    Louise, 80–82
    Maggie, 136
    Mandy, 76–78
    Maria, 114–16, 123
    Mary Ellen, 196–97
    Mrs. Kinman, 232
    Patti, 176–84
    Phyllis, 174–76
    Ralph, 31, 32, 34, 36–37, 38, 39, 40–41,
        42, 44
    Rebecca Burns, 3–12, 14, 15–18, 19,
        100
    Robbie, 21–28, 30–45
    Ronnie, 161–64, 166–68, 170, 172
    Samantha, 81
    Sandra, 238–41
    Sandy, 212
    Susan, 244–47
    Sylvia, 105, 128–29
    Ted, Jr., 161–68, 170–72
    Ted, Sr., 161–73
    Timmy, 105, 107, 120, 128–29
    Tommy, 161–64, 166–72
    Tony, 96
    Tonya, 244–47, 248
    Will, 118
    Williams family, ix–xii
Casey Foundation, 196
change, 80
    biological, 193–94
    metaphor and, 99–100, 102
    by parents, 205–6
    placement as catalyst for, 82–83, 201
    realistic expectations for, 86
    shaming and, 74–76
Chasin, Richard, 237, 241
Chicago Tribune, xiii
Chichetti, D. V., 227
Child Protection Block Grant (1995), 192n
Child Protective Services (CPS), 4–5, 23,
        25, 26, 28, 35, 115
    strengthening of, 220–21
    work environment of, 22
children, 175–76, 194, 197, 217, 228, 229,
        236
    acting out by, see acting out
    "as if" manner of, 27
    attachments of, see attachment
    "bad," 51, 117–18, 120
    biological impairments of, 50
    calls for help by, 113–15, 124

countertransference and, 234
in crisis cycle, 113, 116
developmental age levels of, 96–99
fathers and, 220
goals and, 141–43
"good," 117–18
grief processes of, 48
hypervigilance and, *see* hypervigilance
individuation of, 126
labels and, 117–18
medication for, 204
need for permanency in, 55–57
PINS petitions and, 199–201
in poverty, 195–96
psychological evaluation of, 91–95,
216–17
reasonable limits for, 41
responsibilities of, 206
reunification with, 197–99
review conference and, 150–51
rights of, 196–97
roles in families of, 53, 97–98, 109,
142
safety plans for, 144–45
separation and, 47–48
truancy of, 199–200
violence and, 195–96
welfare for, 196–97
see also family; parents; placement
Children's Defense Fund, 192*n*
Child Welfare Reform Act (1979), New
York, 82, 183
Chrousos, G. P., 193
Combs, G., 85, 100
community
network of positive connections in,
228
parents' beliefs endorsed by, 200
safety of children as concern of, 195
Connors, C. K., 227
countertransference, 234–37
courage, 173, 191, 235
Courtney, J., 223
CPS, *see* child protective services
Cramer, B. G., 193
crime, neglect and, 195
crises, 24
of attachment, 193–94
chronic, 54, 55
excitement of, 56–57
in family services, 206–8
as form of avoidance, 243
hypervigilance and, 126

loyalty and, 125–26
placement and, 110
practitioners' role in, 14, 106, 126, 166
as progressive series of triangles, 232–
34
real, 54, 153, 201
review conferences and, 150–52
serial, 99, 232–34
shame and, 75
split messages and, 111, 112, 237–38
time dimensions of, 117–18
time frames for, 82–83
tracing roots of, 95–96
as way of life, 56
Crowley, R. J., 104

Daro, D., 198, 210
De Angelis, T., 220
De Bellis, M. D., 193, 193*n*
Del Valle, C., 196*n*
denial, as protection, 54, 55, 75, 113
Denn, J., 221*n*
depression, 123, 193, 204
*Diagnostic and Statistical Manual of Mental
Disorders, IV*, 50, 137
Di Leo, J. H., 94
dissociation, 99
Dodsworth, R. O., 56, 89
Dolan, Yvonne, 242*n*
Dorn, L. D., 193
double binds, 109–12
dreams, 101
dual centering messages, 157, 237
split messages and, 119–22
validation and, 124–25
Duhl, B., 100

ecogram, 132*n*
Edelman, Marion, 134*n*
Edelman, M. W., 230*n*
Egeland, B., 193, 198
Einstein, Albert, 187
"either/or," 240, 242
Elliott, S. N., 227
Ellis, B., 223
Epston, D., 225
Erickson, M. F., 198
Erikson, E. H., 97, 107, 121
ethnicity, 134–35
evaluation, *see* psychological evaluation

families in need of supervision (FINS),
201

family
    children's role in, 53, 97–98, 109, 142
    chronic crises and, 54, 55, 82
    community-based services and, 211–
        12
    crises as way of life for, 56
    fathers and, 220
    framing choices for, 243–44
    "gatekeeper" in, 86
    generations of separations in, 56
    loyalty and, 26, 49, 55, 57
    mapping resources of, 83–84
    multigenerational patterns and, 76
    placement and, 84–86
    reunification and, 197–99, 227
    "second," 155–56
    shame and, 75–76
    substitute, 111–12
    teen pregnancy and, 111–12
    temporary living arrangements and,
        110–11
    in therapy, 76–80
    threats, violence and, 28–30
    see also children; parents; placement
family services
    community-based, 211–12
    crisis in, 206–8
    foster parents and, 215–16
    funding of, 206–7
    network approach to, 212–14
    one-call intake service and, 214–15
    permanency specialists and, 216
    zone defense model of, 212
family workers, 136–37
    see also practitioners
Farber, E. A., 193
fathers, 220
    placement and, 86–87
Federal Adoption Assistance and Child
        Welfare Act (1980), 82
feeling thermometers, 93
Ferreira, A., 112
Figley, C. R., 144
Finkelstein, N., 49
FINS, see families in need of supervision
Fisher, P., 227
Fong, R., 134n
Fossum, M. A., 106, 116
Frank, Charles, 117n
Frank, Jenny, 212n
Freedman, J., 85, 100
Freeman, E. M., 220
Freud, A., 197
Fruchtman, D., 94, 219, 227

Galanter, M., 134
game therapy, 103
Gardner, R. A., 103
Garfinkel, I., 220
Garrison, J., 134
"gatekeeper," 86
Gelles, R., 197, 198
gender, respect for, 134–35
genogram format, 85–86, 132n
Gerson, R., 86
Gil, E., 99
Giordano, J. 134n
Girard, J. L., 50
goals, 125, 238, 242
    children and, 141–43
    network intervention and, 141–43
    paperwork and, 224–25
    permanency work and, 141–43
Goldstein, J., 197
Goldwyn, 227
Goodfield, R., 88n
Gottlieb, J., 196n
Gould, M. S., 227
Green, R., 196n
Gresham, F. M., 227
grief, 48, 55
Grinder, J., 127
group care, 202–3
    adolescents and, 146–47
    attachment and, 145–47
    children's behavior and, 204–5
    network approach and, 203
Groze, V., 85

Haley, J., 109, 112, 147
Harlow, H. F., 56, 89
Harlow, M. K., 56, 89
Hartman, A., 85, 132n
Hartman, C. R., 193
Hawaii (Healthy Family program), 210
Hechtman, L. T., 193
Herman, J., 193
Hernandez, M., 219
HMOs (health management organiza-
        tions), 221–23
"holding the crisis," 141
Holt, A., 132n
Home Rebuilders Workgroup, 223
hospitalization, 202–3
House of Representatives, U.S., 192
Human Resoures Department, Texas, 198
hypervigilance, 114, 194
    crises and, 126
    violence and, 54–55

illegitimacy, 196*n*
Imber-Black, E., 100, 134, 225
"imminent risk," 201
independent living, 210
individuation, 126
interventions, xiv, 24, 237
    to counter split double bind, 112
    see also network intervention

Jackson, D., 109
Jackson, D. D., 112
James, Beverly, 103, 242*n*
Jones, E., 210

Kagan, R., 54, 55, 62*n*, 76*n*, 82, 95, 103,
    141, 150*n*, 154, 199, 200, 242*n*,
    243
Kaladjian, G. M., 223
Kantor, G. K., 194, 195
Kaplan, L., 50
Kaplan, P. S., 193
Karpman, S., 163*n*, 232
Kaufman, S. H., 93
Kelly, M. J., 220
Kingsolver, Barbara, 134*n*
Klein, A. F., 54
Klein, J., 200
Klein, R., 80*n*
Kliman, J., 86*n*, 134
Kolb-Latu, D., 210
Kotulak, R., xiii

labels, 118–19, 150
Landau-Stanton, J., 86, 97, 134
Lankton, C., 100
Lankton, S., 100
Lauderdale, M., 198
Lauri, 60, 91
Lawrence, E. C., 97, 100, 116
Lazarus, A. A., 94
Lee, R., 249
Lefter, L., 193, 193*n*
Levine, E. S., 194
Levitt, E. E., 60
Liederman, D. S., 195
Lightfoot, Sarah Lawrence, 134*n*
limits, *see* time frames, limits
Lindemann, E., 54
Linesch, D., 103, 153
Lion King, The (film), 188
Llewelyn, S. P., 193
Louis, M. E., 219
Louis, R., 219

loyalty, 61, 74, 79, 102, 119–20, 157
    cycle of crises and, 125–26
    family and, 26, 49, 55, 57

McCormack, A., 193
McCurdy, K., 210
McGoldrick, M., 86, 134*n*
McMillen, J. C., 85
McNamee, M., 196*n*
Madanes, C., 29, 75, 80, 86, 100, 144, 148
magical thinking, 153
Magura, S., 227
Mahler, M. S., 193
Main, M., 227
mapping family resources
    countertransference and, 236–37
    Hartman's ecogram and, 132*n*
    placement and, 83–84
    safety plan and, 144
Mason, M., 75
Mason, M. J., 106, 116
Masterson, J. F., 109, 110, 126
Mayor's Task Force on Child Abuse and
    Neglect, 198
Medicaid, 207, 222
medication, 204
metaphor, 98–104, 157, 191, 217
    art, drawings and, 103–4
    assessing, 100–101
    change and, 99–100, 102
    dreams and, 101
    first words and, 101
    game theory and, 103
    split messages and, 122–24
    storytelling and, 102–3
Meyer, V. F., 220
Mills, J. C., 104
Minuchin, S., 126
Mitchel, L., 198
Molish, H. B., 60
Morrell-Samuels, S., 210
Morrison, Toni, 134*n*
Murray, H. A., 92

Nace, E., 75
neighborhood resource center approach,
    214
network approach, 228, 237, 247–48
    attachment and, 210–11
    to family services, 212–14
    foster parents and, 215–16
    group care and, 203
    permanency work and, 203, 212–14

network intervention, 122, 132
    being realistic and, 153–54
    extended family and, 145*n*, 157
    goals and, 141–43
    mobilizing, 133–34
    other service providers and, 135–38
    permanency and, 140–43
    placement and, 133–34
    practitioner and, 135–38
    respect and, 134–35
    review conferences and, 149–52
    safety plan and, 144–45, 157–58
    substance abuse and, 143–44
    visits and, 147–49
New York
    Child Welfare Reform Act of, 82, 183
    Department of Social Services, 82
    family service cuts in, 192
    Home Rebuilders program in, 223
Nichols, M., 112
Nichols-Casebolt, A., 220

O'Connor, W., 195
one-call intake service, 214–15
outcome research, 226–27

paperwork, 224–26
Papp, P., 112
parents, 26, 30, 41, 49, 53, 97, 194, 236,
        243
    adoption and, 218
    as advocates, 217–18
    and behavior of 2-year-olds, 108–9
    change by, 205–6
    disabled, 90
    fathers as, 86–87, 220
    PINS petition and, 199–201
    placement and, 89–91
    practitioners as seen by, 120
    retarded, 89–90
    reunification and, 183, 184, 197–98
    review conference and, 150–51
    rights of, 181, 196
    safety plans by, 144
    split messages and, 112
    substance abuse by, 143–44
    visits and, 147–49
    see also children; family; placement
Parsons Child and Family Center, 218*n*
Parsons Prevention Program, 212*n*
Pearce, J. K., 134*n*
Pearlman, L. A., 242*n*
Pearson, C., 193

permanency, 247–48
    acting out and, 204
    adolescents and, 204
    advocacy and, 218–19
    change by parents and, 205–6
    community-based services and, 211–
        12
    effectiveness of, 203–5
    framing choices and, 243–44
    goals and, 141–43
    legislation and, 218–19
    level of care and, 202–3
    need for, 55–57
    network approach to, 140–43, 154,
        203, 212–14
    onset of work in, 202
    outcome research and, 226–27
    paperwork and, 224–26
    specialists in, 216–17
    supportive network and, 203
    time frame for, 206
person in need of supervision (PINS),
        106, 162, 166, 177, 199–201, 207
"perverse triangles," 112
PINS, *see* person in need of supervision
Phillips, K., 193
Pinderhughes, E., 134
Pine, F., 219
Pines, D., 219
Pittman, F. S., 116
placement, 122, 156, 201–2
    as catalyst for change, 82–83, 201
    children's attachments and, 87–89
    crises and, 110
    crisis of attachment and, 194
    criteria for, 50, 51
    determining effective parent-figures
        and, 89–91
    diagnosed disorders and, 50–51
    family and, 53, 84–86
    family's test and, 76–80
    father and, 86–87
    in foster homes, 38–39
    foster parents as cotherapists and,
        215–16
    genogram and, 85–86
    "imminent risk" and, 201
    length of, 83
    level of care and, 202–3
    mapping family resources and, 83–84
    network intervention and, 133–34
    number of children in, 49–50
    parents and, 89–91
    projected stability date and, 52–53

psychological evaluation and, 91–95
real world therapy and, 128–29
and rebuilding attachments, 127–29
record keeping and, 225
and reunification, 197–99
safety and, 53–54
table of strategies for, 71–74
time frame of, 39, 82–83
timeline and, 85–86
as turning point, 52–55, 126–30
violence and, 51
wounded people and, 80–82
see also children; family; parents
poverty, 193, 195–96, 219
practitioners, xv, 193, 208
advocacy and, 217
community-based services and, 211–12
countertransference and, 234–35
crisis in family services and, 206–8
defined, xv, 230n
HMOs and, 221–22
language of managed care and, 221–23
network intervention and, 135–38
outcome research and, 226–27
paperwork and, 224–26
parents' perception of, 120
as permanency specialists, 216–17
personal mental state of, 14, 126, 242–43
and role in family crises, 14, 106, 126, 166
stressful situations and, 231–32
progressive triangles, 232–33
Projective Storytelling Cards, 92
psychological evaluation, 91–95
drawings and, 93–94
family puzzle and, 91–92
feeling thermometer and, 93
projective questions and, 92–93
reenactment and, 91–92
sentence completion and, 94
storytelling and, 92–93
testing and, 92
Putnam, F. W., 193, 193n

Radbill, F. X., 196
Rattray, R. S., 49
real crises, 54, 153, 201
real world therapy, 128–29
reenactment, 91–92
Reid, W. J., 199, 200
respect, 134–35, 235–36

reunification, 183, 184
placement and, 197–99
time frame for, 183n
review conferences, 149–52
agenda for, 150
children and, 150–51
crises and, 150–52
ending, 151
parents and, 150–51
time frame and, 149
Reynolds, W. M., 94
Roberts, J., 59, 92, 100, 103, 225
Roberts Apperception Test, 92
Roosevelt, Theodore, 230
Rossi, P. H., 227
Roth, Sallyann, 237, 241
Rowland, C., 132n
Runtz, M. 193
Russell, D., 193
Ryder, M., 223

Saakvitne, K. W., 242n
safety plan, 144–45, 157–58
Schaffer, C., 219
schizophrenia, 7, 8
Schlosberg, Shirley, 54, 55, 61, 62n, 76n, 82, 95, 99n, 107, 108, 141, 150n, 154, 165, 199, 200, 242n, 243
secondary posttraumatic stress disorder, 14
"second family," 155–56
secrets, toxic, 113, 116, 203
Segal, J., 193
Semidei, J., 223
sentence completion, 94
separation, 47–48
serial crises, 99, 232–34
sex abuse, 3–10, 15–17, 19, 43–44, 76–78, 114–16, 138–39, 148, 161–73, 191, 228, 244–46
biological change and, 193–94
false accusations of, 11
investigative process and, 11
parental rights and, 11
parental threats, violence and, 29–30
typical pattern of, 164
validation and, 10
sexual orientation, respect for, 135
Shackelford, L., 219
Shaffer, D., 227
shaming, 74–76
Silverman-Mose, B., 227
Society for the Prevention of Cruelty to Animals, 197
Solnit, A. J., 197

Sparrow, S. S., 227
Speck, R., 134
spiritual wounds, 80
Spitz, R. A., 47
split double bind, 112
split messages, 109–12, 157, 180–81
    behavior and, 109–10
    crises and, 111, 112, 237–38
    dual centering messages and, 119–22
    "either/or" dilemma and, 240, 242
    exercise for, 241, 249–51
    finding, 237–41
    framing, 119–22
    metaphors and, 122–24
    parents and, 112
    practitioner's mental state and, 242–43
    validation and, 127–28
Sroufe, L. A., 198
Steinhauer, P., 48, 52, 175, 195
storytelling, 59–60, 191
    metaphor and, 102–3
    psychological evaluation and, 92–93
Strauss, M. A., 194, 195
stress, 14, 75, 117
substance abuse, 143–44
substitute family, 111–12
Suomi, S. J., 194

Tan, Amy, 134n
Taplin, J., 132n
Taylor, H., 221
teen pregnancy, 196
    adolescents and, 111–12
    motivations for, 219–20
Thematic Apperception Test, 92
therapists, see practitioners
Thomas, E. B., 194
threats, 28–30
time frames, limits
    crises and, 82–83, 117–18
    fixated, 117–18
    in group care, 203
    for permanency work, 206
    for placement, 39, 82–83
    for reunification decision, 183n
    review conference and, 149
    substance abuse and, 143–44
Titelman, P., 235
toxic secrets, 113, 116, 203
traumas, 113
    biological changes and, 193–94
triangles
    "perverse," 112
    progressive, 232–33

Trickett, P. K., 193, 193n
Trieschman, A. E., 54
Trieschman Center, 195, 197
Trimble, D., 86n, 134
Trocki, K., 193
truancy, 199–200
two-year-olds, 107–8

Uohara-Pratt, B., 210

Valentine, D., 198
validation, 27–28, 122, 132, 243
    dual centering messages and, 124–25
    of positive striving, 124–25
    sex abuse and, 10
    split messages and, 127–28
van der Kolk, B. A., 193
Ventura, M., 234
victim-rescuer-persecutor cycle, 232
violence, xvii, 30, 123, 198, 233
    adolescents and, 51, 195
    children and, 195–96
    crime and, 195
    emotional abandonment and, 51–52
    hypervigilance and, 54–55
    as learned behavior, 195
    parental threats of, 29–30
    placement and, 51
visitation, 37–38, 39
    attachment and, 148–49
    network intervention and, 147–49

Waldman, S., 219
Ward, M. J., 219
Waters, D. B., 97, 100, 116
Watson, F. I., 220
Watzlawick, P., 112
Weakland, J., 109
Wegscheider, S., 75
Weiss, G., 193
welfare, xii, 196–97, 219–20
White, M., 225
Whitehead, B. D., 196
Whiting, R., 100
Whittaker, J. K., 54
Williams, C., 196n
Wingert, P., 219
Wycliff, N. D., 220n
Wylie, M. S., xiii

zone defense model, 212

DATE DUE

JAN 14 2003		
DEC 15 2003		
MAY 15 2008		
		Printed in USA